TELEPEN

UNIVERSITY OF NOTTINGHAM

WITHDRAWN

FROM THE LIBRARY

00 128503 9

D0409710

LIFE'S ALL A FRAGMENT

Life's all a Fragment

by

CHARLES TENNYSON

Life's all a fragment.   No less grandly shows
A shattered vault, abrupt against the sky,
With ivy chevelured and the wild red rose,
A promontory of brick, whereunder lie
Shepherd and sheep in afternoon repose
(O'erhead, like rapier strokes the merlins fly)
—Than undefeated frames of arch on arch that still
Shoulder the Roman sluice intact from hill to hill.

In Memoriam—*Charles Dennis Fisher*
J. S. Phillimore.

With 4 half-tone plates

UNIVERSITY LIBRARY
7 OCT 1953
NOTTINGHAM

CASSELL & CO LTD

LONDON

CASSELL & CO. LTD
37/38 St. Andrew's Hill, Queen Victoria Street
London, E.C.4
and at
210 Queen Street, Melbourne
26/30 Clarence Street, Sydney
Haddon Hall, City Road, Auckland, N.Z.
1068 Broadview Avenue, Toronto 6
122 East 55th Street, New York 22
Avenida 9 de Julho 1138, São Paulo
Galeria Güemes, Escritorio 518/520 Florida 165, Buenos Aires
Haroon Chambers, South Napier Road, Karachi
15 Graham Road, Ballard Estate, Bombay 1
17 Central Avenue P.O. Dharamtala, Calcutta
P.O. Box 275, Cape Town
P.O. Box 1386, Salisbury, S. Rhodesia
P.O. Box 959, Accra, Gold Coast
Calçada Do Carma 55/2°, Lisbon
25 rue Henri Barbusse, Paris 5e
Islands Brygge 5, Copenhagen

All rights reserved
First published 1953

C

Set in 12pt. Bembo type and
printed in Great Britain by
J. W. Arrowsmith Ltd., Quay Street and Small Street, Bristol
F. 353

TO CORDELIA CURLE
CHARLES'S SISTER AND
JULIAN'S GODMOTHER,
IN GRATITUDE FOR A
LIFE-LONG FRIENDSHIP

FOREWORD

So MANY friends have helped me with these essays that I cannot possibly thank them all by name. I am especially grateful to Charles Fisher's sister, Mrs. R. Curle, and his sister-in-law, Cecilia Lady Fisher, for invaluable help and encouragement; to the Hon. George Lyttelton for allowing me to make free use of his admirable essay on Charles; to him and his sister, the Hon. Lady Buchanan Riddell, for permission to use the letters received by them from him; to Colonel P. Hanafin, D.S.O., and Rear-Admiral H. E. Dannreuther, D.S.O., for much invaluable assistance in connexion with Charles's work in the Red Cross and the Navy. I have also to thank the Clarendon Press for allowing me to print the poem *Chivalry of the Sea* from the *Poetical Works of Robert Bridges*, and to the *Oxford Magazine* for permission to print the lines by the late Professor J. S. Phillimore on the title-page.

I record with deep gratitude my special indebtedness to Dr. F. J. Dixon, Mr. H. H. Goodall, Mr. Jesse Gray, Mr. Harold Walker and Mr. A. H. Rose, for the great trouble which they have taken to help me in my researches on J. C. Snaith; to Mrs. F. C. Boon for the loan of many of Snaith's books which I should otherwise have found it very difficult to obtain; to Mr. John Macleay for permission to use his correspondence with Snaith, and to Mrs. Florence Coleman for her very interesting accounts of the old High Pavement School at Nottingham.

In preparing my short memoir of Roy Truscott I have been greatly helped by his sister Mrs. Doris Greenall, and his cousin, Alderman Sir Denis Truscott. To Esme Wingfield Stratford and W. R. Brandt I owe grateful thanks for their reminiscences of Roy's life at Cambridge. Sir Hugh Walpole wrote especially for me the very interesting letter printed on page 117 and I am glad of this opportunity of acknowledging his kindness and of thanking his Executors for allowing me to print the letter. Most of those who have so generously helped me with information about Roy's career in the War are named in the text, but in addition I have to acknowledge with gratitude the very full accounts which were supplied to me by Lieut.-General Sir Travers Clarke, G.B.E.,

K.C.B., and the late Major-General Sir Evan Gibb. My account of Roy's brief career in East Africa is based on an excellent description written for me by Mr. Leonard Leech. Mr. Boyce of Suffolk Lane and Mr. Percy Michael helped me most generously with accounts of his work in the Printing Industry. Without the full co-operation of Ruth Truscott the memoir could not have been written at all, and I keenly regret that she has not lived to see it in print.

CONTENTS

LIST OF ILLUSTRATIONS

CHARLES DENNIS FISHER

Charles Dennis Fisher

THOSE who knew Charles Fisher during his last years at Westminster School and as an undergraduate at Christ Church, felt that he must inevitably rise to the top of any profession which he might adopt in after life. He could, if he wished, become Prime Minister, Commander-in-Chief, First Sea Lord, Archbishop of Canterbury: all that was needed was inclination. When he died in 1916, Lieutenant R.N.V.R., at the age of thirty-eight, with nothing to his credit but revised texts of the *Annals* and *Histories* of Tacitus, not one of his friends would have retracted that opinion.

Charles came from one of those families which are rooted deeply and widely in all that is best in English life. His father, Herbert Fisher (a nephew of John Constable's faithful and discriminating friend Archdeacon Fisher), had himself been a senior student of Christ Church (equivalent to the 'fellowship' of an ordinary College) and is immortalized in Clough's *Bothie* as 'Arthur Audley':

> '*Arthur, the shapely, the tranquil, the strength and contentment diffusing,*
> *In the pure presence of whom none could quarrel long, nor be pettish*'

After his election as student he had been tutor to King Edward VII (then Prince of Wales) during his residence at Oxford, and later, for ten years, his Private Secretary, forgoing a career at the Bar for this purpose. On retiring from the Prince's service he was made Warden of the Stannaries, a legal position carrying a small salary and smaller duties. He was a fine scholar in the literary sense, with a deep love of the Greek and Latin classics, a keen sportsman and lover of the country and a man of remarkable personal beauty, whom King Edward would always hail, on his annual appearance at the Levée, with the greeting:
'Handsome as ever, Fisher, I see!'

3

Charles's mother's mother had been one of the famous Misses Pattle, sister of Julia Margaret Cameron and the beautiful Lady Somers. Through her his ancestors had been linked by blood and friendship with Wordsworth, Tennyson, Thackeray, G. F. Watts, Leslie Stephen, and other great Victorians.

Herbert Fisher and his wife had a large family, all distinguished in mind and feature—many of them also by high accomplishment. The eldest was H. A. L. Fisher, famous as historian and educational pioneer. Two years older than Charles was William Wordsworth Fisher, a very great sailor, who did more than any other single man to save Britain from the submarine menace during the First World War, and would undoubtedly have become First Sea Lord had not death taken him at the comparatively early age of sixty-two. Another of the older brothers was Hervey, a brilliant scholar, crippled from his youth by a tuberculous spine which prevented him from ever bringing his great abilities to fruition. Edmund, an architect of great ability and charm, lost his life as a volunteer in the First World War at the age of forty-two, and the youngest, Edwin, became Chairman of Barclay's Bank. The second son, a brilliant soldier, died young as a result of service in the South African War. The four sisters, of whom one married successively the historian F. W. Maitland and Sir Francis Darwin, and another Dr. Ralph Vaughan Williams, were women of high distinction, integrity and charm.

Charles's childhood and boyhood were spent at Brighton and in the New Forest, where his father had a holiday house. There he developed a splendid physique and a great love of country life and country sports. When, in 1891, he went to Westminster as a boarder from the famous Dragon School at Oxford, he was already a marked personality, having shown himself a fine all-round athlete and obtained first place in the Westminster 'Challenge' scholarship examination. He got his cricket colours at Westminster in 1894 when only sixteen, being singled out by Wisden as one of the most promising schoolboy cricketers of the year, good both as bowler and bat, and he was a leader in the football eleven. In the later years of his school life ill health interfered a good deal with both his cricket and football. Nevertheless he left with a considerable athletic reputation which no doubt contributed to the outstanding position which he held in the School, as did his superb physical appearance, for he was well over six feet tall, immensely

Charles Dennis Fisher

powerful in build, fresh complexioned, chestnut-haired, with a noble profile, brown eyes that sparkled with humour and courage, and a laugh which it is no *cliché* to call Homeric. Although the headmaster, William Gunnion Rutherford, a grim and precise Scotsman, and John Sargeaunt, the leading classical master, had a high opinion of his scholarship, he was perhaps not quite the best scholar in the school, but he had the ability to enjoy what he read, was accurate and fluent in Greek and Latin, especially delighting when he could accomplish a good set of verses, and wrote beautiful English. It was surely prophetic that an essay of his on Patriotism was so outstanding that he had to read it aloud to the whole of the VIIth Form.

He was fortunate in being able to spend his week-ends during term time with the Leslie Stephens in Hyde Park Gate. There he met outstanding people and heard much notable talk which gave him a broader view of life and letters than the daily grind of school life could afford. These week-end visits also enabled him to visit picture galleries and theatres and to develop a genuine love of poetry, but he had not any precocious faculty in verse. Sir Maurice Gwyer recalled that in Charles's last year they both entered for the English verse prize, the subject being the recent siege and relief of Chitral. Just before afternoon prayers the headmaster handed them back their compositions—Gwyer's first, with the comment:

'Well, it's very ba-ad.'

Charles's hopes rose high, only to be dashed when he received his copy with the same criticism:

'It's very ba-ad, too.'

Charles did not take this reverse very seriously, maintaining that his poem included one (no doubt apocryphal) couplet which alone should have ensured him the prize:

> *With lotus and with amaranth crowned they come*
> *Each British bull-dog with his fife and drum.*

Yet in spite of his athletic prowess and his immense capacity for enjoyment, he was to most of his contemporaries rather a remote figure. His splendid appearance and the impression which he gave of great reserves of power and self-control, overawed them a little, and they felt a kind of moral fastidiousness about him and a chastity of intellect which were rather intimidating. Probably this detachment was in part due to his happy home life. The large and intensely affectionate family in which he had grown up and the hours which he spent at Hyde Park Gate, gave him something with which the rough-and-tumble of school could not compete, and he never had the kind of ambition which could persuade him to sacrifice ideals in order to enhance his personal position.

Charles came up to Christ Church, Oxford, in 1896 with the first Westminster studentship (scholarship) and Slade Exhibition. Christ Church was at that time the largest of the Oxford Colleges, and differed from the others through its close association with the Cathedral. In former times all the Senior Students (or Fellows) had to be Canons and therefore clerical, and the Dean of the Cathedral was Master of the College. The Dean was still Master when Charles came into residence, but the Constitution had been altered so as to permit of a majority of non-clerical Fellows. A strong minority had, however, still to be Canons. This tradition led to a certain dualism in the College and some jealousy between the lay and clerical Senior Students, which might have been worse under less broad-minded Deans than Francis Paget (later Bishop of Oxford) and the famous 'Tommy' Strong (afterwards Bishop of Ripon, and then of Oxford), who presided over Christ Church during Charles's period of residence. One excellent result of the Cathedral connexion was the attraction to the College of a certain number of undergraduates of genuine religious feeling, many of whom intended to seek their life's work in the Church.

The College had other distinctive features. There were scholarships reserved to Westminster School, and there was always a strong contingent of Scottish Exhibitioners, mostly men who had had a tough struggle to pay for their education and fought their way to Oxford by sheer hard work and tenacity of purpose. There was a strong rowing set, with a nucleus of Etonians, and there was still a close association with many of the great aristocratic families, although this had been somewhat weakened in recent years, largely as a result of a famous disagreement over a Ball at Blenheim, which the College authorities had forbidden the undergraduates to attend. A number of them ignored this prohibition and were sent down. The action of the authorities was much resented, and the families of some of the men concerned severed their connexion with Christ Church. But the aristocratic and hunting tradition persisted and was embodied in two very exclusive clubs called respectively 'Loders' and 'The Rousers'.

Charles was ideally suited to such a society. His great reputation as scholar, athlete, and Westminster monitor, had preceded him and he bore a name already honoured in the College, of which not only his father but his grandfather also had been scholars and senior students. But all this paled before the impact of his personality—his tremendous physique, his classical beauty of feature, the extraordinary breadth of his interests, his pungent humour and brilliant and spontaneous charm.

It was not surprising that he very quickly made a name for himself. He played in the freshmen's matches at soccer and cricket and soon became a tower of strength in College sport, though his great size and muscular development prevented him from achieving high distinction at football, and probably also kept him out of the first rank as a cricketer. He worked hard, getting a first in 'Mods.' and took an active part in all phases of College and University life. He made friends of all types—athletes, scholars, aristocrats, aesthetes, the playboy and the student, the eminent and the obscure, wherever he could find sincerity and independence.

Perhaps in the University at large he was regarded as primarily an athlete, but his intimates knew that this was a false valuation, for they realized how great were his capacities and how fundamentally serious his nature. Many of his closest friends were keen Churchmen, and several have since attained high ecclesiastical office. But although it was clear that he understood and respected their convictions, he disliked and often delightfully ridiculed the hierarchic and ritualistic elements of the Church, and his attitude on the fundamental issues involved was marked by a curious reserve. His friends could not fail to realize that he had a reverence for truth as fastidious as his scholarship, but he avoided discussion and would never give any indication of his own inner beliefs, so that they, for the most part, came to regard him as a supreme example of the personal charm and moral excellence that can be achieved by an enlightened Paganism.

He was to take 'Greats' in 1900, and this year also saw him fighting for his cricket Blue. It was one of the most famous of all the years of Oxford cricket, when R. E. Forster (who made the record score of 171 in that year's University match), B. J. T.

Bosanquet (not yet known as the inventor of the 'googly'), H. Martyn, one of the best wicket keepers of all time, H. C. Pilkington, C. H. B. Marsham and F. H. B. Champain were available, and it was a high distinction for Charles's cricket that he secured a place in the team, and in a University match when 1,200 runs were scored for 28 wickets, made a quickly hit 26, and took two wickets for 42 runs in Cambridge's first innings—including that of the redoubtable T. L. Taylor, one of the toughest batsmen that Yorkshire has ever produced.

Charles's achievement of his Blue was a great delight to him and to his friends, but it inevitably interfered a good deal with his work, and it was a grievous disappointment when the Greats list came out and he found that he had only secured a Second Class.

It had for some time been generally assumed that he was destined to be one of the leaders of the College and would be elected to a senior studentship at Christ Church as soon as he had taken his degree, but his election did not take place immediately, not because his comparative failure in Greats caused anyone to be preferred to him, but because of a College regulation which laid down that there must always be a certain proportion of clerical students. There was a vacancy for a clerical candidate and Charles had to wait till this was filled. The position was made clear to him and he waited patiently, acting as a lecturer meanwhile. It did not occur to him to seek any other profession. The life at Oxford suited him and he had never felt drawn elsewhere, except perhaps to the Navy. This he had foregone because William, the brother closest to him in age, temperament and affection, had chosen it.

By 1903 the technical obstacle had been removed, and he was elected a senior student and tutor for Pass men. Two or three years later he became tutor for Honour Mods. and in 1907 was appointed Junior Censor—the junior of the two dons responsible for discipline, like the Deans of other Colleges.

In 1908 he was made a Governor of Westminster School, and in 1910 an Almoner of Christ's Hospital. In the same year he became Senior Censor at Christ Church and a member of the Board for *Literae Humaniores*. Meanwhile he had brought out a revised text of the *Annals of Tacitus* for the Clarendon Press, had completed a revised text of the *Histories* (published 1911) and had been commissioned to carry through the critical revision of Books

XI–XVI of the *Histories*, which had been undertaken by Professor Pelham but left unfinished at his death.

The mere facts of such a career (except perhaps the early appointments to Westminster and Christ's Hospital) could no doubt be paralleled by scores of clever young men in any university generation. What they do not reveal is the extraordinary position which Charles had come to hold in his College and in the University before the outbreak of war in 1914. This was due not so much to his athletic or scholarly achievements as to his remarkable character and personality, which ripened and expanded with the passing years, just as these strengthened and filled out his magnificent body.

After his appointment as Junior Censor in 1907 at the age of thirty, there was never any doubt that he was the most important and influential figure in his College. He had friendships 'joyous, varied and intimate' in all circles—'Loders' and 'Rousers'; the scholars and, particularly, the Westminster scholars; the Blues and the Bloods and the toilers—and did more than anyone to harmonize the various still discordant elements in the College, for he loved the varieties and vagaries of human nature, and always seemed, without any conscious effort, to draw the very best out of those with whom he came in contact. In Charles's massive presence the 'Blood' insensibly learned to revise his conviction of his own importance, while the younger and weaker thought of him as a bulwark standing between them and the fears and despairs of youth—as one of these said, 'Something like what the British Navy is to the British people'.

He had no patience with scholars who moaned about the boredom of teaching—indeed, for the majority of them he thought teaching the most useful thing they could do—and when, at the beginning of his career, he had to take on the Pass men because there was no vacancy for an Honours Mods. tutor, he devoted himself to the work with genuine pleasure, recognizing honest effort where he found it, but not sparing appropriate comment on the slovenly or idle. His criticism could be direct and devastating, but it was noticeable that he would generally find an early opportunity of doing the victim some special kindness or giving him some word of special praise to restore his self-esteem.

'Of his teaching', wrote John Murray, his friend and colleague as Junior Censor, afterwards Principal of University College, Exeter, 'it would be hard to say where the moral discipline ended and that of intellect and taste began'. For many it was 'a challenge to clarity and rightness of thought and will, for which the response of nothing less than the whole personality sufficed'. Moreover, 'He had the imaginative insight to make his way into very diverse natures, and a heart big enough for all of them. His likings were strong, his admiration generous, his hate and scorn severe'. To pomposity and insincerity he was ruthless. Yet he himself made no pretensions. Certainly no one could have been more careless of his appearance. He was, indeed, reputed the untidiest person in the University. He wore one kind of suit only—it was made of blue or grey flannel, cut very loose, and the double-breasted jacket resembled a peculiarly shapeless blazer. New suits were always ordered from the tailor by post—never a moment before they were needed. At a time when too many Dons were still shy, austere, remote and unapproachable, he distrusted people who 'lived on too high a plane', and seemed, quite spontaneously and without self-consciousness, to mix with all on terms of perfect equality. But he never failed to make his standards clear. I do not think anyone ever heard him use foul language (he would invent the most mouth-filling expletives for use when his feelings needed relief—such as 'm-m-mother of all m-m-mice!' spoken with terrifying emphasis), and his natural fastidiousness ruled out what is often the most fruitful source of masculine humour; yet more spontaneous laughter never came from undergraduates' rooms than when he was of the party. But, as at Westminster, with the affection which all but the pretentious and self-seeking felt for him, there was mixed a decided feeling of awe. For in spite of a charm and sympathy which seemed so spontaneous, there was always something inscrutable about him—an elusive quality as of something held back in self-expression. This was emphasized by the extreme economy of statement which marked his conversation. Even his humour was never of the verbose Gilbertian kind then so popular, but always concise, simple, illuminating with a flash. Indeed, some thought that his mastery of Tacitus was largely due to a similarity in temperament between editor and author. 'Few men in any age', wrote John Murray, 'can have been more admired, feared, trusted, loved, obeyed, or on better grounds of strength and goodness'.

He had an uncanny instinct for dealing with men. He himself said that his method was quite simple: he gated the rich and fined the poor. But that, of course, was not an exhaustive description. If rebuke had to be given it was short, quiet, measured, and went home. For trifling offences, apt to provoke tedious arguments and irrelevant excuses, he evolved a technique the exploitation of which gave him great amusement, though of course the victim was never allowed to see this. A man who came before him for missing roll-calls would be received, as soon as he entered Charles's room, with the sharply uttered question:

'Jones, you have not kept your roll-calls—WHAT?'

The depth of meaning in the last monosyllable and the flash of Charles's brown eyes which accompanied it, never failed of their effect.

One year he had living above him a German undergraduate (now Dr. Kurt Hahn, the distinguished founder and head of Gordonstown School) who, owing to the effects of sunstroke, was not allowed to go out when the weather was warm. Young Hahn was an enthusiastic high jumper, and to keep himself in form used to practise in his room over ingeniously constructed obstacles. Charles, who sympathized keenly with the young man's misfortune and also with his enthusiasm, put up with its results as long as he could. Then one day he invited Hahn to lunch, and in the middle of a most agreeable meal, suddenly pointed up to the ceiling and said, with a twinkle in his eye, 'Nice and quiet up there now'. That was the only reference he ever made to the subject, but it was enough, as he knew it would be.

Once he had to deal with a young man whose rather uncouth manners and gift of sarcasm had made him unpopular with the rowdy element in the College. One evening, after some unusually convivial celebration, an attempt was made to duck him in the fountain in the middle of Tom Quad. The intended victim, when he saw his enemies converging on him, drew a loaded revolver and fired into the ground between their legs. Charles, who had considerable sympathy with the man and very little with his attackers, sent for him next morning and when he appeared, very sorry for himself and fully expecting to be sent down, asked him quietly:

'I suppose when you fired that pistol you were quite sure that you wouldn't hit anyone?'

'Well', was the reply, 'of course you never can be quite sure, but I am an experienced shot and was reasonably certain'.

'Well', said Charles, turning to go on with his work, 'don't do it again or I shall have to gate you'.

It was the cheerful custom of Loders and The Rousers to come out into the Quad on Sunday evenings and demonstrate the sonorous qualities of their horns and hunting-crops. When Charles felt that the noise was passing the bounds of decency, he would stroll out of his rooms, pipe in mouth, and the expression of his face, without a word spoken, would promptly restore Sabbatical calm.

Sometimes, after a College celebration of exceptional conviviality, he would order men to their rooms. If anyone seemed disposed to stay and argue the point, Charles would calmly take him by the nape of his neck and the seat of his trousers and push him through one of the ground-floor windows; or, if the reveller was from another college, deposit him in the street. Those incapable of locomotion he would carry upstairs (one such was a famous heavy-weight rowing Blue of fourteen stone), undress and put to bed—not forgetting to remind the delinquent suitably of his lapse next morning. Once, it is said, he turned on the revellers the hose which the firemen had brought to extinguish a bonfire in the Quad.

His position in the Senior Common Room was equally outstanding, although among the older Dons there was, no doubt, some criticism of his unconventional methods. In Tommy Strong, with his impish sense of humour, hatred of dogma, ritual, fuss and sentimentalism, and sincere affection for the young, he found an ideal chief—one far more congenial than he might have expected to find in so ecclesiastical an institution.

Traditions of his peculiar humour still linger in the Senior Common Room—such, for instance, as his definition of Haverfield's prayer. Haverfield, a celebrated archaeologist and historian, used to come into the Cathedral very late for the Sunday Service and remain on his knees in preliminary devotion for the shortest possible time. One day in the Senior Common Room someone asked for suggestions as to the form of prayer which he used on these occasions. Charles's suggestion, 'Save Jock!', easily held the field. When, later on, the length of the prayer seemed to have become somewhat extended, Charles amended his suggestion to 'Save poor old Jock!'.

A favourite exercise of his humour was the application to his friends and relatives or acquaintances of the most ridiculously appropriate names, titles, or similes, generally struck out on the spur of the moment with the most delightful effect.

Once A. E. Housman came to lecture on a characteristically arid theme, the Latin spelling and pronunciation of Greek names. The lecture went on for a long time, consisting largely of quotations from a Continental scholar called Snihatta, and the seemingly interminable repetition of the same words with endings varying by a single letter, such as *Ennian, Enniam*. Before the speaker had finished, Charles's massive form was reclining in helpless boredom on his companion's shoulder. When the end came at last he pointed to the lecturer and said. 'Do you know what he reminds me of? . . . The man who measures you from the fork at the tailor's'. Those who remember A.E.H. (whom Charles greatly admired both as scholar and poet) will recognize immediately the ludicrous aptness of the simile.

It was not surprising that Charles's sayings and doings grew into a regular saga at Christ Church and that his occasional public utterances, such as his speeches at the annual 'Censors' Dinner', were eagerly awaited and long remembered. But to his friends at Oxford he was much more than a loyal co-worker and witty companion. They respected his scholarship, which, although he valued exactitude and mastery of detail, sought out instinctively those elements which reflect and make for humanity, while his wide knowledge of the modern and medieval literatures of England, France and Italy added greatly to the scope and value of his classical learning. There was a largeness of soul about him which could not be ignored, and his friendship with such men as George Gordon, J. S. Phillimore, W. P. Ker, Gilbert Murray and Robert Bridges, and the pleasure he took in inviting to dine in his rooms and at the high table visitors from outside Oxford and from foreign countries, brought him into touch with the larger issues of University Life and of the world beyond.

After his death George Gordon wrote of him: 'He should have been immortal. We lighted our little rushlights at his torch, and when we felt womanish and academic, we went to him for a great breath of manliness and life.'

He did not take much part in University politics, and hated anything to do with money. When finance was under discussion at the College Council he would cross his arms on the table and lay his head upon them, with groans of unspeakable boredom. But if a subject moved him his attitude was uncompromising, however strongly friends might be ranged against him. When, in November, 1911, a motion came before Convocation which he believed would ultimately result in the total abolition of compulsory Greek at Oxford, involving a disastrous severance between humanity and science, and a fatal blow to the great Oxford and Cambridge tradition of a liberal and general education for all as a condition of entry, he fought the proposal with all his strength, although it had the strong support of his friend, Gilbert Murray, and the Chancellor of the University, Lord Curzon.

All through these years Charles stuck steadily to his work at Oxford, sometimes complaining that the spring had passed without his having heard a nightingale or seen a young rabbit or a fledgling. Now and then he would steal an afternoon and evening for a long walk over the Berkshire downs, and many of his old pupils still remember his bathing parties in the Cherwell on sultry summer nights.

But it was in vacation time that his personality blossomed most fully. He played cricket a few times for his beloved Sussex in a classic team which included C. B. Fry, K. S. Ranjitsinhji, E. H. Killick, George Brann, P. Latham and A. E. Relf, getting a few useful wickets and once making 80 against Worcestershire; but County cricket was too formal and competitive for him, and later he confined himself to tours with the Authentics and Free Foresters and a round of what he loved best of all—country-house cricket. In such games he was a man whom any captain was glad to have on his side—a bulwark in adversity and often able, when the issue was doubtful, to turn the scale by sheer force of personality.

There were many country houses at which he was a welcome guest. Particularly he loved old houses with old traditions and singularities which refused to give way to the demands of fashion or material progress. Nowhere was he more welcome than at Hagley, the Worcestershire home of the Lytteltons, whose chief, the eighth Viscount Cobham, was his staunch ally. George

Lyttelton, who from about 1904 was one of his closest friends, has written an account of Charles's visits to Hagley, which I will not venture to spoil by adaptation.

Charles was very soon completely at home at Hagley, and became as one of the family. His visits depended on no set invitation given or answered; he just appeared, if possible timing his stay to avoid Sunday, in well-founded mistrust of his self-control under a country sermon. Hagley is a place which might appear to some to possess considerable drawbacks. The Black Country is close by and sends forth a blight over the land when the wind is in the north, and the rain often falls with pitiless concentration when the wind goes to the south. The house itself was built before comfort was much thought of, and had changed little. Unless you were in luck your general impression might be that there was no light, natural or artificial, that the bells didn't ring, nor the clocks go, nor the windows open, nor the taps run. Charles liked it all the better for these eccentricities, which he professed to regard as a completely suitable setting for the occupants.

He strongly disapproved of any change, especially in the direction of comfort, even if it was only a new wallpaper in the bathroom; and to the last he used the original rain-water tap which filled the bath with a rank liquid, coloured by the Dudley flues. He always insisted on having the same room, giving as his reason his fondness for the works of Bishop Pilkington whose volumes line the walls immediately outside. A further reason alleged was that his night's rest was only assured if he knew that no sound louder than the cough of a Worcestershire sheep could come and disturb it. In the hall downstairs there are numerous plaster casts of well-known Greek statuary, which were parodied by Charles with such merciless felicity that their original characters have vanished, and to none of us will Hermes ever recall anything but the bowler-hatted umpire with the bails, and in place of Bacchus we shall only see 'Warner from his bath declaring the innings closed'.

He at once made firm friends with everyone from my Father—to whom Charles with affectionate irreverence gave the name of Chob, later in common though clandestine use—down to my sister Nan's infant John, who saw, with the unerring instinct of three years, that here was the last word in bears, horses, tunnels or playmates in general. Chob's vein of cheerful pessimism in comment and prophecy concerning the prospects of himself, his family, and his friends, had a special appeal for Charles, and he was untiring in his manoeuvres to acquire and store up examples of it, hailing his frequent successes with open hilarity. Their relations remained undisturbed by

the discovery announced at an early stage in the friendship by Chob;
'Charles Fisher, I believe, regards me as a person of great singularity
and is always on the look out for manifestations of it.' Charles would
always seek out Chob's company at Lord's, and, when allowed by
the hostess, at the Hagley dinner table, after which he would triumphantly declare that Chob was 'no older and as good company as
ever'. My father on his part was frequently heard to ask whether
Fisher (Christian names are a modern growth) was not coming soon;
a question not often asked by a host about a guest over thirty years
younger than himself.

The diverse interests of the rest of the family Charles followed with
humorous solicitude, and invested them all with a thick atmosphere
of nonsense, so that the effect was produced that each of us was
gravely playing a part solely for his benefit as audience.

It was at Hagley, I believe, that Charles learnt to play golf. He was
a scandalous golfer for one of natural advantages. He hated all the
paraphernalia of the game, the caddies, the etiquette, the solemn jar-
gon, and made a point of ignoring it all. I can see him striding to the
first tee, pockets stuffed with re-made, re-painted, second- or if possible third-hand balls, all doomed to early oblivion in gorse, pool or
wood. He preferred no caddie, but if one was forced on him, a bag
of heterogeneous instruments, few and rusty, was handed over,
Charles watching closely for any signs of surprise or derision on the
boy's face. Then the drive off—a lurch of the great shoulders com-
prising all known golfing errors, followed by a wholly problematic
flight on the part of the ball. A favourite shot of his was a far-
travelling scurry at right angles to the proper line. 'It's all right,
Georgie, I've opened up the hole for you,' was the shattering
euphemism employed to his partner on such occasions. Similarly, 'I
know the shot you like', braced his partner to prepare for a desperate
brassie shot from long grass instead of the expected easy approach.
A complacent murmur of 'Poetry' signalized the rare co-operation
of hand and eye, perfect flight and direction. He would always play
in a foursome if he possibly could, as providing more company and
fewer opportunities of exposure; if there were any odds he would
be much intrigued with the manipulation of the bisques of his own
side or in attempting by unceasing bluff and gibe to stampede his
opponents into the misuse of theirs. I do not think he ever improved
much. Once, in response to my inquiry after his progress at Hayling
Island, the oracular answer came: 'The Committee have their eye
on me,' but whether with a view to honorary membership or sus-
pension I never found out. He could no doubt have been a good
player, but he disliked rules and dogma in all things, especially in

games; and golf, unless begun in the nursery, is exacting in this respect. It is impossible to picture Charles, text-book in hand, eradicating his faults in a lonely corner of the links!

His keenness to win games was much less than his enjoyment of them, which was immense. But he saw through them and over them and knew exactly their place and value. He was at all times a great walker. One of the best times I ever had with him was a week at the Lakes. We set out from Hagley, greatly stimulated by Chob's tragic forebodings. Charles maintained that the gist of Chob's parting advice as to his recently sprained ankle was, that though hill-climbing was obviously dangerous, a still nastier wrench attended a fall on the level, while most disastrous, because most unexpected, was to turn your ankle while standing still—but that I suspect was *ben trovato*. The lakes were at their best. The inns were empty and we had samples of every kind of weather on a background of searching rain. Charles was thoroughly characteristic. He refused to take more forethought than is required for a walk to church. He scoffed at any suggestion of a ruck-sac. 'We're not going into the wilderness; hot water laid on at every corner.' He had no stick, no nails in his shoes (Burberry slip-ons, as Caryl called them, going off and on without unlacing), and an ordinary suit of the familiar blue flannel. He paid no attention to the map. He seized it from me from time to time, but merely in order to acquire a few more melodious and mouth-filling names to roll over his tongue. That done, the map would be handed back crumpled, sodden with rain, wrong section uppermost. 'Keep to the high ground, then we can't go wrong' was his reiterated conviction which experience was powerless to shatter, and his profound content so long as he was under the winds and open sky was infectious enough to obliterate the importance of such things as rest and regular meals. But he was very suspicious of 'under-catering', and the morning visit to the village shop to lay in provisions for the day was not lightly treated.

The other piece of daily ritual was the dispatching of half a dozen postcards to various friends; many will remember these cryptic communications, of such character with all their terseness that getting one was like a lightning glimpse of Charles himself. Sometimes it might be a telegram, especially when careful timing would point the jest. I cannot resist giving an instance. Once at Cambridge there was an athletic meeting between the University team and the Racing Club of France. I was down to put the weight against one Parouskovopoulos. At the height of the proceedings they were interrupted by the arrival of a telegram for me bearing the pathetic appeal, 'Have mercy on my boy', signed 'Parouskovopoulos *père*'. The Oxford stamp betrayed the perpetrator, but in any case no one but Charles would have instinctively divined that 'My boy' was fifty years old and nineteen stone in weight.

The only other thing Charles was at all particular about was the choice of books, one apiece to read in the evening. He brought a contemporary best-seller, mainly on the grounds that he saw no chance of finishing it unless he had no other with him. I was merely obvious and brought a *Wordsworth*, but Charles read it most of the time, and the best-seller was not only never finished but was left behind to 'shock Canon Rawnsley'. Charles would produce Wordsworthian fragments at frequent intervals in a walk, much as De Quincey for days together used to repeat the words 'And Belshazzar the King made a great feast to a thousand of his lords', just for the pleasure of their sound. I remember one or two fragments.

> *So have I, not unmoved in mind,*
> *Seen birds of tempest-loving kind*
> *Thus beating up against the wind,*

was a favourite. Also some resounding lines from 'To Joanna', telling of Hammer-Scar and Loughrigg and Glaramara and Silver-how, and an imperial stanza of Matthew Arnold's which I had not seen or heard quoted by anyone else:

> *Thin, thin, the pleasant human noises grow,*
> *And faint the city gleams;*
> *Rare the lone pastoral huts—marvel not thou;*
> *The solemn peaks but to the stars are known,*
> *But to the stars and the cold lunar beams;*
> *Alone the sun arises, and alone*
> *Spring the great streams.*

But this was his limit as regards length. How he would have hated to think there was any danger of his being pictured as a spouter of poetry from mountain tops!

Many were the sayings of 'Chob' which Charles delighted to circulate among his friends—mostly so outrageous as to be immediately detected as apocryphal; such, for instance, as Chob's alleged description of W. G. Grace: 'The dirtiest neck I ever kept wicket behind' (for Chob had played county cricket in his day); or Chob's comment to the lady who had hurt herself when a very venerable Hagley chair had collapsed beneath her:

'There are many women's backs, but only one chair like that.'

In almost every house which he visited the same atmosphere was produced—as though each of the inmates 'was gravely playing a game for his benefit as audience'. When he visited George Lyttelton at Eton, this practice was even extended to His Majesty the King, for Charles's bedroom commanded a magnificent view of Windsor Castle. When late for breakfast, he would plead that loyalty forbade him to rise before the King had put a leg out of bed, for which event he watched discreetly from his pillow. A sudden peal from a distant belfry was the King ringing for his boots, and the noisy escape of steam from a South-Western Railway engine produced a sympathetic reference to His Majesty's asthma.

In one country house where he was a prime favourite, the head of the family—not less beloved than Chob, but not less irreverently known to Charles and his friends as 'Old Pott'—was a famous shot, one of his chief titles to renown being that he had sometimes had five pheasants dead in the air at the same time, one from the first barrel of his first gun (then handed to the loader to be reloaded), two from his second gun, and two more from the first gun reloaded and handed back to him. Charles was himself a worse than indifferent shot ('Another one gone to rot', was the legendary comment of the head-keeper when his umpteenth mis-hit flew away over the beaters with a leg down), and he delighted to extract from Old Pott—if possible at dinner on the first evening of his visit—an account of this feat, with an explanation why, to achieve it, only one barrel of the first gun must be used, so as to facilitate quick loading, the whole skill of the feat being in the loading, *the mere shooting being quite easy*. One or two of the guests would be in the secret, but they would only be able to guess that the game had begun from the extraordinary solemnity with which Charles would look at them across the table and the scarcely perceptible flicker of amusement in his eyes; nor did the sobriety of his demeanour allow his host to perceive that he was playing a part in one of Charles's favourite pastimes.

To Old Pott's children Charles was like the most delightful of elder brothers. Many were the fantastic games which they played together, many the impromptu concerts after dinner, when he would sing *Twankydillo* and *The Golden Vanity* and join uproariously in the choruses. For many years there were very few

vacations during which he did not pay Old Pott a visit, and a
stream of postcards and telegrams kept him present in spirit when
he had left. Once when he was staying in the house, the
younger members of the family were engaged in a competition
which involved the sending of a vast number of picture cards
through the post from different offices within a given time. In
order to help them, he took the slowest train which he could find
to his next port of call—in Devonshire—and got out at every
station to post cards back to them, each containing a neat and
appropriate little rhyme. For example, on a card almost entirely
occupied with a photograph of Windermere, there was squeezed
into one corner this couplet:

> *No room! Let us, for both our sakes,*
> *Be thankful for the size of lakes!*

In the Christmas vacation Charles often joined a reading party
of undergraduates which his much-loved friend, Lionel Smith of
Magdalen, son of A. L. Smith, Master of Balliol, used to take to
Bamburgh. The rough Northumbrian coast, fierce seas and
towering old castle, appealed to some deep-seated and powerful
instinct in him, although characteristically he always referred to
Bamburgh light-heartedly as 'the place where you buy socks at
the grocer's', and he was never known to express his feelings for
it more enthusiastically than by saying, after his return to Oxford,
that the cry of the Old Etonian in Tom Quad was a poor exchange
for the wailing of the Northumbrian sea-birds. It was characteristic, too, that he persuaded Mrs. A. L. Smith to lend a cook for
the occasion in order to 'prevent under-catering'. Many events of
these reading parties passed in due course into the Charles Fisher
Saga, as, for example, the solemn entry into the dining-room one
morning of Mr. Quelch (Charles's much-valued scout from
Christ Church) carrying on a tray a golden half-sovereign.
'I think this is yours, sir.'
'Where did you find it, Quelch?'
'In your shoe, sir.'
Some part of the Easter and summer vacations Charles nearly
always managed to spend abroad. His classical interests drew him
often to Italy, and he stayed at Florence several times to study the
Medicean Codex of Tacitus's *Annals* when he was working on the
text for the Clarendon Press. But he travelled widely through

Italy on foot, often with Lionel Smith, visiting Rome, Ravenna, the Apennines, Venice and the delightful cities of Lombardy, Tuscany and Umbria, and passing over the border into the Tyrol and the Dolomites. France, too, he knew well, going more than once to walk in Normandy and Brittany in the spring, and particularly rejoicing in the countryside and old cities of Provence. Spain he seemed to find less congenial, feeling something barren in the splendour of its mountains and something repellent in the character of its people. Possibly he would have changed this view had he explored the south of the Peninsula, which I do not think he ever did.

To give some idea of this phase of Charles's life I will quote the account of another friend who made a tour with him in 1908 through the Tyrol to Verona and Venice and back by way of the Dolomites:

Charles was an ideal walker. He carried no stick or other paraphernalia, and wore nothing more romantic than a grey felt hat, flannel suit and ordinary golf shoes with hobnails, so that the rucksack on his back was the only sign of any purpose more remote than a stroll round his native parish. Some say that in more civilized country he would take nothing but a razor and a toothbrush, as shirts, socks and handkerchiefs could be thrown away when dirty and new ones bought. He did not make a fetish of distance, but was content with an ordinary twenty- to twenty-five-mile day, involving a good two hours for lunch and rest, and a halt for tea (or some equivalent) between 4 and 5 p.m. Moreover, he had no itch for sightseeing; no lust for the picturesque lured him from the allotted path; walking was to him simply the most agreeable mode of travelling, and travelling the ideal way of seeing life. And life meant not churches or pictures, though these meant a good deal, but people and customs, the humours and beauties of the countryside. He loved mountains, but not climbing, which he used to say took him too far away from the ' ἔργα ἀνθρωπων ', and he had, what all good travellers must have, a romance for his food. Indeed, this was one of the few subjects on which we ever differed, for I, being young and inexperienced, was sometimes in favour of a sandwich lunch which would make us independent of the high road. But Charles, if the map showed a promising inn at an appropriate point, would override my suggestions with a genial firmness which there was no escaping. Every day which brought us nearer to Italy our meals became richer and more romantic. What a morning it was when we bought our first kilo of green figs from a swarthy matron

c

at Brescia! Half the joy of Verona was to sit at a little round table on the Piazza and dawdle over '*uccelli*' and *Val Policello*; while at Venice the exploration of dining-places was pursued with no less devotion than the hunt for Tintorettos. On the third day we had the good fortune to discover the Café e Birreria del Sport just beneath the Rialto Bridge, where they fry cuttle-fish with genius, and from that time our pilgrimage was at an end.

I only remember Charles being out of temper once during our three weeks of adventure, and then the cause was culinary. It was after a very tiring and not very successful day, on which we had descended the Stelvio and tramped on a cold, wet evening up a narrow valley behind the Ortlers to Santa Caterina. We had never been hungrier or studied the menu with more picturesque antici-pation. Choice was difficult, but all three voted immediately for '*Minestrone Asciutto*', which figured on the list. 'Dry soup', we said—'that is to say, a thick, or even very thick, soup, well fortified with stock and seasoned with vegetables, spiced, too, in all probability, with a sprinkling of grated cheese. Nothing could be more suited to our condition. We ordered it and sat in blissful expectation. An exclamation from Charles aroused us. We turned, and saw the waiting-maid stagger in behind an enormous dish of steaming macar-oni. This was the only time I ever saw Charles angry. At Vittorio, I remember, he swallowed without wincing a thin, tasteless broth, in which the pale heads and feet of defunct chickens were dismally islanded; but *Minestrone Asciutto* was too much for him. He explained in laborious Italian to the astonished waitress how misleading her menu was. He pointed out that the words used could not possibly imply the thing they represented: that, in any case, the thing was one with which no self-respecting Englishman could be expected to begin his dinner. It was fully five minutes before the humour of the situation dawned on him. From that moment, *Minestrone Asciutto* became a byword, about which his peculiar humour played with unflagging delight.

It was Charles's humour which had first endeared him to me. Some years before I first met him, someone told me of a friend who had been away on a cricket tour. His family, not having heard a word of him for three weeks, were just beginning to feel anxious, when they were reassured by receiving an unsigned telegram 'when last seen the old champion was moving in a north-easterly direction'. The friend was Charles and from that moment I determined to make his acquaintance as soon as possible. When I did so I found the anecdote delightfully characteristic. Charles was not, I think, a witty or brilliant talker, or a great *raconteur*; nor was he in any sense a buffoon, yet his fun depended largely on the cunning use of catchword or patter. But he never used patter merely to amuse. With him it was the natural expression of his exuberant enjoyment of life and of that genial irony which he employed to defend his ideals. At the time of which I write, the word 'monkey' was in high favour with him. He would use it impartially as a term of endearment, eulogy or contempt, as a noun, verb or adjective; it formed the basis of innumerable similes, the starting-point of countless flights of fancy. He would apply it in reverence to Dante, in contempt to some over-cautious professional batsman, in affection to some favourite friend or relative; and always with the most imperturbable gravity. I remember his last words to me as we parted at Toblach and he shook me solemnly by the hand, were:

'Goodbye, my dear boy, and remember, the monkey is a noble animal.'

Another favourite exercise of his fancy was to hit off the characteristics of people whom we met upon our travels by coining nicknames for them or applying to them the names of celebrities or common friends. At the hotel at Ponte di Legno, for instance, our neighbours in the dining-room were instantly christened Caruso, Dr. Hornby and the King of Spades. In every case the name hit off the main features of the personality with such astonishing aptness and at the same time suggested to the imagination so ridiculous a contrast, that it delighted the mind like a successful epigram.

I have another picture of him in which contrast played a most engaging part. From Dezenzano we hired a boat to take us out to Sirmione. I think we chose the boat solely because of the absurdity of the boatman. He was a miserable, wizened and apelike creature, clothed in baggy brown trousers and a wasp-like, black-and-yellow jersey. During the whole of the journey Charles set himself to draw out the whimsical little creature. That noble animal the monkey figured in every sentence, though the application was never clear to our boatman, and the contrast between the latter's impish and innocent vivacity and Charles's massive and ironical calm kept us in fits of laughter.

A foreign walking tour with its variety of incident and freedom from restraint was ideally fitted to bring his humour into full play. And this quality of his was invaluable in tiding us over the untoward incidents with which such a tour is sure to be beset.

I recollect a terrible three hours in the train from Breno to Brescia at the end of a grilling day spent trudging down luxuriant lowland valleys, where, in the rich river meadows, beneath sharply rising rocks that seemed to beat back the sunshine in our faces, swarthy women and children were piling the second hay crop on to small ox-wagons. Just as we were beginning to recover from the fatigues of the day, the train stopped at some holiday resort evidently in high favour with the inhabitants of Brescia. In a second our third-class carriage (one of the loose-box variety) was filled with chattering and perspiring Italians. Every seat was taken two deep, and men and women stood, laughing and gesticulating, on the toes of the sitters. The steaming air was filled with the smoke of the most lamentable tobacco. It was pitch dark and the carriage was lit only by the tiny flicker of an atrocious oil-lamp. On Charles's toes there stood a particularly voluble Italian, in a red cummerbund, with a peculiar straw hat balanced on the back of his head, who shouted incessantly: '*Oh, che bel panorama!*' and cackled with laughter, which was echoed shrilly by the whole of his admiring party. In after years we hardly ever spent an hour together without the phrase: '*O che bel panorama!*' coming to Charles's lips.

In all his enjoyment of travel, his deep and constant love of literature played a great part. In this field, too, he had ranged widely and with the most pleasantly robust appreciation, so that he was always ready with an apt quotation whether from Borrow or Carducci or Wordsworth or Mr. Jorrocks or the *Lunatic at Large*, and every quotation came with absolute spontaneity to his lips, the unforced recollection of a pleasure deeply felt and unconsciously stored up in the treasure-house of memory.

The same delightful buoyancy marked his appreciation of the classics. In this there was a spring of inexhaustible freshness, so that even in the most familiar fields of controversy he was always susceptible to new ideas and new impressions. I remember, for example, how keenly his interest was fired by my description of the fury with which Thoby Stephen used to maintain the thesis that Virgil is a greater poet than Homer, and the *Aeneid* a greater poem than the *Iliad*. The subject lasted us half a morning, and he often recurred to it as though the paradox appealed peculiarly to some vital element in his constitution; and indeed, though he could not bring himself altogether to accept the paradox, this preference for the patient, sane and exquisitely human art of the Roman poet did seem to correspond with some basic article of his intellectual creed.

At the foundation of all Charles's tremendous gifts of mind and character one was always conscious of the solid sanity of John Bull. I recollect that at Venice he steadfastly refused to admire the exuberance, richness and tremendous vigour of Paul the Veronese. The spark of vulgarity which lurks even in the most brilliant compositions of that master, seemed to outrage his sense of propriety. Yet his taste in art was catholic enough. Long before Augustus John became fashionable a delightful drawing of his hung just by the door of Charles's sitting-room at Oxford, 'to make the young Etonian sit up', as he was fond of explaining.

His favourite among all the Italians was Piero della Francesca, whose gravity of form and intensity of feeling seemed to touch him more closely than the work of any other painter. When in London he spent many a half-hour contemplating the great 'Nativity' and 'Baptism' and many of his Italian tours were largely devoted to the pursuit of Piero's work.

The mention of London brings to one's mind pictures of Charles's family life. His father died in 1903 and his mother moved soon afterwards to 25, Cheyne Walk, just east of Oakley Street; later, when the size of the family was reduced by marriages, to a smaller house in Phene Street two hundred yards away. Mrs. Fisher was one of those wonderful Victorian women in whom remarkable physical beauty was matched by a spiritual beauty no less intense. In her youth she had been a favourite model of G. F. Watts, and though she was now sadly lamed as a result of an accident and worn by the cares of a large family brought up on very modest resources, her essential beauty of form and character was still undimmed. Five or six of her children were generally to be found in Cheyne Walk, and great was the joy when William and Charles could be there together. They met all too seldom during these years. Charles would visit William in his ship whenever he could and had acted as best man at his marriage to Cecilia, daughter of the Vice-Provost of Eton, Francis Warre Cornish, whose exquisite scholarship, so delightfully mated with his wife's witty and wayward genius, extended a gracious influence far beyond the limited world of Eton and Etonians. William generally managed to get to Oxford when the United Services played the University at Rugby football, and many will remember the sight and sound of those two huge figures towering above the crowd and shouting against one another in friendly rivalry.

The two brothers were remarkably alike both in form, feature and character. Charles looked like a sailor and was an enthusiastic member of the Navy League. William had been on the point of sitting for a Winchester scholarship when the chance to enter the Navy offered itself. He still kept up his classics and had been known to hold long conversations in Latin with a Yugoslav

Professor at Split. Both had depths of character realized only by the very few who were allowed to penetrate their singular reserve, and even this reserve was hardly realized because of the geniality and zest for life which their whole personalities so warmly radiated. Both had the same brilliant humour and when they were together each stimulated the other to extravagant efforts. For their mother they had an unbounded devotion and reverence, which they delighted to disguise in a cloud of ridiculous banter, calling her by the most absurd nicknames, crediting her (to the amazement of those who did not know this peculiar family convention) with the most fantastic and outrageous adventures, and surrounding her with an atmosphere of chaff, the very extravagance of which was really a measure of their deep affection and respect.

No one meeting Charles in London or at Oxford at this time could have felt that his was anything but a useful and happy life, yet as the years passed his friends began to realize that it was not capable of exercising to the full his great abilities and energy. He contributed irregularly to the *Saturday Review* and *Oxford Magazine*, but although he wrote a clear and distinguished prose, it could not express his whole personality; he was too reserved and too fastidious. He could write verse as concise and pointed as a Greek epigram, yet, so far as I can trace, only one short original poem by him survives:

The Doctor

I hear the carriage-wheels along the drive;
The trees that border it, they say, are green:
But I shall never pass that way alive.
It is the doctor's carriage: he has been.

'A week to live, and probably no pain':
The sentence he so gently gave is grim.
Just at the door he looked at me again.
How strange! I always used to laugh at him.

In 1912, at the request of George Gordon, he delivered in the Examination Schools a lecture on Petrarch, which was published after his death with an admirable foreword by H.A.L. It is a learned, humane and comprehensive study, with occasional

flashes of Charles's characteristic humour. He knew Italian literature well and found much that was congenial in Petrarch's
humanism, his love of the Pagan classics and the integrity of his
scholarship. Dante, I think, appealed to him considerably less. Of
the English poets Wordsworth was perhaps his favourite, and he
had an unexpected fondness for T. E. Brown, shrewdly noting
that the short lyrics by which Brown is chiefly known in antholo-
gies are by no means his best work. The reasons for his love of
Brown appear clearly in the following extract from a lecture which
he wrote, though I do not know whether it was ever delivered:

> He had, it is true, great joy in life, and it was a sane joy, a larger
> and more acute joy, a more boisterous joy than Wordsworth's. But
> at the same time he felt the sadness that Wordsworth felt, and the
> sadness, as with Wordsworth, was more deeply embedded than the
> joy. . . . Various in his themes, full of surprises, volcanic, irregular,
> but above all perhaps even in his humour, sad. Of his poems he says
> in one of his letters: 'Like everything I have ever written they are
> for myself, to be murmured inwardly, a solace of a sort. No one will
> ever know anything about them. For greater effort I have no heart,
> no stomach.' . . . There is no poetic attitude struck, no professional-
> ism. His poetry is just an expression of the man and nothing more.

Another favourite was Hardy, whose fundamental sadness
seemed to echo some basic element in Charles's constitution, for,
in spite of his apparent light-heartedness he had a strong vein of
melancholy. More than once he expressed to friends his dread of
living beyond forty, and I find in a letter, which must have been
written before 1903 and seems to refer to his father's congratula-
tions on his birthday, the words: 'He knows as well as I do that a
birthday is a sad day, so no more of it'.

'This', he wrote in an essay on Hardy's poetry, 'so far as I can
interpret it, seems to be the Cosmic Scheme to which Hardy
clings. We must live in an ill-built house: though some of the
rooms are all right, the drains are bad and we have to rest satisfied
with the architect's apologies. He built it long ago and has long
since gone out of business, but he is very sorry.'

Very characteristic of Charles is his summary in this essay on
the development of poetical language:

> Let us distinguish three rough periods in English poetry. First there
> is the Classical period from which Wordsworth appeared. Words-
> worth wished for a plainer kind of language, but the language he

advocated was prim—the kind of language which one may suppose that Canons in residence speak with fluency. It is not mobile. It is stiff; a step onward no doubt from the traditional language, but as things worked out, though the language of living men, it was not a very living language. The New School have altered this. Language has become their servant. Each can deal in his own way with it. The emancipation started by Wordsworth has ended in complete freedom, and (some would complain) in complete licence. So it comes that the language of this poetry is not the traditional language of poets, Wordsworth's enemy, nor the spoken language of ordinary men, Wordsworth's friend. For them the language of poetry is the language of the individual poet. In the hands of the inferior man this individualism is mannerism, and mannerisms are bad. In the hands of the man of power this individualism is distinction. The language is full-blooded and idiomatic: it is a part of the man, and the man moves freely up and down it because it is his own. . . .

All this suggests that Charles could have made an admirable critic, but his nature was too positive to be content with criticism.

Had there been more prospect of absorbing work at the University, he might have been content to go on there indefinitely, but the headship of the College was closed to him because he could not accept the dogmas of the Established Church, and therefore was not able to take Holy Orders. Even in scholarship, where he was so fitted to excel, he was met with disappointment. The fashion of the day was for a picturesque and romantic approach to the Classics—particularly for a type of translation in which (as he once wrote in an article in the *Morning Post*) 'the translator triumphs at the expense of the translated', producing 'smart ephemeral' journalism, which gives little idea of the dignity and force of the original. Charles's taste was too refined, and his knowledge too thorough, to allow him to pander to these tendencies. One result was that, in 1907, when the Clarendon Press wanted a new translation of Tacitus, the work, for which Charles was so admirably fitted, was given to W. H. Fyffe.

All this inclined him to look for openings elsewhere than at Oxford.

In an undated letter to his mother (which begins characteristically: 'Just come out of Chapel, and a sermon by our oiliest Canon on pain'), he mentions an invitation to stand for Parliament for Isleworth, which he had rejected—though in terms which suggest that he did not regard a Parliamentary career as entirely

out of the question—and in 1909 he made a definite effort to find
another sphere of work. In that year the Headmastership of
Clifton fell vacant, through the transfer of David to Rugby.
Charles's work on the governing bodies of Westminster and
Christ's Hospital had given him a great interest in the public
schools and he decided to apply. William Temple was also a
candidate and was strongly backed by Bishop Perceval, who was
Chairman of the Governing Body. In due course the candidates
appeared before the selectors, when Charles was so strongly
pressed by Perceval about his religious opinions that after a time
he declined to answer any more questions. Unfortunately his
characteristic honesty had already given an impression of a
greater lack of sympathy with the religious point of view than he
really felt. No one who heard him read the Lessons at Christ
Church could doubt the depth and sincerity of his reverence for
the life and teaching of Christ, and he probably had a sounder
knowledge of theology than some of those who attacked him;
but now, when he was asked what his attitude would be in the
event of any strong development of religious feeling in the School,
he merely replied: 'I should not do anything to oppose it'. With
equal honesty, when asked what experience he had of teaching
boys, he replied: 'Eight days with the Lowest Form at Winchester', and roared with laughter. These replies lost him the
appointment, although in spite—perhaps because of—them there
was a strong minority for appointing him. One of his supporters, angered by Perceval's attitude, attacked Temple strongly
on something which he had written about Plato, and his candi-
dature also was rejected.

Two years later, when the Headmastership of Marlborough
fell vacant, Charles applied for the post. He was again unsuccess-
ful, a clergyman securing the appointment.

After these failures Charles was forced to the conclusion that
the highest positions in the public schools were closed to him no
less than the Deanery at Christ Church. But he had to endure a
still more grievous frustration. He had many friends among
women, both old and young. To the daughters in some of the
families where he was a frequent visitor he was like the most
delightful and affectionate of elder brothers; yet, so far as his
friends could see, he had reached the age of thirty-four without
any serious love affair. He had, however, for some years been

deeply attached to the sister of one of his closest friends, though he had never spoken of this, even to her, because his acceptance of the Censorship at Christ Church precluded him from marriage. In the summer of 1911 he decided that he would wait no longer. He spoke, and discovered that the attachment was mutual. But he soon found himself confronted with serious difficulties. He had long made up his mind that he would never continue at Oxford as a married man, since this would mean giving up the Censorship and abandoning his unique position at Christ Church, which was largely due to his intimate relations with the undergraduates, and could only be maintained by a bachelor living in College. On the other hand, after his failures at Clifton and Marlborough, he did not know where to look for a career which would enable him to offer his wife the kind of life to which he considered her entitled. In these circumstances he could see no near prospect of marriage, and as he knew that another man, for whom he had a great liking and respect, was in the field, he came to another of his sudden decisions and withdrew his claim. The decision caused him acute suffering, for it involved one whom he never ceased to consider the finest woman he had known and the only one with whom he could contemplate a partnership for life. But he was convinced that the course which he was taking would be for her greater happiness, and although, as he wrote to his mother, his withdrawal seemed to leave him nothing worth living for, he could not be induced to retract it. As a result, although none of his friends seem to have realized this, he became more and more restless at Oxford. He still liked his work there and knew that he was doing it well, but there is no doubt that from this time he was ready to accept any work providing opportunities of worth-while service which might be offered him.

War

In 1914 the call came.

When war broke out on 4th August, Charles was incapacitated by a sharp attack of phlebitis. As soon as he could walk he took steps to find out what active contribution he could make to the war effort. Chob was consulted and reported to have expressed the opinion that it didn't much matter what branch of the Services he chose, as he was sure to be killed almost immediately anyway. In the end, circumstances decided the question for him.

Neither the Army nor the Navy would accept him, for he was thirty-six years old and the soundness of his leg was questionable, and after considerable difficulty he succeeded in getting accepted as an orderly and interpreter, with the rank of Private, in a Red Cross unit which was to proceed immediately to France. There is some evidence that the Dean resented his decision to leave the College for non-combatant work at a time when many of the younger members of the staff were joining the fighting Services and the whole life of the College was being thrown into confusion. But for Charles the call was irresistible. He had for years been subconsciously longing for a life of action, and he could not bear to remain behind 'teaching the refuse' when so many of his friends were gladly risking their lives. Although he might have been paid for his services, he flatly declined this and even insisted on paying for his outfit. Nor, in view of the Dean's attitude, would he ask for more than the minimum amount of money from the College. 'Of course', (he wrote), 'all my money as Censor will go, and really I shouldn't mind if the rest went too. I quite see that I am doing Christ Church no good by going away, and I don't see why I should ask for more than that my place should be open to me when I return. So then the Salaries Board is quite free to use my pay for any other purpose—and I dare say there may be pinches elsewhere—and I shall feel no grievance whatever'.

On 6th October he wrote an uproarious letter to George Lyttelton:

> Any more for the *Skylark?* You will be amused to hear that I go to France at the end of this week or the beginning of next as an interpreter and orderly in the Motor Ambulance Corps. I am busy buying clothes such as the Stourbridge 'bus-drivers wear. I shall be prepared to carry you out of the trenches when the time comes and take any last messages.

He went down to Folkestone on 11th October and reached Boulogne on the 13th with a party consisting of a retired admiral, a medical student from Bart's, an Oxford friend and a number of chauffeurs.

He arrived in France at a crucial moment. During the first three weeks of October the Allied forces, of which the British formed part, had found themselves compelled by the fall of Antwerp to attempt the holding of a line running south from the sea along the river Yser (to which the much-worn Belgian Army was in process of withdrawal), through Dixmude, Menin, Lille and La Bassée to Arras. Attempts were being made to break through the enemy's line at Menin and Lille, and the Germans were desperately trying to regain the initiative which they had lost when their first rush towards Paris had been foiled. The attempts at Menin and Lille proved abortive and the Allies had to abandon these towns, but they retained Ypres. Here came into existence the famous salient in their ultimate line, which bent eastward round the town and then ran southwards through Armentières and west of Lille, La Bassée and Lens, making another curve eastwards below Lens so as to take in Arras. This line was to be the scene of much bloody fighting during the next eight months, the Germans, who were greatly superior to the Allies both in numbers and artillery, making strenuous efforts to break through along the Yser in the north and at Ypres, La Bassée and Arras. The attempts to break through the northern sector were foiled before the end of the month, first by the fire of the monitors sent by the British Admiralty to attack from the shallow coastal waters, and secondly by the flooding of the Yser region by the Belgians.

On the twenty-second the Germans attacked at La Bassée and Neuve Chapelle, to the south of Ypres. Here the line was held by the British who, on the twenty-eighth, were reinforced by Indian troops. The enemy gained some ground, but after about three weeks their attack was weakened by the diversion of some of their forces to assist in the attack on Ypres.

Meanwhile an assault had been launched against the French at Arras to the right (south) of the British line. This attack, though it destroyed much of the ancient town of Arras, did not succeed in dislodging the French.

The most serious of the enemy's attacks was that launched against the Ypres Salient on 21st October. This salient was held entirely by British troops with French territorials on their left. The fighting, which lasted for four weeks (until 18th November) is recognized as one of the most remarkable achievements in the history of the British Army. Between Armentières and the sea the Germans had 402 battalions as against the 267 of the Allies. They had at all stages an immense superiority in guns, and they staked all they had on the attempt to break through at Ypres and failed; but the losses on both sides were enormous, almost equalling the complete losses of North and South in the American Civil War. Whole British battalions practically disappeared. Among the officers there fell one divisional general, two brigadiers, a dozen staff officers, while eighteen regiments and battalions lost their colonels. It was an almost continuous and crazy mêlée in which units became hopelessly mixed, officers had to fling into the breach whatever men they could collect, and subalterns and N.C.O.s suddenly found themselves thrust into positions of vital responsibility. In such conditions the coolness and initiative of the British regular soldier made him more than a match for the iron discipline and fanatical courage of the German troops, greatly superior in numbers though these were.

Fate decreed that Charles, who a few weeks before was being pushed about Tom Quad and 'Peck' in an invalid chair, should find himself closely involved in these terrible events. From Boulogne he went first to Rouen, and then to St. Omer, about fifty miles from the line. By the 20th of October a hospital had been opened at Wimereux and wounded were pouring in. It was a depressing initiation. The men were worn out with the appalling strain of the first weeks of war, when they had been battling against such overwhelming odds. 'They look absolutely finished, like hunted animals', Charles reported; 'not a single man wants to go back to it again'. There were rumours, too, of trouble in the A.S.C. and of British prisoners having to be escorted by French troops. During the succeeding weeks Charles's ambulances—a convoy of thirty cars—were engaged in collecting wounded from various points. First at Hazebrouck, twenty-five miles from the line; then at the grim little town of Bailleul, twelve miles nearer; then at Nieppe, Armentières and Kemmel, almost in the fighting line at the southern end of the great battle for Ypres.

Bailleul was the unit's headquarters from 28th October until 20th November, and the closer Charles came to the scene of action the higher his spirits rose. On 1st November, after an afternoon under fire at Wulfenghen behind Messines, he wrote: 'I have changed my occupation for the better and life is now really worth living'; and on the 4th, when a fierce attack on Allenby's forces at Messines and Wytschaete was in progress: 'I have never enjoyed myself more'. Every night during these vital weeks the unit used to go up to the various dressing-stations immediately behind the line—and in those days there was no second line—and clear the wounded under fire. It was dangerous work, and a friend who saw Charles at Bailleul, where his immense form was blocking up the whole of the lower half of a ground-floor window in the main street, noted that he seemed to sniff the unattractive air of the town with approval for that reason. Now and then he had narrow escapes. A shell came down at his feet, burying itself without exploding; shrapnel and rifle bullets whizzed past his head out of doors and in the unit's mess-room. 'None of these incidents', said one of his fellow-workers, 'seemed to do anything but amuse him'. He was always up at six, generally after sleeping on the floor, and he hardly ever washed. 'I believe it is more wholesome to remain filthy', he wrote in a letter home; 'this I know is Hervey's opinion'. His letters and diary are full of vivid notes: villages packed with refugees, and horses nibbling the grass in the churchyards; a small French boy who sticks to him the whole of one day and can only be detached by being given two pears and told to take one to his sister; a group of Sikhs crouching before a golden wood in the sun and almost indistinguishable from it in colour; a van, with the legend in enormous letters 'THE WORLD'S APPETIZER', stranded in the middle of a field with shells bursting round it; a parson conducting a service for four aviators in a turnip field; French soldiers blazing away with their rifles at enemy aeroplanes, and the English Tommies sardonically advising them to fix bayonets; dead bodies being shipped off in packing-cases from Bailleul Hospital; the girl in the *estaminet* pouring out beer for the English Tommies and saying '*Santé*' to each as she hands him his mug; General Smith-Dorrien in the street at Bailleul addressing the few surviving N.C.O.s of the Lincoln Regiment who are crowding round him on the pavement; a French soldier with the calf of his leg blown away, drinking champagne; another, who had lost both his legs, unconcernedly smoking cigarettes. . . .

Coming back to his billet on 9th November, Charles finds the family weeping in the dark kitchen, having just heard that one of the sons, whose little children are living in the house, has been killed on the Ypres front. In the evening the children are still engaged in long prayers for the quick return of their father from the war. Charles offers to leave and find another billet, but he has already endeared himself to them and they will not hear of it. He is able to arrange transport for the widow to visit her husband's grave, but is refused leave to go with her owing to the pressure of work. She returns with harrowing stories of the condition of the Belgian Army, who are resting shoeless, bootless, and some with nothing but trousers. A few days later the unit moves from Bailleul to Lillers, some miles to the south-west, leaving the family, in spite of very jumpy nerves from continuous firing, determined, like so many others, not to abandon their home, and praying nightly to Joan of Arc to defend them from the Germans and for the eternal repose of the lost son.

Their failure at Ypres convinced the Germans that they would not be able to break through the Allied lines and that it would be more profitable to divert some of their troops to the Eastern front. Both sides now set about improving their trench systems, for the violent battles of the autumn had allowed no time for this, and a period of temporary stalemate ensued. But the Allies, although they were still very short of munitions and in no position to attempt a large-scale offensive, developed a system of local attacks in order to maintain the morale of their own forces and prevent the enemy from concentrating against any part of the line, or detaching too many troops for the Eastern war.

In December, Charles was involved in one of these diversionary attacks at Wytschaete, working till three-thirty one morning, then the whole of the day and night till ten next morning, and starting again at four in the afternoon. Four days later he was at Givenchy, where another British attack had begun. Streams of wounded poured along the road, so dirty that they looked as if they had been buried for weeks. A village had to be evacuated and the unit's baggage and the wounded removed under fire. One of the cars got stuck in a ditch when trying to avoid a shell-hole, and was only extracted after enormous labour. Then there was a summons to the advanced post at Givenchy. On the way one of the cars got smashed by a collision with a mule-cart and had to be towed. The unit arrived with all lights extinguished and did their job with bullets rattling against the telegraph posts and splashing at the feet of the stretcher-bearers. That 'day' lasted from two-thirty p.m. to eight-thirty a.m. and the cars came back peppered with bullets and shrapnel.

On Boxing Day Charles claimed to have carried the heaviest

man in the British Army out of the trenches on his back. He refused Christmas leave ('it doesn't seem worth while. Something might always happen when one was away') and wasn't depressed by a spell of atrocious weather, reinforced by Chob's reported prophecy that the winter was going to be an unusually long one. He was cheered by finding a stretch of country very like the South Downs, where all the pigs were white, and by a photograph of Robert Bridges and Walter Raleigh drilling on the New College cricket ground. Bridges was a faithful correspondent and sent parcels of chocolate and cigars. His French hostess noticed that Charles never kept such presents for his own consumption, but always distributed them among the wounded men under his care. When a man was too badly hurt to help himself, Charles would put a cigarette or a sweet straight into his mouth.

He was now the recognized leader of the convoy under the commanding officer, and on 9th January was appointed adjutant, which apparently gave him the rank of officer, though when questioned about this for official purposes, he would reply with a laugh that he had never been able to understand what his rank was.

On 22nd January the convoy moved to Hazebrouck, no doubt to be in readiness for the fighting which was expected to develop round the Ypres salient in the spring. At first his work led him southward and he had some exciting experiences, staying out the whole of one night alone, searching, in the end successfully, for a wounded man on the Mont Noir, near Bailleul. He never spoke of his adventures, and this one only became known to his hostess because he came home with his shirt deeply stained with blood. After a month or so it became clear that the convoy's main work in the near future was to be in connexion with the fighting round Ypres, and Charles persuaded the General to allow a section to be moved into the town under his charge, arguing that if the cars continued to ply from Hazebrouck, their destruction by the infamous roads was certain, whereas their destruction by shell-fire in Ypres was uncertain. The move to Ypres was made on 20th February, though some of the men concerned protested because no special provision had been made for their wives and dependants before taking them to such a dangerous position, for the town had been intermittently shelled by the Germans all the winter. The convoy found quarters with considerable difficulty on the outskirts of the town in and near the Asylum, which was being used as a British Hospital. Charles himself had to be content with a miserable room, entirely unfurnished except for a bed, and his first afternoon there was enlivened by a continuous stream of shells, many fragments of which struck his roof. For the next three weeks the bombardment steadily increased and he had much interesting work to do, visiting various points on the Salient, often under fire in the forward trenches. He enjoyed visiting the neighbouring villages, where until the war the English were practically unknown; now most of the children could whistle 'God Save the King' and 'Hitchy Koo', and some even knew both the words and tune of 'Tipperary'. Like the rest of the troops he revelled in the return of spring, noticing that the soldiers sang now as they came out of the trenches, which they never did in the winter. In his letters he records seeing a kingfisher on the Canal and the currant bushes coming out along the banks. The song-birds had all been driven away by the firing, the only music being 'of the home-made variety, "It is not mine," etc., and the chattering of magpies'. The first cowslip and brimstone butterfly are duly chronicled and one letter is written 'sitting within spitting distance of a primrose'. One afternoon he enjoyed a few hours' ratting in the Dickebush stream, and the approach of summer was heralded by catching practice with turnips for the benefit of the convoy's cricket XI, of which he was, of course, the mainstay. Much of his time was occupied in carrying the wounded from the Ypres Hospital to hospitals further from the line, for example those at St. Omer, Calais and Dunkirk. He had learned to drive now and often drove the cars himself.

Though his sleeping accommodation was rough, he was fortunate in being billeted for meals with M. Henri Vanderghote, the manager of the Ypres Gas Company. The house was a sad one, since the eldest son, a boy of eighteen, had been killed only a month before. But it was still full of children, for the Vanderghotes had two nieces staying with them in addition to four daughters, aged 21, 16, 13 and 10, and one son aged 8 called Joseph, a solemn child, whom Charles immediately nicknamed 'Augustus Cicero Cornelius Felix', and engaged to come to England as his secretary after the war. Charles's fondness for the children immediately endeared him to the parents, and in a very short time he had become an adored member of the family.

D

Chaque fois qu'avec son phlegme et sa bonhomie habituelle il venait dans notre cuisine [wrote M. Vanderghote] c'est a dire au moins dix fois par jour, il n'avait d'aise que lorsqu'il avait pu dénicher un des deux enfants, et par fois les deux ensemble; et alors ce furent des cajoleries, des badinages, des tours d'acrobats, de tambourinage a ne pas en finir, et tout cela accompagné de plaisanteries, d'imitations comiques de mots flamands qu'il prononçait à sa manière, ce que faisait rire les enfants et même les grandes personnes a se tordre; et, au dessus de tout, ce franc et bruyant éclat de rire qui avait le don de derider les fronts les plus assombris, surtout quand a ces moments là le bombardement allemand faisait rager dans notre voisinage.

He was equally beloved by the elder girls, whom he delighted to tease with light-hearted practical jokes and to bewilder by solemnly proposing the most fantastic activities for them in his most correct and laborious French.

Sometimes when the family was assembled at supper he would suddenly be observed standing, silently and solemnly, in the door-way, dressed in one of the girls' aprons and a hat with long white feathers, or in a lady's matinée coat with a baby's bonnet on his head—and always with his pipe in his mouth, and his pockets full of sweets for the children and cigarettes for the elders. When he was at home for supper he delighted to concoct a soup for the family, the recipe for which he pretended to guard with the most jealous care, except for the obvious fact that it involved a liberal injection of curry powder, sent from England. Generally he would bring three or four of his comrades from the convoy, who would act as his assistants, pouring in the ingredients and stirring the pot till they panted with exhaustion, while he encouraged them with characteristic gibes and exhortations.

It was no wonder that during the few weeks of his stay at Ypres Charles won for himself a very warm place in the affections of M. Vanderghote and his family, for they realized that the chief aim of all his fun and raillery was to help them to forget the bitterness of their recent loss and the horror of the doom which every day drew sensibly nearer to their native city.

The crisis began on 17th April, when the British opened their famous attack on the slight elevation of the earth's crust about three miles south-east of Ypres, which was dignified by the name of 'Hill 60'. This tiny eminence, slight as it was, had considerable importance because it commanded a wide stretch of the German trenches on the low-lying ground which surrounded it. It was now to be the scene of one of the most famous battles in our military history.

In anticipation of the British attacks Major P. J. Hanafin (now Colonel Hanafin, D.S.O.) had been sent with the 14th Field Ambulance and stretcher-bearers to the support trenches and warned to be prepared for 200 wounded. He amplified these instructions and prepared for 350. At about seven in the evening of the 17th, the British exploded mines on the Hill, secured the top of it and entrenched themselves with machine-guns. Next day at 7.30 am. the Germans made a strong counter-attack in mass formation. They reached the British trenches in spite of heavy machine-gun fire, but were driven back after severe hand-to-hand fighting. For three days the German attacks continued, for the position was vital to them if they were to hold their ground in the south-east sector of the Salient. A whole division was thrown at the Hill, which was exposed to heavy artillery fire and asphyxiating bombs from three sides. For four and a half days the defenders, hemmed in in a space not exceeding 250 yards by 200, went through hell, and at the end Hill 60 was still in their possession.

As a result, the estimated casualties were greatly exceeded. Before 7.30 p.m. on the 18th over 1,000 had been collected, and Major Hanafin sent repeated appeals to Divisional Headquarters for more stretchers and bearers. H.Q. sent out an appeal for volunteers, and Charles immediately answered the call. For three days and nights he worked incessantly, forming the highest opinion of Major Hanafin, 'who,' he wrote, 'stands out above all the men I saw and I saw some pretty good ones,' and he greatly admired many of the Major's men, particularly a little red-faced sergeant, who was 'never perturbed or pale, always fresh as the dew in spite of a succession of sleepless nights and great physical fatigue; always absolutely quiet and not only directing most efficiently, but working harder with his hands than anyone else— always pipe in mouth'.

Meanwhile, on 20th April, a heavy bombardment of Ypres began. This was plainly the forerunner of an all-out attack on the Salient, and Major Hanafin and his ambulances were moved, as soon as they could be spared, to a farm on the outskirts of the town. Then came something which marked a new epoch in land warfare. On the 22nd, at 6.30 in the evening, the Germans on the northern sector of the Salient launched their first gas attack. Nothing like this attack had ever been endured by any troops before and the effects were devastating. The gas kept close to the ground, filling even the trenches. Its effect was to choke the lungs with fluid and cause sudden and acute bronchitis, and those caught by it suffered horribly. With starting blinded eyes and blue swollen faces they struggled helplessly for breath. The natural tendency was to run back, which simply meant that the sufferer followed the deadly wave instead of letting it pass by him. The casualties of that first attack, against which, as it was totally unexpected, the men had absolutely no defence, were severe and horrible to see. Fighting, with heavy German bombardments, continued all through the 23rd, and at 3 a.m. on the 24th a second gas attack was launched. Still there were no instructions as to methods of defence. But many of the men protected themselves instinctively, though of course not adequately, by tying wet handkerchiefs over their mouths and noses.

The battle for the Salient raged for more than a month, with further gas attacks on the 2nd and 24th of May; with asphyxiating shells which were only less horribly deadly; with mass infantry attacks, and continuous artillery bombardment to which we had as yet no adequate reply. But the use of gas was never again so destructive as during the first two attacks, for the men were now provided with respirators, which gave fair, though by no means complete, protection.

All through these terrible days Charles was working continuously and with a renewal of the exhilaration which he had felt during the first days at Bailleul. The risks to be faced, the excitement of surmounting apparently insurmountable difficulties, the deeds of heroism and unselfishness which he saw on every side, and the feeling that he could throw himself unreservedly into the service of his suffering comrades, carried him triumphantly through exertions which those who saw him at work felt to deserve a dozen Victoria Crosses.

He worked straight ahead day and night, losing all count of time and meals, lying down fully dressed for an hour or two when there was a chance, and bracing himself for the next effort with a sluice of icy water from a tin. Men who did not know who he was, spoke of seeing his tall figure, beautiful and imperturbable as a Greek god, leading the stretcher parties day after day into the most dangerous places; and so apparently reckless was his driving over the shell-swept and shell-pitted roads that he became known as 'Mad Charles, the motor man'. All one night he worked with a score or more of badly gassed men whom he had collected into a churchyard, going from one to the other, doing what little he could to relieve their sufferings. Soon afterwards he was sent to evacuate wounded from an area which was so exposed that he could do no more than hurriedly select the most hopeful cases, and on his way to the clearing-station had more than once to deposit the men in ditches by the roadside till the violence of the bombardment had abated.

It was not long before he received another appeal for help from Major Hanafin. The officer in charge of the ambulances between St. Jean and Potige, a mile or so to the north-east of Ypres, reported that he could not get his vehicles past the fire-swept roads near those villages. Major Hanafin sent four wagons under one of his most experienced N.C.O.s, but the man came back in about an hour saying that it was impossible to get through the barrage of artillery and machine-gun fire. Charles at once came forward with one of his comrades and asked to be allowed to try. Hanafin replied that his orders were only to use Charles's ambulances between the dressing-stations and the central clearing-stations, but that, if the drivers wished to volunteer and clearly understood the risk, he would consent. In a few moments Charles came back to say that all his drivers had volunteered. He set off at once with four wagons and not only got through and brought back a load of wounded on that trip, but went on all that evening and all the ensuing night until the advanced dressing-stations and regimental aid posts were completely cleared.

By the beginning of June the German effort had spent itself. The British had been forced back, but the enemy's attack had failed, for we still held the Salient.

There followed some days of comparative quiet. Ypres was a city of the dead, a mere cluster of ruins and rubble. The Vander-ghotes had fled, their house and the adjacent Hospital razed to the ground. Charles's Headquarters had been evacuated to Poperinghe. But he did not follow them. There were rumours of further acti-vities, and he built himself an elementary wigwam outside a wood full of nightingales. At night frogs croaked and owls hooted, and for company he had the mice, which ran cheerfully in and out of his hut and over his recumbent body. He woke to the scent of beanfields in the sun and enjoyed the first bathe of the year—in a stagnant pond at the hedge-side.

Then, on 6th June, he went home for a week's leave.

THE NAVY

There was an inevitable reaction after the tremendous events of the Battle of the Salient. Weeks passed without any work of interest and Charles began to feel a desire for more responsibility than he could expect in the Red Cross, where the volunteer workers had, according to the prevailing regulations, to be put under the direction of subordinate doctor officers, many of whom had no experience of administration or the management of staff. He had the satisfaction of knowing that his work had received some official recognition, for he had been mentioned in dispatches by the Commander-in-Chief, Field-Marshal Sir John French, for 'Gallant and distinguished conduct in the field'—an honour which his comrades thought quite inadequate for his achievements but which he, with his usual humility, accepted as more than he deserved. Moreover, the Commander-in-Chief who had visited the convoy during the critical period, had written an enthusiastic letter to its Head saying that he had never seen such organization and such effective work carried out by civilians and would not have thought it possible had he not seen it himself. The first words of the recipient on reading this letter were 'This is all for Fisher, not for me'.

Charles now wrote to William telling him of his desire for a change of work, and the brothers agreed that he had best try for a commission in the R.N.V.R. as his leg might prevent his acceptance for the Army. At the end of July he left for home with a strong letter of recommendation to the Admiralty from Sir Arthur Lawley, the Head of the Red Cross in France, telling of his extraordinary work in the Ypres fighting and describing him as a born leader of men. Soon after his arrival he was offered a commission in the Grenadier Guards, which he refused as it would have involved a long period of training, (as he himself put it, 'The Grenadiers made no concessions for age or horsemanship'), whereas in the Navy he could get to work immediately. William was delighted to have his brother safely out of France with the prospect of a commission in his own beloved Service. Charles was equally pleased, though he professed to see himself 'spending the rest of the war in the North Sea with his head over the side'. Indeed, both the brothers were in high spirits, treating the whole affair as a tremendous joke, 'as indeed it is,' said Charles, 'until the whiting begin to nibble my bones'.

Charles went to Portsmouth towards the end of August for a very rapid training in H.M.S. *Excellent*. The change from his Red Cross work was startling. Many of the other men in the course had been wounded at the Dardanelles. 'All have eyes like hawks,' he wrote, 'and have seen a good many odd things. Their language is very picturesque and they regard me as a harmless lunatic.' He was immediately recognized, by his name and likeness to William, and came in for a lot of chaff from officers who had been examined by William in earlier days and now threatened to work off old scores on William's brother. After thirteen days (during which he had three examinations) he was summoned by wire to H.M.S. *Invincible*, a battle cruiser then refitting in Belfast, where he joined her on 6th September as Lieutenant R.N.V.R. By the beginning of October the ship was round at Rosyth, the base of the Battle Cruiser Squadron, where she was to be stationed for the next eight months, with occasional visits to Scapa, where William's ship, the *St. Vincent*, had her Headquarters, for gunnery practice.

Charles threw himself with enthusiasm into the new life. A ship, as he wrote to his mother, is a floating laboratory with a foreign language of its own as difficult as Greek, and he had much to learn. At first he felt 'about as much use to the ship as the Welsh goat is to the Welsh Guards,' and said that he had to be led about her like a blind man. But he made such rapid progress that within a few days he had a division of seamen committed to his charge and was given an important duty in the fire control of the main armament. To his division he was in much the same relation as is a captain to his company in the Army, being responsible for their inspection and general welfare. One of his functions was to look over their indents for clothing, and his first essay at this was cheered by the item: 'One pear drours'—'a good and delicate start'. He also had to censor correspondence and was amused to find the sailor an even greater letter-writer than the soldier and much more sentimental—a quality further proved by the sailor's 'fondness for the fruitier hymns'. He made an early attempt to arouse an interest in literature and sent to Oxford for some of his friend Sir Walter Raleigh's broadsheets. However, he had to admit that these were generally above the heads of the ordinary A.B., who couldn't be expected to take much interest in 'Lovelace with the original spelling or a passage from Meredith about a wood in Spring Time', and he soon had recourse to supplies of good novelettes. But the seamen's picturesqueness of expression delighted him, and he chronicled with joy such phrases as 'not worth a bloody hatful of crabs', describing something intrinsically worthless. Some of the boys in the ship he found 'absolute clinkers, humorous and sharp as needles'. He felt he would never be able to look at a slovenly Oxford scout boy again, though he admitted that the comparison was hardly a fair one, 'for the scout boy has little to rise to, while the stripling in the Navy has the vision of an almost indefinite ascent'. His job in controlling the gun-fire was a very vital one, having to be carried out on the fore-mast a hundred feet above the water line, and involving, as he described it, 'a steep climb up the monkey ladder for one of my build into a hole about large enough for a hedgehog'. In this 'hole' he had charge of the 'rate of change' instrument, by which the officer in control adjusts the constantly changing distances between his ship and the enemy, as the two steam rapidly towards, away from, or across one another. The job required quick observation and sound judgment and was of primary importance, for by transmitting the continually changing range correctly to the gun positions the officer could do a great deal to ensure accuracy of fire.

His fellow-officers were amazed at the speed with which Charles picked up the complicated technique of a great warship. In a few weeks he seemed to have mastered what most men take ten years to acquire.

The eagerly anticipated meeting between the two brothers took place not long after *Invincible* reached Rosyth. One morning, when *St. Vincent* was at Invergordon in Cromarty Firth, William, to his intense surprise, suddenly saw *Invincible* steaming into harbour. He dashed off at once in a picket boat and there was Charles, who happened to be officer of the watch, 'stalking the quarter-deck with a telescope under his arm and looking as if he had been a naval officer for about half a century'. William being a captain, had to be piped over the side, but when the two gigantic brothers confronted each other on deck, the stateliness of the ceremony completely broke down 'under the stress of family emotion' and 'the mariners were dissolved in helpless laughter'.

William was at this time the youngest captain commanding a battleship in the Grand Fleet. The prestige of his early achievement, his splendid bearing, courage, ability and leadership, made him a prince among his fellows, and his pride and delight in his younger brother's success were evidence of his own modesty and generosity, no less than of Charles's essential greatness. *Invincible* was so busy that they could not spend as much time together as they would have liked; but William fetched Charles away twice for golf, and was delighted with the praise of him which he heard on all sides. Charles was already quite at home in any conditions and any weather, and the captain of the ship said how he *relied* on him, who knew so well what shell-fire and danger were, to keep those around him cool and brave when the test came. 'He likes the ship and, by gum! the Invincibles appreciate him, too!' was William's concise summary of the position.

One night the brothers dined with the Rear-Admiral of the First Battle Squadron, who was deeply interested in Charles and urged him to dine again the next night. 'When Charles talks, of course everyone else is dumb', wrote William. But although his captain had given him leave, Charles felt that he ought to go back to his ship; so he and William sallied out together in regular lifeboat style, with oilskins and sou'-westers, through a howling gale and torrents of rain, in time for Charles to keep the middle watch (midnight to 4 a.m.), with no prospect of a meeting on the next day—the last of *Invincible*'s visit.

The winter and spring of 1915–16 were extremely trying for the British Grand Fleet, watching from Eastern Scotland for the badger on the opposite side of the North Sea which refused to come out of its hole. The men chafed for action and no one more than Charles. Very indicative of his state of mind were memorial notices which he wrote for the *Oxford Magazine* of two old pupils, Gerald Legge and Fleetwood Thorne.

> The Hon. Gerald Legge, Captain in the Staffordshire Regiment, was last seen on a slope in Gallipoli, wounded and cheering on his men, having refused to be carried in. There can be little doubt that he died where he lay.

Gerald Legge came to Christ Church from Eton. He never took his degree, for his interest lay not in books but elsewhere. He was one of those men who, with all the comforts of civilization at their disposal, yet rejected them all. Long dinners and London life he disliked, and was far happier collecting specimens for the Natural History Museum in Africa and the Outer Hebrides. As an ornithologist he made a considerable name for himself. Any time left over from this passionate pursuit he gave to the Boy Scouts in his native county, and no offer of a cheerful cricket match could lure him from his task. Then he was swept off to the war in Gallipoli. He wondered whether it was decent to take such delight in the squalor of trench warfare. But he cheered himself by the thought that he cheered others. Cheer others he certainly did, and he impressed them too, if they calculated the privations he had suffered and the things he knew and then reflected on the modesty and simplicity of his character.

F. Fleetwood Thorne, Captain and Adjutant of the 4th Battalion of the Grenadier Guards, having nursed one of his fellow-officers through the night at Loos, was afterwards hit in the head and might have saved himself had he not refused to leave a drummer-boy whom he endeavoured to carry in.

Anyone who saw Thorne casually would have noticed at once his anxious and almost diffident manner, but few would have guessed the resolution which lay concealed behind. He always seemed to himself to be confronted by difficulties beyond his capacity to bear, but, as on his last day, he always surmounted them all. At the beginning he was hampered by ill-health and was kept in England, to his great disgust. But when once set free he crowded much into the little space allowed him. His conscience was never kind to him and he did everything with all his might. The end, however bitter, is surely exactly right for one who always forgot himself in his efforts to do the best for others.

Charles was delighted when towards the end of the year he heard that Major Hanafin had been awarded the D.S.O.—'a gorgeous fellow'. His own feelings of frustration he relieved in a succession of characteristic letters to George Lyttelton.

Oct. 13—After this war I shall never want to see the dawn again however beautiful, though perhaps when and if there is a dawn at Haggles, I might bestir myself once more.

Nov. 25—Face I trust permanently discoloured by exposure to 'God's wind' (Bishops of London, Ely and Birmingham). I am getting very thin and could dive without contact through the left leg of your pyjamas. In fact after the war we might do a circus turn together to that effect—I on a horse with spangles and you in dress clothes with a whip in the arena. My God, when shall I wear a bowler hat again or get up in the morning at a reasonable hour without any duties to perform!

Decr. 28—A good damp day at Hagley, I expect, dispelled by rabbit pie, tobacco and logs from the ancestral trees, always excepting the largest leaning cedar tree in Worcestershire. We spent a fairly jovial Christmas. Catering and song. I had the morning watch and saw the holly tied to the tip of the masts, feeling all the while that I couldn't have done the job better myself. . . . There are about three of us in this ship who intend to take H.O. after the war. I should like to pass away in a Worcestershire Rectory, having helped to determine the date of Deuteronomy. . . . Routine here broken slumbers, stout and beer—sometimes separate, more often mixed. . . . When it is all over I shall go to bed for about five years and just get up for meals. This is not incompatible with my other resolve of becoming a Worcestershire divine.

Good Friday—A fine and constant rain in these parts, which may be good for the land but does no good to the sea. The Classics are going to be forced up the spout after this war, so it seems, tho' I don't know what harm they have done. If some of our Generals had been eminent classical scholars there might have been a case against Nepos and Aesop.

He was, as always, able to extract plenty of amusement from his surroundings, particularly from one tiny and intensely serious midshipman, whose confidences gave him unfailing delight.

'Between you and me, sir, I only really like a whisky and soda when feeling a little below par.'

'Privately and strictly between ourselves, there is a good deal to be said for the Roman Catholic religion.'

'Sir, I have been thinking of what is life's greatest tragedy—unrequited love!'

At 6.30 one morning the poor little fellow came up to Charles with a green face but a most impressive salute and told him that he might be sick at any moment. Asked what was the matter—he didn't know. What had he eaten the night before? Salmon. Was it tinned? He didn't know, but would inquire. 'And now,' wrote Charles, 'comes out the maturity of his views on life. He returned

and said that the salmon had been tinned, as he had asked the
mess-man, and he was very grateful to me for my suggestion. "I
am no longer uneasy, now that I can put my finger on the cause."
Another salute and he was gone.'

He was delighted with the gift of Robert Bridges' *Spirit of
Man*, though he thought that there was too much Hopkins in it
and that the passages from Aristotle were not the best that could
have been chosen. 'The old devil says very drily all that need be
said', was his admiring comment on the Poet Laureate's preface.

Soon after Easter Charles got a few days' leave and it was clear
that the long weeks of inaction were beginning to tell on him. He
spoke of trying to get out of the Navy into the Army. There
seemed such an endless amount to learn in the Navy: even the
midshipmen knew more than he did and he wanted a life of
action, not study. He felt that he was 'too old to climb up ladders
in a high wind and then squeeze through impossible holes at the
top'. He was thinking of his life after the war, too—making it
plain to some of his intimate friends that he would never go back
to Oxford. To William's wife, Cecilia, he talked of seeking some
wider sphere, where there was work of real importance and
difficulty to be done, as for example in South Africa or Ireland.
One evening when alone with his mother, he spoke quietly of
religion, leaving her with the conviction that, whatever he might
say about Churches, rituals and dogmas, he held deep down in his
heart the essentials of the Christian Faith. He had never spoken so
freely to his friends and family before, yet he left them with a
sense of foreboding—his sister Adeline Vaughan Williams with
the feeling that he did not really wish to survive the war, and
William with the realization that he was the sort of man who was
bound, sooner or later, to give his life for his country.

JUTLAND

At the end of May *Invincible* and *St. Vincent* were both at Scapa.
Charles had already decided to accept a commission in the Rifle
Brigade which had been offered him. William was doubtful
whether the Admiralty would allow the transfer after Charles had
been given nearly a year's training and become a really useful
officer, but he fully sympathized with Charles's point of view.
In the Navy he would never be able to rise to any higher

responsibility, whereas in the Rifle Brigade, though he would have to start as a subaltern, he might rise to almost anything. The brothers had two days' golf together ('huge haw-haws all the way round') and William had never known Charles in better form and higher spirits. He felt that he was seeing 'the real Charles emerge at last . . . not one single weakness and not one single enemy', and that the new Charles would never be content to go back to Oxford but would find some much wider sphere of action.

On the 30th William went over in his galley and fetched Charles for a walk on his favourite island. It was a perfect afternoon—hot sun, blue and dancing waters and the corn waving green in the fields. William knew every crofter on the island and their families (his 'constituents' Charles called them) and it delighted him to see Charles swapping yarns with the men, chaffing the women and playing with the children. The crofters stared open-mouthed at the two enormous brothers, so genial, brilliant, high-spirited and humane.

While they were still together—at about 7 p.m.—came a message that the Fleet was putting to sea. They went off at once in the same boat and William sent Charles on to his ship. The great moment, which all had awaited so long, had at last arrived.

About noon Admiral Jellicoe had been warned that the German High Sea Fleet might sail early next morning. By 10.30 that night of May 30th the British Grand Fleet was dashing across the North Sea in three sections—one under Jellicoe from Scapa, including the Third Battle Cruiser Squadron, *Invincible*, *Indomitable* and *Inflexible*, one under Jerram from Invergordon and one under Beatty from Rosyth.

The excitement of that wild eastward race against time will never be forgotten by those who took part in it. Eyes sparkled, faces beamed, and rumours and messages flashed to and fro.

By 11 a.m. on the 31st Jerram had joined Jellicoe. By 2.40 Jellicoe had news which convinced him that Beatty, who had a shorter distance to cover than the other two sections of the Fleet, should be in touch with the enemy by 4 p.m. He prepared for action and increased speed. At 3.55 Beatty reported that he was in contact with five of the enemy's battle cruisers, and the Third Battle Cruiser Squadron, which was already, owing to its superior speed, twenty-five miles ahead of the rest of Jellicoe's ships, was ordered to push on and help Beatty, who was desperately contending with superior numbers. Half an hour later it became clear for the first time that the whole of the German High Sea Fleet was out and a great battle inevitable.

At about 5.45 p.m. the Third Battle Cruiser Squadron came in contact with the enemy, well ahead of the rest of Jellicoe's fleet. They saw that Beatty was heavily engaged, trying to hold the German fleet until Jellicoe's ships could come up. The odds were against him and he had already lost the *Queen Mary* and the *Indefatigable*, though this they did not know at the time. *Invincible* was leading the Squadron, and Charles was at his post in the central top when three enemy light cruisers appeared, apparently cut off from their main body. The Squadron engaged them, and in nineteen minutes the leading German ship blew up with a tremendous explosion. The other two enemy vessels were some distance away, and, as it was very foggy, the Third Battle Cruiser Squadron left them for the large battle cruisers behind to deal with, and piled on coal so as to come up with the main enemy fleet, which could be faintly discerned through the fog. In less than half an hour *Invincible*, leading the British Squadron, was about 8,000 yards from the German ships, which included the *Derfflinger*, a much more powerful ship than herself. *Invincible* engaged her immediately, her very first shot striking *Derfflinger* rather high on the deck. Ranges were adjusted and the firing continued at the highest pressure. By now the ships behind on both sides were engaging with all their might and the cannonade was tremendous, *Invincible*'s shooting, which Charles was helping to direct, being so accurate that Rear Admiral Hood who was commanding the squadron sent a message through to the Gunnery Commander, Charles's close friend, Commander (now Rear-Admiral) Dannreuther: 'The firing of the *Invincible* is excellent. Keep it up as fast as possible. Every shot is telling'.

The message was transmitted by voice pipes all through the ship, and the excitement grew higher and higher, more and more jubilant. For the *Invincible* had as yet suffered only negligible damage and it seemed that at any moment she might put *Derfflinger* out of action. Commander Dannreuther, who had passed the Admiral's message through to Charles, saw him a minute or two later in his little 'hedgehog hole' working his instrument and transmitting his directions, his eyes sparkling and a smile on his lips. Then, at 6.34 p.m. a heavy salvo landed in the middle of the ship. Huge tongues of flame burst out of her sides, and with a succession of terrible explosions she broke in two. In a few seconds nothing was left to mark the last resting-place of the mighty cruiser and her one thousand and twenty-six British dead, but a pall of black smoke in the sky and two huge sections of battered and twisted metal towering up out of the glassy water.

Charles had not lived to be forty.

The Chivalry of the Sea

(Dedicated to the memory of CHARLES FISHER, late Student of Ch: Ch: Oxford)

Over the warring waters, beneath the wandering skies,
The heart of Britain roameth, the Chivalry of the sea
Where Spring never bringeth a flower, nor bird singeth in a tree:
Far, afar, O beloved, beyond the sight of our eyes,
Over the warring waters, beneath the stormy skies.

Staunch and valiant-hearted, to whom our toil were play,
Ye man with armour'd patience the bulwarks night and day,
Or on your iron coursers plough shuddering through the Bay,
Or neath the deluge drive the skirmishing sharks of war:
Venturous boys who leapt on the pinnace and row'd from shore,
A mother's tear in the eye, a swift farewell to say,
And a great glory at heart that none can take away.

Seldom is your home-coming: for aye your pennon flies
In unrecorded exploits on the tumultuous wave:
Till, in the storm of battle, fast-thundering upon the foe,
Ye add your kindred names to the heroes of long-ago,
And mid the blasting wreck, in the glad sudden death of the brave,
Ye are gone to return no more.—Idly our tears arise:
Too proud for praise as ye lie in your unvisited grave,
The wide-warring water, under the starry skies.

ROBERT BRIDGES

June, 1916

JOHN COLLIS SNAITH

John Collis Snaith

THREE OR FOUR afternoons every week between the years 1930 and 1937 a tall, gaunt middle-aged man, with very thick steel-rimmed spectacles, used to walk from the Hampstead Garden Suburb to the Garrick Club, where he had a cup of tea, without sugar, and some dry toast and butter, studied the financial papers, sometimes played a rubber of bridge and then walked home again. In summer, when the weather was fine, he would vary this procedure by spending an occasional afternoon at Lord's, where from the pavilion he watched the cricket with the critical attention of an expert. He seldom opened a conversation, though he was courteous and self-possessed when spoken to, and would on certain subjects express himself with a humorous ferocity—for example, the absurdity of erecting a statue to the Duke of Devonshire in Whitehall, or of the law, which, for a nominal payment of seven shillings and sixpence per annum, conferred upon the dogs of London certain privileges in respect of its pavements that Society at large had, for some little time past, ceased to claim. At intervals he would retire and give himself a shot of insulin, for he had been a diabetic for about fifteen years. In appearance he resembled a hungry and rather diffident eagle, and there was something about his walk which suggested a slow left-hand bowler beginning his run up to the wicket. This was John Collis Snaith—a name fairly well known to the reading public of the day, for he had, during forty years of authorship, published thirty-five novels, most of which had enjoyed comfortable sales in England and even more in America. He had been happily married for eighteen years, losing his well-loved and devoted wife (Madeline Armstrong, a niece of Dame Nellie Melba) in 1931, and when he died of accidental insulin poisoning in 1936, he had by judicious investments accumulated a fortune of over £40,000.

But his real life had ended thirty years before, and it was only a shadow that shuttled so unobtrusively four days a week between the Hampstead Garden Suburb and the Garrick Club.

John Snaith had been born in 1876 at 45, Lamartine Street, Nottingham, the eldest child of Joseph Dawes Snaith, owner of a small wholesale paper business in the city and a gypsum mine—or plaster-pit, as it was called—a few miles away. Joseph Snaith was a good-looking, smartly-dressed man, who by his reserved manner and carefulness in money matters gave the impression of being better off and more efficient than he really was. He had married Elizabeth Walker, member of a family well known in the lace trade, whose handsome face and figure, fine taste in clothes and unusual choiceness of speech earned her amongst her friends and relations the nickname of 'Queen Liz'. Neither she nor her husband had any interest in literature, but Joseph Snaith had one passion which was to have an important influence on his son's life. He was a devotee of cricket. Before coming to live in Lamartine Street he had played regularly for the village of Plumtree, and as soon as he settled in Nottingham he became a member of the Nottingham Commercial Club, which was largely run by the famous cricketing family of the Dafts. Joseph Snaith believed in giving his children a good education to enable them to make an early start in the world, and Jack and his two brothers and one sister were all sent at six or seven years old to the best private school in Nottingham, that belonging to the Misses Hipkin of Shakespeare Street. From there Jack went, at the beginning of 1885, when he was just nine, to the High Pavement School, in the heart of the Lace Market just behind the Unitarian Chapel. The School, which was famous for its sound commercial education, had been founded in 1787 by the wealthy Unitarians of Nottingham, who were mostly lace manufacturers and took the best of the boys into their counting-houses in due course. The lace industry was closely connected with the Continent, and much attention was given to the study of French and German, although neither Greek nor Latin formed part of the curriculum. More important for little John Snaith was the emphasis laid on the teaching of English. The boys were well grounded in history and given some introduction to the works of great English writers. Every year a play of Shakespeare, one or more of the Waverley novels, and poems by contemporary writers were carefully studied, long passages having to be learned by heart and recited in school. On speech days plays, or parts of plays, in English, French and German were performed by the children, and there was a careful study of grammar and of the origins of the English language. All this part of the school's work appealed strongly to little John and he very early developed a fertile imagination and an extraordinary command of words, his essays and compositions being often passed from hand to hand and read aloud in class. The school had no playground, its two long rooms standing, as they still do, one above the other on the almost precipitous slope which looks across the railway from behind the Unitarian Chapel, but twice a week the boys, dressed in scarlet Garibaldi coats, were marched by a drill sergeant from the Lace Market to the Castle Green for physical training, a sight still remembered by many inhabitants of the ancient city. This lack of playground did not, however, discourage Jack from the development of his inherited passion for cricket. At about the time when he entered the High Pavement School the Snaith family had moved from Lamartine Street to a roomy red-brick house (Number 68) which Joseph Snaith had built in West Bridgford Road, almost opposite the entrance to the famous Trent Bridge cricket ground. From this time onward Jack was one of a band of boys who played regularly on any convenient piece of waste land which might be available, particularly on a stony triangular patch almost under the shadow of what is still known as 'George Parr's Tree' from the frequency with which that Nottingham hero's famous leg-hit came rattling among its branches. When Parr died in 1891, two years after John had left the High Pavement School, a branch of the tree was placed upon his grave in Radcliffe churchyard. The 1880s were the Golden Age of Trent Bridge cricket, for Nottinghamshire won the County championship in 1883, 1884, 1885, 1886 and 1889, and numbered amongst its legendary heroes besides George Parr ('the Lion of the North') such mighty men as 'Old' Clarke, Richard Daft, Alfred Shaw and Mordecai Sherwin, first of the great modern wicket-keepers.

In the last decade of the nineteenth century Nottingham was a city well qualified to stir the young imagination. Built on a rocky height above the broad river Trent, its streets and surroundings showed a remarkable blending of the Old and the New. Overlooking the city from a precipitous cliff 130 feet high was the famous Castle, built by William the Conqueror, dismantled, after successfully withstanding many an assault, by the Parliamentary leader, Colonel Hutchinson, and finally burned down by the mob during the Reform Bill riots of 1831. Hard by was the site, still called *Standard Hill*, where Charles I raised his banner in 1642 calling on all good subjects able to bear arms to attend him.

In the middle of the city was the ancient market place, reputed the largest in England and covering an area of five and a half acres. There was still held every October the famous three-day Goose Fair, an orgy of prizefights, shooting alleys, freaks, fat ladies, magic mirrors, haunted houses, coconut shies, flying machines and roundabouts, with Bostock and Wombwell's travelling menagerie as its crowning feature. No one who saw the last night of the fair will ever forget its flaring lights and the uproar of squibs, ticklers, squeakers and hurdy-gurdies, with the youth of Nottingham winding in and out of the dense crowds in long sinuous lines, hands on shoulders, singing, shouting and playing on rattles, mouth organs and every kind of instrument which ingenuity had devised for the devastation of the human ear.

Wealth and poverty jostled each other in Nottingham. There was the Park with its spruce villas and elegant gardens, homes of the industrial magnates, for the city had long been the centre of the lace and hosiery industries, and now two great pioneers were creating, in Boots, the cash chemists, and the Raleigh Cycle Company, new Nottingham industries of world-wide fame. In sharp contrast were the squalid slum areas of Sneinton and the Lammas Lands, and the grim colliery villages at Eastwood and Wilford. But the old feudal life of England was still very much in evidence. In Bridlesmith Gate was an ancient house, said once to have been a palace of King John, who had hanged twenty-four boys under fourteen years old as hostages on the Castle Hill. Lord Middleton's huge and florid sixteenth-century mansion of Wollaton, with its deer park, stately terraces and noble avenues, was on the very edge of the town. Colwick Hall, once the unhappy married home of Byron's Mary Chaworth, now a public *café* and restaurant, was only a threepenny steamer trip from Trent Bridge; and Byron's home at Newstead Abbey only ten miles away. At Clifton, adjoining West Bridgford, there was a maypole on the green, and the gouty squire drove the few yards to church every Sunday in a carriage and pair, with shining horses and liveried footmen. Belvoir Castle, which could be seen from the Castle Hill, was a favourite outing for Nottingham folk; and Sherwood Forest, with its legends and relics of Robin Hood, and the ducal palaces at Welbeck, Clumber, Rufford Abbey, Hardwick and Thoresby, lay a few miles to the north; while southward were Melton Mowbray and the great hunting country of the shires. The arts, too, had their legends. Byron's influence was strong, for he had lived in the city and nearby at Southwell, as well as at Newstead, and after his romantic death at Missolonghi his body had been brought to lie in state at the 'Blackamoor's Head' in Pelham Street. And Romance hung about the memories of two other Nottingham boys, who had died before their powers could reach maturity—Kirke White and Richard Parkes Bonington.

Little Jack Snaith absorbed all these influences as greedily as he did those of Trent Bridge, but their romance meant nothing to his father, who had no idea of keeping him at school beyond the age at which it was normal for Nottingham boys to seek employment in the commercial offices of the city. In pursuance of his conviction that boys should 'get out into the world early and learn the value of money', he removed his eldest son from the High Pavement School in June, 1889, when he was thirteen years old, and got him a job in the Midland Railway offices just opposite the present Midland station.

Jack must have been a singularly inept clerk, for his thoughts were generally far away from the offices of the Midland Railway. His caustic tongue, which spared no one, and swift bowling, delivered with a completely circular sweep of the left arm, had now firmly established him as leader of the band of boys who met for cricket on the patch of ground by George Parr's Tree. In winter, football and hockey were pursued with equal fanaticism; and about the year 1893 or 1894 he founded, in conjunction with Jesse Gray (afterwards a pioneer of Nottingham education and honoured by having one of the new Primary Schools established under the Butler Act called by his name), the Bridgford Athletic Football Club which is still prominent in League football as the South Nottingham Football Club. Jack was the first Chairman of the managing committee, and surviving members remember vividly his blistering comments on those who came late for the meetings ('the night shift', as he called them) or failed to pull their weight in the matches. But he was a silent, moody boy and

when not playing one of the games he loved led a solitary life,
fishing at Beeston Weir or wandering, with a book in his pocket,
about the high wooded banks and open heaths which bordered
the still beautiful Trent, for already literature was his passion.
Even at parties he would get into a corner by himself to read, and
in the evening his lean form was generally to be seen in the library
of the Mechanics' Institute poring through thick-rimmed glasses
over the novels of Fielding and Smollett or the tales of Scott and
Robert Louis Stevenson. It was then that he laid the foundation
of that immense reverence for the great creative writers of
the past which was to influence him so profoundly in later
years.

Neither his parents nor his brothers shared his passion for books,
or realized what strange ambitions were fermenting in his brain;
but his mother's mother, old Mrs. Walker, who lived only a few
yards away from 45 Lamartine Street, had long been conscious of
the unusual gifts of her eldest and favourite grandson. She was
now a confirmed invalid, confined to her room for long periods
by bronchitis and asthma, and her great delight was to get Jack
to read to her on Sunday afternoons, which he did with gusto,
commenting freely on what he read. One evening she said to him
'Jack, you seem to know so much about it, why don't you write
a story yourself instead of reading other people's?' The family
tradition is that Jack was fired by his grandmother's remark to
take a step on the verge of which he had long been hesitating. He
immediately set about a short story which, to his great delight,
was accepted for the Christmas number of one of the Nottingham
newspapers. I have not been able to confirm this, but it is certain
that within a year or two of leaving school he had begun work
on his first novel, the plot of which was gradually elaborated in
talk with young Robert Radford (later the famous bass singer
of Covent Garden Opera House) when the two boys walked
together each morning over Trent Bridge to their respective desks
in the city. Progress was duly reported to Grandmother Walker
on Sundays, but this was necessarily slow, for the boy's office
hours were long and in the summer cricket absorbed most of his
spare time. It was quickened by a fortunate accident. In 1894 he
broke his leg playing football, and the necessary period of inaction
enabled him to devote some weeks of continuous effort to his
writing. Even so the book took something like four years to

complete. Great was the excitement under George Parr's Tree when it was known that Jack's book had been accepted by a London publisher, Messrs. A. D. Innes & Co., of Bedford Street, by whom it was issued in December, 1895, under the elaborate title:

MISTRESS DOROTHY MARVIN

Being
Excerpta from the Memoirs of
Sir Edward Armstrong, Baronet,
of Copeland Hall in the
County of Somerset

Edited into modern English.

It was not surprising that the boy, with his slight experience of life and his literary enthusiasm, should have chosen a historical subject for his first novel, especially as he was beginning at a time when Stevenson had given the historical novel fresh life and popularity. But it was surprising that he should not have gone to Nottingham and Sherwood for his theme. Instead he turned to the West Country, which he had never visited, for his imagination had been stirred by what he had read of Monmouth's rebellion, and by long talks with a friend who came from Cheddar to visit his parents and who knew well the country round about Taunton and Sedgemoor. The book was a singular concoction, written (except for a few passages where the speed of the action ran away with the young author) in a style which R.L.S. would have condemned as 'tushery', for Jack's love of words led him into some distressing exuberances—'ponderation', 'bibaceous', 'inertion', 'besoddened', 'rememorate' being amongst the abortions of his pen. But the 430 pages were crammed with exciting incident, and the sequence of events was managed with a skill remarkable in so young a boy, whose formal education had ceased at thirteen. Moreover, although he had as yet little knowledge of human nature, he showed a distinct flair for the literary exploitation of character on more or less conventional lines, and in at least one brief scene there was displayed that intense emotional power which was to give to three of his later books an extraordinary significance.

Both in England and America (where it was published by

Messrs. Doubledays of New York) the tale met with a surprisingly good reception, considering that it was by a totally unknown author. In the Midlands the tone was set by a review in the *Nottingham Guardian* by John Macleay, afterwards for more than twenty years the distinguished editor of the *Liverpool Daily Post*, who called attention to the book's striking merits and predicted a fine future for its young author. After this its success in the Midlands was assured. It was more remarkable that several important London critics gave the young author a good word, including the *Spectator* and the *Academy*. The *Athenaeum*, on the other hand, condemned *Mistress Dorothy* as rambling and verbose beyond description, full of verbal anachronisms and carried out in a style based on reminiscences of *Robinson Crusoe* refreshed by a perusal of Robert Louis Stevenson and his imitators. Snaith never forgot the debt which he owed to Macleay for the good word which had launched his first book so successfully and given him encouragement to proceed on his chosen career. Nor did he ever forget the remark of another critic who observed that the author of *Mistress Dorothy Marvin* had evidently not had the benefit of a university education. He had long resented with some bitterness his father's refusal to let him stay at school, and this comment seemed to confirm his fears that lack of early education might prove a serious obstacle to the realization of his high ambitions.

The success of his first book made Jack Snaith a marked man—or boy—in Nottingham. People began to look with interest at the tall, carefully-dressed figure, with pale, gaunt face, straight black hair and slightly stooping shoulders, which stalked morning and evening along the West Bridgford Road. They would have felt something more than interest had they realized what wild dreams and aspirations were beginning to smoulder behind that serious façade. His position was strengthened by his growing reputation as a cricketer in that cricket-loving county. Just about the time his book came out he was made a member of the Notts Forest Amateurs, a club which had been in existence since 1879 and was well known throughout the Midlands and the North. There he met the great J. A. Dixon, who had been captain of the county team since 1889, and his two brothers—C. P. Dixon, several times doubles champion at Wimbledon, and F. J. Dixon, who was practising as a doctor in London. J. A. Dixon knew J. M. Barrie, who had been from January, 1883, until March, 1885,

on the staff of the *Nottingham Journal* and an enthusiastic attendant
at Trent Bridge, and got him to read *Dorothy Marvin*. Barrie was
interested not only because of the book's promise but because of
the author's growing reputation as a cricketer, and an interview
was arranged, when Barrie strongly advised young Snaith to go
on writing but not to undertake another book for two years,
devoting the intervening time to the study of Greek and Latin.
This advice, following the critics' reference to his lack of a university education, naturally impressed John, and in the spring of 1896
he began to study Greek with a young university graduate in
Nottingham, Cyril Shelbourne, afterwards a leading figure in the
educational life of the city. However, this scheme soon had to be
given up, for the long hours which he was working at the railway
office and the intensity with which he pursued his English studies,
made it impossible for Snaith to attempt so new and difficult a
subject with any hope of success.

In November, 1896, he was elected to a new literary society,
rather unfortunately called the *Nottingham Sette of Odde Volumes*,
which had been formed by the city librarian and included two or
three of the leading professors at Nottingham University College.
The first paper which he read to the Society showed that an important new influence had entered into his life. In the last few
months he had—perhaps on Barrie's recommendation—discovered George Meredith, who had just closed his career as a novelist
with three of his most controversial works—*One of our Con-
querors* (which he himself described as 'a strong dose of my most
indigestible production'), *Lord Ormond and his Aminta* and *The
Amazing Marriage*. For young Snaith the discovery was staggering.
Here was a blend of tragedy and comedy more moving, a romantic atmosphere at once more human and more poetic, than any he
had yet experienced, and a style compressed, flashing and pene-
trative, which seemed able to illumine the darkest recesses of the
spirit. It was not surprising that his first contribution to the Odde
Volumes dealt with Meredith, whom he acclaimed as the kin of
Cervantes, Fielding, Scott and Balzac. Fired with his new discovery, he forgot Barrie's caution and set about a new book (to be
called *Fierceheart the Soldier*) on which he meant to lavish every
ounce of power that was in him. He was still fascinated by the
romance of English history, and this time chose as his setting the
Young Pretender's invasion of 1745. His hero was Sir James Seton,

a retired general living in a remote house in Cumberland, a mild-mannered, uxorious, dandified little man of seventy-two, famous for the elaboration of his wigs and the charm of his manners, whose deeds at Blenheim, Ramillies and Malplaquet thirty years earlier had won him international renown. Indeed, it was said that had it not been for his stubbornness and scrupulosity, he might have held the position won by the great Duke of Marlborough. With him still lives his old and failing wife, to whom he has been married for forty-six years and for whom he entertains a chival-rous devotion, reciprocated by her with a passion of admiration never clouded except by the loss of her two elder sons, who had joined the Army with their father's encouragement and lost their lives in battle on the same day. Her one surviving child is a son, Tom, a handsome, dashing, romantic, lovable fellow, as obstinate as his father, who is in disgrace for kicking over the traces in London, where he has been squandering money at the clubs and gaming-houses and with the ladies of the town. The other member of the household is the General's niece and ward, Molly Appleby, who is engaged to Tom, a true heroine of romance, beautiful, candid, with a brilliant natural charm and infinite courage. Sir James Seton is a fanatic, and his dominating passion, which takes priority even over his love for his wife and son, is patriotism, a stubborn, unreasoning, quixotic devotion to the House of Hanover and the British Constitution. The Sancho Panza to this Quixote is the rector of the parish, the Reverend John Blount, a naïve, untidy, quarrelsome, tactless, warmhearted, blus-tering old bachelor, formerly chaplain of the general's regiment and his companion in many campaigns. The two meet nightly, to the disgust of Lady Seton, who dislikes Mr. Blount, to play chess and quarrel about the general's weakness with his son, whose follies Mr. Blount considers to be entirely due to his not being allowed by his mother to join the Army.

Upon this quiet household bursts the news of Prince Charlie's landing in Scotland. In spite of Lady Seton's tearful protests, the two old men set off quixotically together to offer their services to Sir John Cope, only to find that he has been disastrously beaten at Prestonpans. While examining the battlefield with professional interest, they are captured and brought before the Prince, where, to his rage and horror, the little general finds his son in high hon-our with the rebels, with whom he has thrown in his lot from convictions just as stubbornly held as his father's devotion to Hanover. The old man is so outraged that he endeavours to shoot his son on the spot, and swears that if he ever sets foot in Cumberland he will have him arrested and executed as a traitor. While Sir James is still under detention at the Pretender's Court at Pinkie House, comes a message to say that his old wife is dying. He and the rector give their parole and hasten back to Cumberland, to find that she has vowed to keep herself alive until she can take leave of her husband and son, and shows every sign of being able to do so. Her husband, with his stubborn, headstrong patriotism, insists, against the protests of his niece and the rector, on his duty to tell her the truth about her son, although he agrees that this will probably kill her. He goes up to her room to do so, while the two others wait in terrible anxiety below. In a scene of extraordinary tension, he fails. The words which he believes will kill his wife, stick in his throat. Something has now to be done to account for Tom's continued absence, for his father refuses to get him home to take leave of his mother. He therefore tells her that Tom has again yielded to temptation in London and been packed off on a long sea voyage as a punishment. When, however, she implores him to bring Tom back from the voyage to say goodbye to her, he refuses, as indeed he is compelled to do, and his dying wife, annihilating the devotion of six-and-forty years, sends him out of her room, saying that she will never see him again unless he agrees to bring Tom back.

The old general now retires to drown his sorrows, so far as he can, in Madeira, while Molly and the rector, without his knowledge, send a message to Tom bidding him, at any risk, to return to say farewell to his mother before she dies. The message reaches him, shortly before Culloden. He is captured and brought south under guard by the English Captain Wiseman after a splendid fight against odds in the bedroom of an inn where he has taken refuge.

He tries his best to persuade Wiseman to take him to London by way of his home in Cumberland, so that he may say farewell to his mother. But Wiseman is a man who thinks only of his own interest. He is soldier enough to admire Tom's fighting courage, but neither sentiment nor sympathy can affect him and he refuses. On the way south, however, Tom contrives to escape. Wiseman realizes his object and calmly diverts his troops to the Setons'

home in order to intercept him there. Tom, though wounded
and sorely weakened, manages to get through. The rector and
Molly smuggle him in to see his mother, thinking they have
eluded his captor. But Wiseman has, without their knowledge,
coolly watched the whole proceeding. When Tom enters his
mother's room, he creeps in behind him intending to arrest him
there. But what he sees and hears is too much for him; cold-
blooded cynic though he is, he is completely overcome by the
scene between the wounded son and his mother, who, on hearing
Tom's full story, forgives him, blesses his father for his effort to save
her from the knowledge of her son's disgrace and falls back dead.
The book ends with the lovers escaping, with the shattered Wiseman's connivance, in a smuggler's boat, blessed by the old rector,
who is more than half in love with Molly himself.

Fierceheart was a brilliant conception and gave the young author
excellent scope for the scenes of tense emotion of which his first
book had shown him capable. It was carried out with great
fertility of invention and a wealth of vocabulary, metaphor and
allusion which proved how much he had profited by his reading
during the preceding two years. Very remarkable—in a boy who
had had no formal classical education—were the aptness and
variety of his classical allusions, particularly those drawn from
Greek mythology and literature. These suggested that even before
his abortive attempt to study with Cyril Shelbourne, he had succeeded in puzzling out some of the great works of the Greek poets
and philosophers in their original language, and that already
Homer, Sophocles and Plato were beginning to have a profound
influence on his mind. But although the writing was much
cleaner and stronger than in *Dorothy Marvin*, the effect of his
Meredithian intoxication was in some ways unfortunate. There
were passages of rare force and poetic beauty, but others where
the dialogue seemed stilted and unnatural, and some scenes which
should have been moving and powerful, were obviously beyond
the young man's capacity, and missed fire.

The reviews were, on the whole, favourable, both in England
and America, although the London press paid little attention to
the book, with the exception of the *Athenaeum* which, while cen-
suring the young author for his loquacity and tendency to moral-
ize, praised his originality and strong imagination, and prophesied
that if he would cultivate a simple style and refrain from putting

his own observations into other people's mouths, he would yet achieve something considerable.

The sales were fairly good, although not nearly so good as those of *Mistress Dorothy Marvin*. However the publishers (again A. D. Innes & Co.) had given Jack excellent terms, and his consciousness of the great advance which he had made on his first book decided him to take the plunge, resign from the Railway Company and devote himself to literature. But he knew that with a stronger educational background and a greater mastery of his craft he could have made *Fierceheart* a far better book, and he began for the first time to realize the full wisdom of Barrie's advice. He therefore decided to put off further publication as long as he could and to devote a year at least to self-education, enrolling for a part-time course at University College, Nottingham, for the session October, 1897, to July, 1898. The lectures available covered subjects from which he was sure to derive very great advantage—Spenser and his contemporaries; Shakespeare's plays, with special attention to *King John* and *Hamlet*; Wordsworth and the *Essays of Elia*; the general history of the Tudor period; and courses on the History of Greek and English philosophy with special reference to ethics.

Even more important to him was the social side of the College life. He was still rather a solitary figure in Nottingham—his description of the hero of one of his later books as 'gloomy and dreamy when not merely formidable' no doubt had a covert reference to himself as a young man—but the publication of *Fierceheart* brought him new and valuable friends, the most important of whom in future influence was Frederick Carruthers Boon. Boon had won an open scholarship in mathematics to St. John's, Cambridge, but family circumstances had compelled him to come down after his first year, and when Snaith joined University College he was working there for his degree, teaching part-time at the High School to help in maintaining himself. He was a man of very wide interests and abilities, a most inspiring companion and the most loyal of friends. He brought back to Nottingham the Cambridge habit of simple hospitality, and many interesting men used to gather in his rooms of an evening, such as Samuel Corner, the first mathematical master at the High School, Benjamin Heald, afterwards Chief Justice of Burma, and Professor F. S. Grainger, head of the Departments of Classics and Philosophy at

University College. Grainger was a fine scholar who had been trained as an architect, and for his unusual combination of knowledge was chosen to edit Vitruvius's famous architectural treatise for the Loeb Library. He also wrote one or two books of considerable reputation in their day. Even more important to his work at the College were his wide range of knowledge and inspiring personality, for he delighted to give all that he had to the young men with whom he came in contact. Snaith was a regular visitor to Boon's rooms and learned much from his association during these formative months with such distinguished minds. With Boon, who went soon after 1898 to become a mathematical master at Dulwich, he formed an enduring friendship.

He also threw himself more readily than might have been expected into the undergraduate life of the College, and with the stalwart Jesse Gray helped to make a very light soccer team one of the best that ever represented it. The match in which (largely through the skill and dash of these two men at full back and half back) the College defeated the hitherto invincible Nottingham Park team, before a crowd of 3,000, on the Nottingham Forest ground, is still remembered.

Young Snaith also took a lively interest in the Students' Association, maintaining stoutly the Liberal traditions of his family, and causing much merriment at the mock election held by the Association in the winter by his caustic cross-examination of the Labour candidate on the Truck Act, which the candidate vaguely supposed to be something to do with the railways. He helped to produce a Christy Minstrel show organized by the undergraduates, writing many of the songs and skits himself, and he contributed to the College magazine, *The Gong*, a lighthearted review of *Hamlet*, treated as the audacious production of a youthful contemporary, in which he endeavoured good-humouredly to wipe off some of his own score against the critics.

All through the months of his university study he had been a regular attendant at the meetings of the Odde Volumes, speaking on journalism, on Byron and on Keats, and being chosen to reply to the toast of Literature at the annual meeting. His addresses always impressed those who heard them with their originality and force, and it seemed that his policy of self-education was on a fair way to success.

Unfortunately his financial position made it impossible for this

JOHN COLLIS SNAITH

pleasant student life to continue. Since he had left the railway office he had found it difficult to work satisfactorily at home. His father had resented his decision to sacrifice a safe job for the precarious career of a novelist, and it was difficult for him to bring his new friends to Bridgford Road. He had therefore moved into rooms at No. 11, Burns Street, kept by Sam Corner's sister, an exceedingly intelligent and well-educated lady, who was keenly interested in his work. But the new life was expensive and the receipts from his first two books were almost exhausted. It therefore became urgently necessary for him to cut down expenses and devote himself to remunerative work. He had for some time been working on a story (suggested by the College course on the Tudor period), in which he aimed to develop still further the intensity of emotion and characterization which had fitfully illumined *Dorothy Marvin* and *Fierceheart*. The main theme was to be the struggle for power between Thomas Cromwell and a northern nobleman, the Earl of Cardellan, a satanic figure of ruthless and unconquerable will, who owns an impregnable fortress on the Northumbrian coast, from which he plans and directs an international conspiracy with the object of overthrowing King Henry VIII and putting himself on the English throne. Cardellan lives, remote and unapproachable, with a few fanatical followers, including his meek and pious wife (whom he has never forgiven for her failure to provide him with an heir), William Brandon, his unacknowledged bastard, and Lady Katharine Carstairs, a beautiful, brilliant and unscrupulous girl, who is his mistress and with whom Brandon, not knowing the connexion between her and his father, falls in love. Snaith devoted the full and unrestrained force of his imagination to this tale, developing with a new intensity, in the character of Cardellan the vein of titanism which had flashed out here and there in his earlier books. The last scene, which he had sketched out, reached an almost maniacal frenzy. Cardellan lies dying in bed high up in the castle keep. His wife has just died in giving birth to the long-desired heir and the old man is dandling the new-born infant on his knees. The King's troops are approaching the castle and he has planned the escape of Brandon, with the baby and Lady Katharine, by a secret passage which leads to the sea, where a ship awaits them. He himself will meet death in his stronghold. Katherine is mad with jealousy and disappointment, for she had hoped to supplant the

F

weak and pious wife, becoming Cardellan's queen and the mother by him of the next King of England. The birth of Cardellan's son has robbed her of his love, and the love which she might have known for William has been frustrated by the disclosure of her relation with his father. The two are in the old man's room, and she persuades Cardellan to give her the child to fondle. He, though conscious that her love for him has turned to hatred, is driven by his overweening confidence in his own power to do as she asks. But her frenzy is stronger than his will. With clenched teeth and face vacant of all feeling, she fixes her gaze upon him and slowly and deliberately twists the child's neck until it is dead.

The book ends with the King's troops battering at the castle gate, while storm howls and lashes at the keep where Cardellan still lies fondling the dead child, with William Brandon at his side. Katherine comes in, cold and mocking, to say farewell. Brandon, who after a night of prayer and horror has come to regard himself as the appointed minister of God's vengeance, takes a burning brand from the hearth and gives it to Cardellan, who instantly applies it to the hangings of his bed. Katherine tries to rush from the room, but Brandon seizes her and holds her. She implores and struggles, choking with the smoke, and in her agony biting his hands till the blood flows, while the old man lies mocking at her through the torment of the flames. At last Brandon flings her on to the bed where Cardellan and the dead child are burning together, and rushes from the room, locking the door after him, to escape in the ship and dedicate the rest of his life 'to charity and the service of the world'.

Snaith never finished this book. There is no direct evidence of the reason for this, but in the light of later developments I think one can assume that the primary cause was a change in his angle of vision. The knowledge and experience gained during his year at University College had given him new ideas and ambitions, which historical romance could no longer satisfy. His mind was turning from the past to the present and future. He was becoming painfully aware of the immense problems, both social and spiritual, with which the rapid development of the industrial era was confronting humanity, and conscious of a growing desire to make his own contribution to their solution. He felt that he had the capacity for work worthy of this great ambition, but he knew that at present his experience and technique were not adequate for the task. For the time being, therefore, he must publish as little as possible, confining himself to work well within his scope, and just so much of it as might suffice to keep the wolf from the door. It was significant that in the *Odde Volumes*, according to the rules of which all members had to be known exclusively by pseudonyms, he chose the name of 'Potboiler'.

By the time the session at University College ended he had a potboiler ready. This dealt with the escape and pursuit of a prisoner from the '45 who is rescued by the heroine, daughter of the nobleman in whose stables he is temporarily imprisoned while being taken south by his captors for trial in London. The style and atmosphere of the book, which was called *Lady Barbarity*, derived from its author's recent study of the plays of Congreve, and some of the scenes, particularly those between the harebrained heroine and her cultivated, cynical father, would not have disgraced the dramatist on whom they were modelled. But on the whole it was—as Snaith himself well knew—a perfunctory performance. However, the *English Illustrated Magazine* bought the serial rights (December, 1898, September, 1899) and Messrs. Ward, Lock & Company, who had taken over the business of Messrs. Innes, gave him excellent terms, as did his American publishers, and the book sold well on both sides of the Atlantic.

This success launched Snaith with good hope on the next course of self-development which he had laid out for himself and which was to last for three years. During the winters he lived quietly at No. 11, Burns Street, reading and writing. Living was cheap, for he paid only a pound a week, and the one extravagance which he allowed himself was in his clothes, which he always chose with care and had made by a good tailor. He had almost given up football, which his spectacles made rather difficult, and his principal winter recreation was a game of chess in the evening. He talked much about literature with Miss Corner, who regularly criticized what he had written from the point of view of grammar and style. Sometimes he would read a chapter to a few friends who came to visit him. All this could, however, only supply part of the development which he needed. He needed also something to take him out of himself and expand his knowledge of and sympathy with his fellows. Here his strange passion for cricket came to his aid. Hitherto he had practically played only Saturday matches, though no doubt he had spent a good deal of time in practice and in watching at Trent Bridge. By 1899 his reputation had so much increased that he was chosen to play for the Colts Twenty-Two against the County, and on the Dukeries tour of the Notts Forest Cricket Club (an older club than the Notts Forest Amateurs) when the famous Yorkshire bowler, Bobby Peel, was a member of the side. For the Notts Forest Amateurs Club he took 43 wickets for an average of 12 and did the hat-trick against Leicester Town. In 1900 he played for Notts County against the M.C.C. early in May (scoring 21), and against the West Indies in July, scoring 18 runs and taking 4 wickets, and for the Colts on May 24-25th. His horizon now began to expand. He joined a London club called the Fireflies, which had an annual week at Skegness at midsummer, and played through most of June and August with another London club, the Incogniti, touring the West of England and visiting Cambridge. So that with the Notts Forest week at Skegness (where in one match he took 7 wickets for 12) he was fully occupied with cricket from the beginning of May until the middle of September.

In 1901 he joined the Druids, a club which had originally been entirely composed of Harrovians and had an annual week at Skegness immediately after the Eton and Harrow match. With this new club, the Fireflies, Notts Forest Amateurs, the Incogniti, Skegness and district, the Authors (for whom in the following year he took all 10 wickets for 32 against an eleven got together by that famous Harrovian, the Rev. E. Stogden) and J. M. Barrie's famous team, the Allahakbaris, 1901 was very fully occupied.

These activities brought him into touch with many men of various types, Old Harrovians and Old Etonians, Oxford men and Cambridge men, squires, authors, actors, artists, doctors, lawyers, land-agents, and parsons. The Skegness week of the Druids was always extremely hilarious. One long-standing event, for example, was a donkey polo match on the sands, for which all the children's donkeys had to be requisitioned. Some of the team were famous practical jokers and John himself was not infrequently their victim. With all this he fitted in surprisingly well. His quiet strength of character earned him general respect and he showed a gently bubbling humour under his cloak of reserve. The Dukeries Tour gave him a glimpse of the life of the great

English country houses at the end of the reign of Queen Victoria. At many the visiting team were lavishly entertained. At Clumber, the Duke of Newcastle's chaplain, a first-class player, led the home side. At Thoresby, Lord Manvers and some of his guests generally played, as did Sir Joseph Laycock at Wiseton Hall. At Rufford, Lord and Lady Savile, and at Welbeck the Duke of Portland, would come to the pavilion to talk to the visitors. With the Authors and Allahakbaris Snaith met Conan Doyle, E. V. Lucas, Augustine Birrell, Owen Seaman, A. E. W. Mason, E. W. Horn-ung, P. G. Wodehouse and other masters of his craft. All his cricket he took very seriously, whether it was for Notts County or the Allahakbaris. One friend who played with him records that he was the only player he ever knew to wear an M.C.C. cap; and another remembers how one Sunday in Barrie's garden, near Farnham, when the traditional match of Gentlemen (left-handed) against Ladies was being played with customary hilarity, Snaith smote Mrs. Barrie on the ankle with a fast yorker and was with difficulty restrained from claiming l.b.w.

Barrie thoroughly enjoyed Snaith's idiosyncrasies. It happened that while he was playing for the Allahakbaris an exciting account was published by the novelist and traveller, Hesketh Prichard (himself a fine cricketer) of an expedition to the forests of South America in search of a mysterious animal known as 'the Giant Sloth'. Barrie immediately invented a shy and formidable and even more mysterious animal, 'The Giant Snaith', about which he delighted to weave grotesquely appropriate fantasies in his slow, rich Scottish drawl.

It is not easy to estimate convincingly the real place which cricket played in Snaith's inner life. It was strange that during these all-important formative years he gave so much time to it and that he pursued it so long and so steadfastly. His knowledge of the game, both theoretic and statistical, was encyclopaedic, and to many of his friends it seemed that to become a first-class player was his principal ambition. Certainly during the summers of his stay in Burns Street no other activity was allowed to take precedence.

His cricket history was a curious one and gave E. W. Hornung, who often played with him for the Authors team, the idea for his description of Jan Rutter's cricket in *Fathers of Men* (published in 1912).

He made his name as a medium or slow-medium left-hand bowler, and on certain types of wicket had the power of bringing the ball in very quickly off the pitch time after time, just bail high, with a 'naturally unnatural' break from the off, which was fatal to second-class batsmen; but against first-class players there was a lack of variety, so that he was liable to be quickly mastered and rendered innocuous. His keenness was shown by the way in which, before his short, quick professional run up to the wicket he would pull his cap fiercely down over his eyes, making a kind of gash in his back hair through which the skin of the scalp showed. This keenness proved his undoing. Suddenly his bowling left him. In trying to cultivate a different type of ball so as to secure the variety needed for first-class cricket, he lost his natural length and spin, while his new ball proved ineffective, for it betrayed itself by a change of action and, moreover, was very uncertain in length and direction. His bowling never recovered from this setback but he suddenly came out as a fine forcing batsman and hit many centuries in local cricket. Later he consolidated his technique and became a solid and reliable opening or first-wicket batsman. He seems not to have been ambitious to become a county cricketer or he would have followed up more strenuously the promising *debut* which he made in 1900. On the other hand, I do not think he played purely for relaxation, or for the help which the social side of cricket could give him in expanding his knowledge of life and manners. Probably he felt the need of some strenuous physical activity to counteract the excessive intellectual and emotional strain which his creative work imposed on him, And there may have been a more subtle influence. In *Henry Northcote*, published in 1906, he describes how the hero, whose self-centredness and refusal to submit to the conventions and taboos of the herd had exposed him to all kinds of brutal and offensive reprisals from his schoolfellows, decides, since he is too proud to employ the methods of those whom he feels to be his mental, moral and physical inferiors, to avenge himself by outstripping them all in 'one of those stupid and unmeaning exercises', his contempt for which had been a potent cause of his unpopularity—Rugby football. This passage may be a sublimation—no doubt in a very extreme degree—of another instinct behind Snaith's curious devotion to cricket, the desire to show the Philistines that a dreamer and a mystic could challenge them in their own field.

Externally his attitude to the game was normal enough. In 1899, in addition to *Lady Barbarity*, he published a lively story called *Willow the King*, which has often been referred to as the best cricket story ever written. It relates to a cricketing family in the Midlands, not unlike the famous Forsters of Worcestershire, and the most striking character is the cricketing sister, Laura Mary Trentham, known as 'Grace' not only because of her uncanny skill at the game, but also for her flagrant unscrupulousness and the cunning with which she interprets the rules to her own advantage. The crisis of the book is a single-wicket match to which the hero (a mediocre player) challenges Miss Grace, the wager being her hand in marriage. When on the verge of an easy victory, Grace staggers her family, and the challenger, by knocking down her own wicket.

Willow the King had an importance for its author beyond its immediate popular success. It was his first attempt at a contemporary subject, and it showed him that he was well able to provide the lively characterization and atmosphere which such a subject needed, thus encouraging him greatly in his ambition to take his place in the great fellowship of Meredith and Hardy.

The period of apprenticeship lasted until the autumn of 1902. *Dorothy Marvin* was published by the *Windsor Magazine* in 1900 as a Christmas supplement and this with *Lady Barbarity*, which was dramatized and put on in New York—I do not know with what success—and *Willow the King* brought him in enough money to keep him for three years. By that time he was ready with two more potboilers. One, *The Wayfarers*, was published by Ward, Lock & Co. early in 1902. 'A blasphemous production', its author called it, for it contained a brilliant drinking scene in which his boyhood hero, Henry Fielding, played the leading, but not altogether creditable, part. Except for this the book was valueless. The other tale appeared in Arrowsmith's *Christmas Annual* for 1901. Snaith was by this time sick of writing potboilers and the story, which he was under contract to deliver by August 1st, had not even been begun a week later. None the less, it showed a technical mastery which made it the most effective of all his historical romances, although not on the same plane as *Fierceheart*. It was fortunate that he had at the back of his mind a subject on which he had begun work, or begun at least to think, two years before. This now took shape under the title *Patricia at the Inn*. It concerned the wanderings of Charles II after the battle of Worcester, and the scene was laid in a desolate inn on the west coast. The fugitive King's supporters have arranged that he shall come to this inn in disguise, and wait until he can be taken off in a ship by a desperate smuggler whom they have paid for the purpose. The King comes and gets engaged by the innkeeper as a servant, and to the same place come a Royalist peer, Lord Farnham, sorely wounded in the battle, with his wife. While they are waiting for the smuggler, the cunning and avaricious innkeeper recognizes Charles and sends for the commanding officer of the Parliamentary forces who are scouring the country in search of the King. There ensues a period of appalling suspense, while the innkeeper waits in anguish to see whether the smuggler or the Parliament men will arrive first, and whether he will be able to save his own skin and win the traitor's reward on which he has set his greedy heart. He has, of course, to keep his intentions from the King and the Farnhams. Charles realizes his danger and the innkeeper's duplicity, but he stays on dallying, jesting, and making love to Lady Farnham, while her husband lies in bed tortured by jealousy and physical pain. The innkeeper waits down below in an anguish of avarice and suspense. His ineradicable reverence for the King's person, the extraordinary effect of Charles's enigmatic personality, the fear of losing his expected reward if the King escapes, the horror of taking the reward of Judas if the King is captured, terror lest the smugglers arrive before the Parliament men, make him almost frantic. At last the Parliament men arrive, the inn is surrounded and they go upstairs to seize the helpless fugitive. But Lady Farnham, by a last desperate trick, makes them believe that her sick husband is the King and the disguised Charles her servant. With the officer's permission she sends Charles out to fetch something from her horse's holsters in the stable, and he passes serenely out to freedom under the very nose of the innkeeper, who is too dazed to give the alarm. By the time Lady Farnham's trick and Charles's escape are discovered, the unfortunate man's mind is so unhinged and his spirit so broken that he submits almost with relief to being hanged over his own inn sign.

By the beginning of 1902, Snaith was ready to settle down to what he intended to be the first stage of his real life's work. *Patricia* and *The Wayfarers*, although practically ignored by the London press, had been well paid for and he did not need to worry about money for some time to come. His cricket tours and the acquaintance he had made with all types of people in the different parts of the country which he had visited, had greatly increased his understanding of life and character, and though he still felt the need for improvement in his literary technique, he realized that the surest way to improve this was by continued practice at the highest level of which he was capable. During the years 1902 and 1903 he played comparatively little cricket except for the midsummer weeks of the Fireflies and Druids at Skegness, and at some time in 1904 or 1905 he found himself a *pied à terre* in London at the house of Dr. F. J. Dixon, who was now practising at Dulwich. During the next few years he was to owe much to Dr. Dixon's understanding friendship, and the arrangement had the additional advantage of bringing him once more into touch with Fred Boon, who was now a master at Dulwich College. He spent many evenings at his old friend's house and more than one passage in his later books shows the intense pleasure which he derived from Mrs. Boon's playing of Chopin and Beethoven.

He worked hard through 1902, 1903 and early 1904 at Nottingham, Skegness (where his family now had a holiday cottage) and at Dulwich. The theme which he chose was the familiar one of an old county family gradually succumbing to the exigencies of modern materialist civilization. The Brokes had been owners of Covenden since before the Conquest, and although ruin and bankruptcy now stared him in the face, the present owner, Edmund William Carysfort Baigent Broke, remained as much rooted to the soil as one of his own oaks. A tall man, with an immense spread of shoulder, and legs and arms as massive as the branches of a forest tree, his ruddy, stolid face was only differentiated from that of a well-to-do farmer by the amazing nose which jutted out from the centre of it like a formidable fifth limb. Superficially he seemed no more complex in character than in physique—a placid, beef-eating, beer-drinking human animal without a thought beyond sport and agriculture. But the real passion of his nature was pride—pride in his country, in his lineage, in his position, and in his family. In this quality were rooted his intense and naïve affection for his children and the strong sense of duty, which was the basis of his simple, feudal code of morals.

Broke's chief pride was in his six daughters, and it appeared to be accentuated by their extraordinary lack of individuality.

Though their ages ranged from sixteen to twenty-four, they seemed as like one another as a litter of puppies—'Every small detail of them fashioned strictly after some arbitrary pattern, like servicemen's tunics or policemen's boots or helmets.' There was no denying that they were distressingly plain, and their plainness was in no way mitigated by the keen wistfulness of the foxhound in their faces, nor by the famous Broke nose which stood out in the middle of each as unmistakable as the knocker on a door. Indeed, the only compliment that could be paid to them was that they were beautifully clean—a quality pathetically emphasized by their clothes, which were old, shabby and mis-shapen and drooped dankly on their lean flanks. But in the hunting field they were classics. 'Damn it, they could take a donkey over Leicestershire', was the comment of an admiring relative.

In mind there seemed as little to differentiate them from one another as in body, for they were their father's children and followed his ideas with unthinking and unswerving devotion. But in strength of character, the eldest, Joan, stood out above the others. Staunch and uncompromising as they all were, to Joan's staunchness and courage they all bowed in homage. Only one of them showed any deviation from the norm—the youngest, Delia. There was something about her which shook her sisters' confidence, something delicate and impressionable which seemed to be reflected in her long eyelashes that turned up so oddly at the ends, and the queer filmy look which gave her bright blue eyes a quality both strange and unfathomable. Moreover, she alone of the sisterhood sometimes ventured upon an original idea. Mr. Broke had voiced the opinion of them all when he once said that if she had been a boy she might have grown up a Radical.

Of their mother all six girls went in awe. At first sight there was nothing to suggest extraordinary qualities in this red-faced, rather countrified, woman with her mellifluous voice which seemed able to adapt itself to any subject without notably embellishing it. But one could not be long in her company without noting the cold twinkle in her blue eyes, the dazzling smile which would, every now and then, transform her features, the extraordinary ease with which she controlled every situation. It was her unremitting vigilance that had kept the house of Broke off the rocks for five-and-twenty years. No detail of management was too small for her; no possibility of material advancement too remote.

Her daughters she drove as a skilled whip drives a team of horses. As for her husband, in any given situation she was tolerably sure how he would act and how she would be able to manage him. Only his pride baffled her; its depths were unplumbed.

The eternal vigilance and the eternal struggle to which she was condemned had hardened Mrs. Broke and coarsened her a little. The armour needed for her defence had stiffened her affections and blunted her maternal instincts, which found an unrestricted outlet only in one direction. To her son Billy she had long extended an indulgence which from her daughters was inexorably withheld. She, no more than anyone else, could withstand the attractions of Billy—the candid charm of his pink-complexioned, blue-eyed face, in which even the Broke nose seemed to be an embellishment; the large equipoise and symmetry of his magnificent physique; his free, merry, affectionate, lighthearted, casual ways. Billy had only to ask and it was given to him. One forgot that he was little gifted with brains and too often sublimely oblivious of the interests of anyone but himself. As befitted the heir of the house of Broke he was in the Blues, and, being in the Blues, he must do as the Blues did. If he wanted five hundred pounds for polo ponies, he must have it. He must get his clothes in Savile Row and play bridge in St. James's, even if his mother had to scrimp and screw more agonizingly than ever to meet the consequences.

And, indeed, Billy was her last card. She knew from old Mr. Breffit, the Cuttisham land-agent, who was deep in the secrets of every great family in the county, that she had come to the end of the Broke resources. And Mr. Breffit, in whom snobbery was sublimated almost into a religion, reverenced the Brokes as the very symbols of Britain's feudal majesty. It was only by his help and liberality that she had been able to hold on so long. Now there was no hope left except in the arrangement of a brilliant marriage for Billy.

In the nick of time, Maud Wayling, a beautiful heiress and one of the most courted young women in society, falls in love with him and he suddenly finds himself treated as though he were engaged to her. There are paragraphs in the papers; friends congratulate him; Maud is asked for long visits to Covenden when he is expected to be home on leave. But unfortunately Billy doesn't care for Maud—she is too reserved and too 'clarsy' for him. He protests in vain to his mother; then, without a word to her, marries a girl from behind the counter of a milliner's shop in Bond Street. This escapade seems to make ruin inevitable, but the indomitable Mrs. Broke rises to the occasion. She visits the girl in the dismal slum where she lives with a poor, broken-down old maiden aunt (a visit which makes her realize, for the first time and with a dreadful shock, the appalling gulf between the lives of the rich and the poor), finds her innocent, refined and charming, though of course penniless, moves her to a cottage at Covenden and tries to reconcile her husband to the event. But his pride is touched. He casts off his son as a traitor to his class. This is the beginning of a series of calamities which fall upon the Broke family with the fatal inevitability of Greek tragedy. Delia and her tutor, the son of a bookseller in Cuttisham, fall in love with one another. The young man calls on Broke to ask for her in marriage. Broke fiercely assaults him and throws him bodily out of the house. Delia runs away from home and marries her lover. She, too, is disowned by her father. Mr. Breffit puts forward his son as a suitor for another of the girls. This is too much for Broke, but in his desperate strait he agrees that one should marry a consumptive duke who is desperately seeking an heir in order to keep his disreputable brother out of the title. Then Joan, the staunch, the invincibly loyal, is killed by a fall in the hunting field, and within a few weeks news reaches Covenden that the gallant and delightful Billy, who has, of course, had to leave the Blues, has lost his life in South Africa fighting against the Boers as a sergeant in the Rhodesian Light Horse. The news comes not long after the Broke family has learned that old Mr. Breffit has died, leaving half his fortune (a quarter of a million pounds) to Billy, and that Billy's wife down at the cottage is expecting a baby, though there is little likelihood of her surviving its birth.

Mrs. Broke has now, within the space of a few weeks, lost four of her children. Those weeks have reduced the robust and stubborn squire of Covenden to a grey-haired, shuffling, incoherent old man; but his stubbornness seems as invincible as ever. She realizes that the only hope of preserving his and her own sanity for the years that may remain to them, is to reconcile him to his daughter Delia and his son's widow. To her alarm, Delia now shows an obduracy as dire as her father's. While Billy's wife lies dying in the little cottage, the tremendous woman wrestles with her husband and her daughter. After bitter struggles and bitterer humiliations she succeeds, and the book ends with a picture of Broke sitting in the cottage clasping his tiny grandson with one arm and his daughter with the other, while the sweat pours unceasingly down his haggard face.

Broke of Covenden was massively constructed and carried out with a masculine force and probity and a strong ironic humour which gave life and poignancy to the tragic scenes; the chief characters stood out with an extraordinary vitality; the atmosphere of life in a hunting country was convincingly suggested, and the whole book had a scope and range which were extremely impressive. It was immensely long—over 580 pages— and it was at one stage even longer, as it contained a rather prolix preface in Meredithian vein, which the publishers very wisely persuaded the author to omit, although he succeeded in getting it reinstated in subsequent editions. No doubt the book could have been improved by a few other omissions, for Snaith was still too much addicted to the Victorian novelist's habit of interrupting the action with his own moralizing, and he was carried away, here and there, by the exuberance of his own humour, particularly in the person of Mrs. Broke's brother, The Right Honourable Charles Chevenix, thirteenth Baron Bosket, an incredibly credible sporting peer who acts as a kind of comic Greek chorus to the tragedy. Moreover, some of the characters were too farcical, and the style tended to prolixity. But these were faults of inexperience, pardonable in an author who was making his first appearance in a difficult field, and did not much detract from the strength of the achievement.

The book was published by Messrs. Constable at midsummer, 1904, and was very well received by the critics. The *Saturday Review* and *Academy* reviewed it favourably during July, as did *The Times Literary Supplement*, which spoke of it as a clever book broadly conceived and executed with vigorous amplitude of detail. The *Spectator* of August 20th gave it a whole column. All the critics, however, emphasized the ironic comedy of the book and none seemed adequately to appreciate its tragic power or the poignancy of the contrasts which it drew between privilege and poverty, revolution and tradition, materialism and spirituality. Snaith himself was not dissatisfied with his achievement. He felt, and frankly said, that *Broke* was almost in the highest class, and he was disappointed that the critics seemed unable to realize this. It was, however, appreciated by many men whose opinions he profoundly respected, such as J. M. Barrie and Augustine Birrell. Conan Doyle in his literary causerie, *Through the Magic Door*, wrote: 'I do not say that the book is a classic, and I should not like to be positive that it is not, but I am perfectly sure that the man who wrote it has the possibility of a classic within him'. Sir Edward Grey was so much struck with the book that, although he had never met Snaith, he wrote asking him to lunch. Snaith invested in a top-hat, a frock-coat and an eyeglass for the occasion, but unfortunately no record remains of what passed between the two men.

That summer Snaith played more cricket than during either of the two preceding years, having an average of 27 for ten innings for Notts Forest and scoring three centuries for other teams. Then in the autumn he returned to Dr. Dixon's house at Dulwich and set about his next book.

The undoubted success of *Broke* did not induce him to attempt another novel in a similar style. His powers had expanded greatly while he was working at *Broke*, and he now had things to say which he could not express through the traditional novel form. As he himself said, he wanted 'a new notation'—some form which would permit him stronger contrasts, a greater spiritual range and more untrammelled imagination. *Broke* had sold well, second editions being called for almost immediately both in England and America (it was reprinted several times afterwards in both countries), and he could afford to take a risk with his next book. He worked hard at this through the winter of 1904-05 and the ensuing summer, playing very little cricket, except for three weeks at Skegness in June and July.

The theme of his new book, *Henry Northcote*, arose naturally out of the spiritual experience which had gone to the making of *Broke of Covenden*, Snaith's realization of the terrible contrast between the lives of the rich and the poor and of the despair which he felt to be threatening the world through the destruction of its spiritual ideals by a rapidly-spreading materialism. He saw his fellow-countrymen (to quote one of the characters in *Henry Northcote*) as 'teeming millions of helots, whose ferocious energies had coloured half the globe red', and who 'with hunger in their faces and fever in their eyes' were awaiting a new deliverance.

The governing classes had failed. The new deliverer must come from below, as Jesus had come; 'only that could prevent [mankind] from dashing out their brains against the blank wall that had come to stand before them'.

The book was to be a representation, half mystical, half realistic, of the powers which such a deliverer would need and the dangers which would confront him. It would also be in some degree a sublimation of Snaith's own spiritual history—his intense ambition to create a great imaginative masterpiece and the temptation which he felt to shirk the terrible expenditure of spirit which such an effort required, and to remain satisfied with a more easily won and much more lucrative popularity.

Henry Northcote, the man who is mystically called to make the great attempt, is a young barrister starving in an attic in Shepherds Inn, the oldest and craziest of the old buildings abutting on Fleet Street. His mother, the penniless widow of a country clergyman, an unlovely but august figure, of martial bearing, large bones, red face, coarse hands and strong country speech, has slaved and starved herself to give him an education which would enable him to carve out for himself a great career at the Bar. But although he has waited and toiled for seven years, his chance has not come, and in order to give himself practice in advocacy, he goes, every afternoon, to address the crowd at the Marble Arch. As he sits one evening shivering in his garret, a tattered figure from the gutter who has heard him on his soapbox, comes to urge him in mystical language to make the great renunciation and become the world's second deliverer. The visitor is 'a member of the governing classes, with the accent of Eton and Balliol, who has seen and felt too much to be able to govern', but he perceives in Northcote the potential saviour. When he has gone, Northcote suffers a terrible crisis of the spirit. He knows that he has the ability and force needed by the man who is to be the new deliverer, but his being is full-blooded, turbulent, tormented by desires, yearning to express a complete moral, intellectual and physical life. He cannot rise to the great renunciation. Suddenly he realizes that he has only to make the final choice—to kneel down and press his face to the rickety table at which he is seated, and the worldly opportunity for which he craves will be granted him. He falls on his knees and, in a wild turmoil of the spirit, presses his eyes to the rough boards. At that moment he hears a step on the stairs and a man enters his room. It is Mr. Whitcomb, the famous criminal attorney, come to offer him at the last minute a brief for the defence of Emma Harrison, a common prostitute, who is charged with murdering the man with whom she had been living, in order to secure the enjoyment of a small legacy which she believes he has left her in his will. Whitcomb is the antithesis of Northcote, middle-aged, successful, cynical, sensual, the incarnation of common sense and normal desires. He takes the starving young man out to sup at a luxurious restaurant and explains the case to him. It is one which really admits of no defence; the evidence is clear. The only chance is to plead insanity, and evidence has been arranged for the purpose. But this Northcote will not accept. He insists on a free hand and promises that if he is allowed to do exactly as he likes, he will secure a complete acquittal. After long and stormy discussions, the solicitor is compelled, much against his will, to give way.

The thirty-six hours between the meeting of the two men and the calling of the case at the Old Bailey—their discussions so oddly redolent of Plato, Thomas Love Peacock and Stevenson's *New Arabian Nights*; Northcote's wild night ramble through the streets, his brain bursting with ideas for his projected address to the jury, which he ultimately tries out on two stolid and suspicious policemen in the early hours of a winter's morning at the bottom of Sydenham Hill; his Socratic dialogue with his precise, bewildered, long-suffering charwoman whom, on the strength of Mr. Whitcomb's cheque, he invites to share the first decent breakfast he has enjoyed for months; his grim and mysterious interview with Emma Harrison in the squalid prison; his revulsion of feeling when he realizes that he will never again know 'the chastening brutality of want', and that he has sacrificed the spiritual splendours of his inheritance for the kind of success which is 'the birthright and the measure of the meanest natures'; his alternations between towering confidence and abysmal reaction— are all described with extraordinary intensity and a wealth of convincing detail.

At last comes the trial. Northcote, in spite of Whitcomb's continued pressure, declines to put forward the plea of insanity; he has no witnesses to call and he cross-examines none of the witnesses for the prosecution, who testify to the woman's purchase of strychnine, the finding of strychnine in the dead man's body, and her attempts to prevent the summons of medical aid. When, however, another prostitute is put into the box to speak of the accused's relations with the murdered man, he, with diabolical skill and by sheer force of personality, compels her to recant what she has said as having been extorted from her by the pressure of the police, and to invent—or half accept and half invent—an entirely fictitious account of the accused's history, which makes the strongest appeal to the sympathy of the jury. Then, having insinuated into the minds of the jurors this faint glimmer of a possible doubt, he sits down to listen to the Crown prosecutor's address, for, having called no evidence himself, he is entitled to have the last word and so can withhold his own address to the end. That address when it comes is surely one of the most astonishing and moving pieces of prose in modern English. At the crisis of it he calls on the jury to imagine—almost compels them to believe —that in their place is empanelled another jury composed of those mighty representative spirits of which the twentieth century is heir—Plato, St. Augustine, St. Francis of Assisi, Shakespeare, Goethe, Molière, Dante, Washington, Cromwell, Kant, Spinoza, Newton, Giordano Bruno, Voltaire. He pictures that jury filing into the box and choosing its foreman. The choice is made in a moment, and a slight, strangely garbed figure with pale, luminous features moves into the foreman's place—a half-stifled sob of surprise, a sort of shudder of recognition, passes over the crowded court. It is Jesus of Nazareth. What, asks the young advocate, would the verdict of that jury be when asked to do an erring woman to death? Finally he reminds the court of a terrible miscarriage of justice which had resulted, only a few short months before, in the hanging of an innocent man. The evidence of the real criminal had been decisive against the accused, for the young and inexperienced counsel for the defence had failed to bring out a flaw which, if realized, must have invalidated the case for the prosecution. On this case Northcote founds a terrible and cynical masterstroke.

'These facts are green in the minds of you all. But there is a coincidence connected with this atrocious story and the grievous case which is engaging your attention. The counsel for the prosecution in both cases is identical. He stands before you framing yet another of those objections with which he has endeavoured to impede the cause of humanity. I point my finger at him, and challenge him to

G

deny the truth of the statement I am making. And by a perfectly logical and natural extension of this coincidence, the judge who sent the butler to his doom, is seated above you now in all the panoply of his office. I leave him now to deal if he is able in a like manner with this poor Magdalene, who may or may not have fallen by the way.'

Northcote sat down after having spoken for nearly three hours. The December darkness had long fallen upon the court. The feeble gas jets seemed to enhance the shadows that they cast. The intense faces of the overcrowded building, bar, jury, populace, all electrified, seemed to belong to so many ghosts, so pale, shining, and transfigured did they gleam. . . . . .

None had foreseen the cruel, terrible, yet melodramatic climax to which the advocate was leading; and when it came over the minds of those present, all of whom in the course of the speech, even the most hardened officers of the court, the ushers, the chaplain, the javelin men, and the newspaper reporters, had passed in one form or another through all the anguish of spirit of which they were capable, pity and horror were mingled with their overwrought surprise. As the advocate stood with his huge and livid face turned upwards towards the judge, with an ineffable emotion suffusing it, and the old man, with tears dripping quickly on to his ermine, put his two fat, white hands before his eyes, terror and bewilderment seemed to pervade the court.

The advocate sat down with parched lips. The hush that ensued was so long that it seemed it would never come to an end.

It was broken by a commotion among the public benches. A woman who had fainted was being carried out at the back of the court. The incident served to unloose the electricity which was pent up in the atmosphere. A voice from the solicitor's well was heard to pronounce the word 'Shame!' In an instant it was answered by the multitude with a volley of the wildest cheers that was ever heard in a court of justice. All the ragged, tattered, despised, broken, and rejected units of the population, those humble, hungry, and inarticulate creatures upon whom Jesus himself had wrought his magic, upon whom he had depended for countenance, took up the challenge, and with their wild and hoarse cries flung it back upon him who had uttered it.

For a time the scene was one of consternation. The judge was but a poor, senile, old man from whom the tears were leaping. Every official looked towards him for his prop and stay, but all there was to see was feeble and inept old age. The Clerk of Arraigns, as pale as a ghost and trembling violently, was spreading his hands before an alderman. Policemen stood dismayed, and officers of the court, who had grown old and despotic in its service, looked towards one another helplessly, seeking for that authority which none had the power to exercise.

At last order is restored and the judge begins his summing-up. But he is a broken man; his summing-up is weak and inconclusive and the jury, after an absence of only nine minutes, returns a verdict of Not Guilty. Emma Harrison is free and Northcote finds himself assured of that worldly success for which he has bartered his spiritual heritage.

That, of course, is not the end, though it is a point at which any writer might have been tempted to stay his hand. The concluding scenes of the book are terrible, cynical, courageous. The young author did not shirk inevitable consequences. Even after the terrific trial scene there is no sense of anticlimax.

Henry Northcote, when brooding over the great task which he has undertaken, says that at thirty a man of genius should give a masterpiece to the world. When Snaith published this book he was just thirty years of age and he might well hope that he had produced a masterpiece. The book, of course, had weaknesses—particularly in the important opening chapter, which is in many places clumsily and pompously written, and lacks the extraordinary sense of reality which invests the rest of the book. In the character of Northcote, Snaith had succeeded in giving an impression of titanic power for which it is difficult to find a parallel in British literature, and the subsidiary characters are all put in with a touch extraordinarily light and vital. In *Broke* he had created the atmosphere of Society in a hunting country with remarkable verisimilitude. In *Northcote*, although legal procedure is sometimes travestied, the atmosphere of the Bar and the Courts of Justice was suggested even more effectively. In fact, the whole book was a considerable advance on *Broke*. It was better constructed; the style, in spite of occasional lapses, easier, more supple and more finely rhythmic; the feeling more intense; the thought deeper. The greatly increased range of emotion showed how the author's mind and sensibilities had developed since he had established contact with men like Barrie, Grey and Birrell, and seen something of the more thoughtful sections of London Society.

For one, at least, who has re-read the book again and again during the past five-and-forty years, its appeal has grown steadily stronger; but for many contemporary critics the notation was too new. When it was issued in April, 1906, only a few of the leading periodicals mentioned it at all, although it is true that on the whole the references of these were favourable. The *Academy* condemned it as having no art and no architecture, while admitting that it contained some striking scenes and was studded with admirable points of observation. The *Scotsman* called it brilliant and fascinating. The *Athenaeum* said that the matter was startling, the book overpowering and defying criticism—a possible masterpiece. Snaith's faithful friend, John Macleay, wrote an understanding criticism in the *Liverpool Daily Post*. The *Times Literary Supplement* discerned in the young author very exceptional gifts—a ruthless directness of vision, a searching sense of social anomaly, a large view of the human comedy and a very unexpected macabre vein. '*Broke of Covenden,*' wrote the reviewer, 'brought Mr. Meredith to mind. *Henry Northcote* summons the august and mighty shade of Balzac. It is no small feat for a young man who has bowled for Notts and who began his literary career with a high-spirited and romping story of the cricket field, to throw such shadows of great masters over his books and withal to owe to them nothing but the influence that a master has on a pupil who brings intelligence to the lecture-room.'

That perhaps was as good a critical welcome as so unusual a book by so young a man could hope for, and it might be thought to augur well for Snaith's future success. The book itself, however, indicated certain dangers. One of the reasons which prevented the completion of *Cardellan* may have been the excessive mental strain which such highly emotional writing imposed on the author. Looking back at *Northcote* in the light of later events, one can perhaps see signs that more than once while he was at work upon it Snaith's mind nearly broke loose from its moorings. For example: in the description of Northcote's wild midnight rush through the streets of London, after his first meeting with Whitcomb, and in that of the trance-like state in which he makes his final decision to summon the genie of opportunity.

> He was not in a dream, because his eyes were open, he knew where he was, and he was in possession of the sense of hearing. But he had surrendered the control of the will; and although he was on his knees with his face pressed to a dusty table before a dead fire, the mind was become divorced from the body and was cast into the

vortex of indescribable scenes. It drifted about among them help-lessly. It bore no relation to actors or events. All was the weirdest panorama, crammed with hurry and wild inconsequence; and yet the spectator was filled with an exhilaration which was as remote from the province of reality as a drunkard's delirium.

He began to make frantic efforts to fix and locate this phantas-magoria. He stretched every nerve to catch the import of a word that was spoken; he craned his whole being to wrest a single incident from this wild confusion. He strove as tensely for a thread of meaning as though he were fighting against the operations of an anaesthetic, but he could reclaim nothing from the chaos in which he was en-gulfed. He was like a drowning man with the heavy yet not un-pleasant rush of water in his ears.

Here surely the young author was describing a personal exper-ience of a gravely disturbing kind. But if he had any such exper-ience, with his usual reserve he kept it to himself, not telling even Dr. Dixon in whose house most of the book was written, or Fred Boon whom he was seeing several times a week. Nor did he speak to them of the new plane on which his thoughts were moving. They saw no change in what seemed the placid, self-controlled and reticent routine of his existence, as he worked solidly on in his room, emerging only for lunch and dinner and a quiet game of chess or an hour of Mrs. Boon's music in the evening.

Snaith did not expect success for *Henry Northcote*, and he was not unduly depressed at its reception by the critics. This was reflected in the sales, which were very slow. But *Broke* was still in demand on both sides of the Atlantic and a new edition of *Fierceheart* had just been issued in America, so that he felt justified in spending the summer playing cricket at Nottingham and Skeg-ness, having the satisfaction of scoring 104 not out against Leices-ter in June and showing an average of 26 in eighteen matches for Skegness and district. About the middle of September he began work on the book, which was to be the complement as well as the successor to *Northcote*. In *Northcote* he had shown the super-man, who might have been the leader of a new spiritual revival, refusing to make the great renunciation and selling his soul, like a new Faust, to a bland and cynical Mephistopheles in the guise of Mr. Whitcomb. In the introductory chapter Northcote says to his mysterious visitor that most people regard Christ's mission to earth as having partially failed; to which the visitor replies that the world awaits a second such failure to save it from itself. Snaith's new book was to depict in a highly mystical way the career and quality of such a second failure. It was also, like *Northcote*, in some degree a sublimation of his own inner history—this time of the mystic and spiritual elements in his nature which tempted him to withdraw into the hermitage of his dreams, shunning the human contacts without which his genius could never be fully fruitful.

To achieve his aim it was necessary for him to carry the 'new notation' a stage further. In *Northcote* the mystical element had been kept apart, very much as the magical element is in the *Peau de Chagrin*; for Northcote himself, although a figure of titanic power, is essentially a human being and contending with human problems. William Jordan Junior, who gave his name to the new book, was to be essentially a creature of allegory. He is introduced as a boy of about twelve years old, a strange figure with a form of elfin slightness; hands frail as gossamer; vivid eyes very deeply set and a face which is of angelic beauty and full of the solemn wonder of childhood, yet marred by one gross physical blemish, an open and never-healing wound in the middle of his right cheek. The boy lives with his ageing father, whose name is the same as his own, in a tiny bare room in a poor London street behind a shop crammed with old books, the infrequent sale of which provides their scanty maintenance. No stranger is ever allowed to pass from the shop into the inner sanctuary, where the boy spends his time earnestly studying the works of the 'ancient authors', those great philosophers and poets of antiquity whose work had meant so much to Snaith himself. The old man is chiefly occupied in poring over a huge tome, a thousand years old (known as *The Book of the Ages*), in which his forefathers have written with their own blood a record of their vital experiences and beliefs. Every now and then he takes from a cupboard a knife, a bowl and a stylus, fills the bowl with his blood and endeavours to write in the book, which he is never able to do—to his infinite sorrow, for it is foretold in the book that when one of 'the dynasty' fails to add his testimony to it, the dynasty will come to an end. The boy is so timid that he will not go upstairs to bed unless his father goes with him, and he dares not lie in bed unless there is a light burning at its fullest in the room. He dares not go out into the streets without his father, for he is terrified of the fierce and cruel 'street persons' who seem always to be staring at him with their rude eyes. He is even afraid to go abroad with his father for fear that they may lose themselves in the great city and never find their way back to the little room, which is their sanctuary. Yet, in spite of his timidity, he has a deep inner conviction that he is destined to be one of the great ones of the earth, and he knows that he must understand all things and face all things if he is to achieve his destiny. His father realizes his determination and has given him the name of Achilles, as a tribute to his courage and a reminder of the trials which he will have to face. The book owes its power and its poignancy to the extraordinary vitality with which Snaith succeeded in investing the symbolic figure of William Jordan Junior, whose tragic struggle with life in the great city of London it describes. The boy goes to a strange, phantasmal school where the aged master, who calls his pupils by the names of personages in the Homeric poems and the dialogues of Plato, is hardly less a creature of allegory than William Jordan himself. But the other boys are all quintessential human boy, and William Jordan's sufferings at their hands have an agonizing reality. Equally real are the miseries which he endures when following the 'street-people' out of doors in order to learn their strange language (for he and his father always speak together in a pure and exalted kind of biblical English); when struggling to earn money for the maintenance of the little room by holding the heads of huge and restive cart-horses in the streets; or when seeking employment as a 'bright boy' in city offices. At last he secures a position as 'handy youth' at Messrs. Crumpett & Hawkers, publishers, in Trafalgar Square. There he is given in charge of a wizened and precocious youth, called Jimmie Dodson, who combines with an unerring instinct for his own advantage the unshakable assurance and irrepressible humour of the true Cockney. At first, Jimmie's only interest in William Jordan is to exploit and make fun of his innocence and timidity, but gradually he finds his affection, and even admiration, engaged in a way quite unintelligible to himself. The two become inseparable companions. In Crumpett & Hawker's office Jordan is only saved from the results of his incompetence by Jimmie's protection and his own innocence and disarming courtesy. Jimmie introduces him to the bar of the Brontë Arms, where his *fiancée*, Chrissie, the blonde, benign, exuberant barmaid, is the presiding goddess, and induces him to attend a party at the Peckham home of his father, Police-Sergeant Dodson, given to introduce Chrissie to his friends and relations. There William Jordan meets (and is overwhelmed by) the magnificent Hermione Leigh, star of the ballet at the Alcazar Music Hall, John Dobbs, who plays the fiddle in the orchestra, and Joe Cox, who, if his friends' hopes are justified, is destined to become the best slow left-hand bowler in Surrey. There is a disastrous day at the Oval where Joe Cox is being tried for Surrey County against Notts, and William Jordan is stricken by the sun, after which a visit to the Alcazar followed by stout and oysters with Hermione sends him back to the little room a dishevelled and bewildered human fragment, with his self-confidence and trust in his old beliefs and ideals grievously shaken. An even more disastrous day is spent at Margate, where Jordan becomes intoxicated with the excitement of his first sight of the sea, and nearly drowns the whole party by attacking one of Jimmie's friends who insists on playing a concertina in the boat in which the party is rowing on the bay. The broad humour and rich vitality of these crowded scenes, and the pathos and mystical beauty of William Jordan's life and character, intertwine like two themes in counterpoint, each enhancing the other and creating a complete and harmonious whole. Then comes a change. One day William Jordan hears that unless twenty pounds can be found forthwith the little room will be taken away. But without a miracle there is no prospect of the money being available. Then the miracle happens. He is sent up to the senior partner's room at the office. The room is empty, but there on the table are two piles of ten golden sovereigns each. Muttering words of despair and terror, he puts the pieces of gold in his pocket and hurries from the room, only to find when he reaches home that during the day a casual customer has bought one of the old books in the shop for the fabulous sum of three hundred pounds. In spite of the frantic and successful efforts of Jimmie Dodson to divert suspicion from him, he insists on confessing his crime, gives himself up to the police and is condemned to six months' hard labour.

Thus ends the first stage of William Jordan's mystical journey through life. The second, his six months in prison, is left without description, but the vital effect of it is seen when he comes out through the prison gate and finds Jimmie Dodson waiting for him on the pavement. He is a changed being: his eyes are wide and bright; his once stammering and hesitant speech is firm and clear. 'I am entered upon the third phase,' he says, 'on the third and the last. The time is brief. I hear already the first faint lappings of the waters of oblivion in my ears. But I have acquired a store of knowledge. I went out in anguish and bewilderment. I return in self-security. If only the strength be given to my right hand in these last days, I shall commence author.' From now on William Jordan spent his days in strange places; without pain, without trepidation he walked fearlessly among the crowded streets, reading the faces of those he found there; or he would go afield to the country lanes and woodland places to read the face of Nature. In the evenings, Jimmie Dodson, though he was mortally afraid of compromising himself socially if seen with a convicted criminal, would tap on the shutters of the shop and the two would go out into the streets together. For weeks William Jordan worked in a Mission Hall in an East End slum, bringing to this work something which none of the other devoted workers had brought to it before. Then one evening, while he was talking to the head of the mission, he coughed and a spray of bright red arterial blood appeared upon his lips. 'Nature's mandate,' he said, with his secret and beautiful smile; and the next morning he set out westwards alone, and without money, staff or bundle, on a last mysterious pilgrimage. For a year he wandered through field and woodland, over wold and mountain and by the shores of the ocean, in mystic communion with Nature, with the wise and simple mountain peoples and with those who wrest a reluctant nourishment from the bare ground and the intractable sea. As the year waned his sight began to fail him and he reached the great city at last, ragged and half-naked, with long matted hair hanging down upon his shoulders and almost blind. There an adventure befell him which showed how much he had changed since the days when his attempts to hold the great drayhorses outside the warehouses of St. Paul's Churchyard had driven him half-mad with terror.

It happened as he turned into a familiar thoroughfare, a street long and narrow, and wondrously busy with a great press of people and traffic, that he suddenly became aware of a strange clamour that was arising before him. Cries of consternation resounded on every side; they overcame the shrieks of the piercing winds as they swept round the houses and shops. With his dim eyes the wayfarer could perceive the drivers of the vehicles make frantic efforts to escape from an on-coming danger that threatened them.

Suddenly there came through the failing light of the afternoon the great form of a horse, a huge animal attached to a heavy railway van. There was no driver, the reins were dangling loose; with tossing mane and wild nostrils, the mighty horse was devouring the road-way with furious strides. It escaped a tramcar as by a miracle; it crashed into a milk-seller's cart, and sent milk-cans with their con-tents rolling in all directions. Yet still it kept its course unchecked, a menace to all whom it passed.

The passers-by, huddling together as far away from the kerb as they could squeeze themselves, were then astonished by a strange sight. A ragged, half-naked beggar, hatless, coatless, without shoes and stockings, and with long matted hair which fell down upon his shoulders, moved off the pavement. He appeared to turn his back upon the mad thing that was approaching him, and then, with a leap of superhuman courage and address, seemed to fling himself at the head of the infuriated brute as it grazed his bare ankles with its hoofs. He was seen to take the reins in his grasp, and, leaping along at the side of the horse, began an attempt to control its furious speed that was little short of miraculous. In the struggle he was several times carried completely off his feet, and borne yards at a time with-out touching the earth. And though man and brute and vehicle swayed and rocked in all directions, no obstacles intervened to shatter them; and at almost every yard he was borne the man seemed to gain a firmer purchase on the brute.

For half the length of the thoroughfare the titanic struggle was waged between the man and the brute on the slippery, circumscribed and narrow road. At times it seemed that the man must be hurled away from the brute altogether; at other times it seemed that he must be flung beneath the hoofs of the brute and trampled lifeless; while, again, in the frantic efforts of the animal to be rid of its burden, it seemed that they must both be hurled through the windows of the shops.

Ere long, however, the fury of the horse began to spend itself. And as it did so, with the man still retaining his grasp of the reins, two policemen, stalwart and hardy and finely-grown men, stepped from the pavement, and, lending their aid at a timely moment, the poor animal was brought under control.

Among the witnesses of the incident was a tall, bronzed man, with closely-cropped hair, who was dressed with remarkable care, and whose bearing was that of a soldier. At his side was a slight, youthful, handsome woman, who was breathless with excitement.

'Upon my word,' said the man, 'that is the best thing I ever saw. That chap deserves a medal.'

The woman, with a strange, dancing brightness in her eyes, looked up wistfully into the face of her companion. 'Get him one,' she said.

Stimulated by their generous curiosity, they walked up to a spot where a small crowd was rapidly collecting around the unkempt and extraordinary figure that was almost naked.

'Better take his name and address,' said the tall, bronzed man to the two police constables in a slow and calm voice which caused them to touch their helmets.

The tall, bronzed man then proceeded to survey the circle of interested bystanders at a dignified leisure, and said in the same tone, 'Suppose we send round the hat?'

Removing his own immaculately-ironed silk head-gear, he proceeded with an air of exaggerated self-possession, which the conspiracy of the circumstances rendered bizarre, to drop several pieces of gold into its interior, and then, standing bareheaded, so that the sleet glistened upon the pomatum of his hair, handed his hat to a man near to him, who was of a similar type to himself. However, while this gentleman, also with extraordinary nonchalance, was adding further pieces of gold to the hat, this somewhat impressive munificence was frustrated.

The half-naked beggar appeared suddenly to realize that he was the cynosure of all eyes. He gave a gaunt look all about him, and then, with a motion of indescribable rapidity, he passed through the ring that had been formed. With a swiftness so great that his flight could hardly be followed, the mists of the evening received him.

The bare-headed man gave a glance of courteous deprecation, which almost took the form of a personal apology, to the man who was placing pieces of gold in his hat.

'Rather a pity,' he said; 'rather a pity to let him go.'

'Yes, a pity,' said the other, wiping a speck of sleet off the brim of the hat very carefully with his glove, and handing it back.

As with an air of disappointment the crowd dispersed reluctantly, the slight, youthful, handsome woman turned with an eager gesture to the owner of the hat. Her cheeks, under their powder, were the colour of snow.

'Did you—did you see his face?' said she in quick, nervous accents. 'I shall carry it to my grave. It was—it was the most beautiful face in the world.'

The owner of the hat gave the woman a little smile of affectionate indulgence, in which, however, pride was uppermost, and handed her very carefully into a hansom.

When Jordan at last reaches the little room, he eats and drinks, and then, ragged and unkempt as he is, falls asleep in a chair by the fireside with his naked feet stretched out towards the embers. At midnight he awakes and, with pens and paper which the old man has brought while he slept, sits down to write. Five days and five nights he writes steadily, at first with controlled passion, then with his large and bright eyes rolling in a frenzy of terror, and then again with a face radiant with joy. Every evening Jimmie Dodson comes to look at him from the shop, for he may not cross the threshold of the little room; and every evening he goes away convinced that he will never see his friend alive again. When he comes at the end of the sixth day, the strain on him is so great that he almost hopes to find the writer dead. But William Jordan has finished his writing and is asleep.

The next evening Jimmie finds the sleeper awakened, and now for the first time he is allowed to cross the threshold of the little room and clasp his friend in his arms. Then comes the question of giving William Jordan's masterpiece to the world, and Jimmie is commissioned, to his horror, (for the work is to him totally unintelligible) to place it in the hands of Messrs. Crumpett & Hawker, preserving in inviolable secrecy the name of the author. The work is a poem, entitled *Reconciliation*, in a novel kind of English hexameter, three times the length of *Paradise Lost*.

Messrs. Crumpett & Hawker, of course, decline to touch it. But Dodson, whose great abilities have now won him a high place with the firm, persuades them to publish 250 copies at the author's expense and send fifty to the principal periodicals for review. The firm's attitude has to be kept from the dying poet, who is now stone blind, and Dodson and the old man set about raising the two hundred pounds needed to pay for the book's production. In Jimmie's opinion the contents of the shop are not worth two hundred pence, and the only hope seems to be in the sale of the thousand-year-old *Book of the Ages*, in which, by a strange irony, the old man has that very day at last succeeded in writing his chapter. After infinite labour and employing every kind of misrepresentation and deceit, Jimmie succeeds in raising the sum required; the poem is printed and the three bound volumes placed upon the poet's knees. Now comes a new difficulty. The dying man longs to hear what reception his work is having from the critics and the people. The review copies have gone out, but no single criticism appears. The publishers are under no obligation to advertise, and not a copy is sold. It is easy for Jimmie to give the blind man convincing reports as to the eagerness with which the public are buying and reading his masterpiece; but when he asks for a review to be read to him, poor Jimmie can only make a frenzied effort to invent a favourable review himself, which, as he has found the poem totally incomprehensible, is a difficult task. In the evening he presents himself in the little room with some clumsy sentences scrawled in a dirty reporter's notebook, and gives them to the poet's father to read. Then a miracle happens. The old man is inspired, and breaks into a marvellous rhapsody in which he analyses at length the theme and execution of William Jordan's masterpiece, appraises the immensity of its achievement, and concludes with a prophecy that centuries hence, when civilization itself has sunk to be a mere shibboleth of the age of 'Reason', the half-divine, half-barbarous music of the unknown poet of *Reconciliation* will prove the only *via media* between the epoch of ample vision and the fantastic shadow world of the long ago.

When he has finished, the poet's face is starlike in its lustre. He stretches out his hand and tries to speak, but he has no longer the power to do so. The old man lifts Jimmie Dodson's dirty notebook to the lips of the dying man, who presses them to it with a joyful gesture and falls back dead.

The next day, while the old man is working in the little room, comes a tap on the closed shutters of the shop.

Upon the threshold of the shop he discovered an elderly, grizzled, grey-bearded man, a total stranger to him. The face of the stranger was of great resolution.

No sooner had the old man opened the door of the shop and beheld this unexpected appearance, than the man upon the threshold looked into his eyes. Suddenly he swept the hat from his head, and his grey hairs fluttered in the icy January wind.

'I think, sir,' he said in a harsh, strange accent, which yet was that of awe, 'I think, sir, I stand in the presence of the poet.'

The old man recoiled a step from his visitor in mute surprise.

'Forgive me, sir,' said his visitor, 'forgive the importunity of the vulgar, but I am hardly to blame. I have come all the way from Aberdeen to look upon the poet. You see, I have been a reviewer of books for the *Caledonian Journal* for fifty years, but a month ago I received a book from which my pen has refrained. But I have not been able to refrain my eyes from its author. To-day, upon my arrival from Aberdeen, I went direct to the publishers, who at first denied an acquaintance with the poet's name, but ultimately I found a young man in their office who sent me here.'

'The poet is not I,' said the old man humbly.

The visitor appeared surprised and incredulous.

'If you are not the poet, sir,' he said, 'I am sure you are a near kinsman.'

The old man peered at the grim features of his visitor with his half-blind eyes. 'You appear to be simple and gentle,' he said softly. 'Perhaps you will follow.'

The old man led his visitor into the shop, into the little room, which was now deserted, and thence up the stairs, into the small chamber lighted with dim candles, in which the poet lay.

As soon as the visitor beheld that which was therein contained, he sank to his knees by its side. He remained in that attitude a long while.

When he arose the aged man was gazing upon him with his half-blind eyes. They confronted one another like a pair of children.

Suddenly the visitor leaned across the bed in an act of further homage to the lifeless clay.

'Why do you do that?' said the white-haired man at his side.

'Why do I do this?' said the other, and his powerful spreading northern speech appeared to strike the walls of the tiny chamber. 'Why do I do this? I am afraid, sir, it must be left to my great-great-grandchildren to answer your question.'

Thus ended the most singular and the most powerful of all Snaith's books. It is not a novel—rather is it a poem, epic in its scope and lyrical in its intensity, a Divine Comedy, in the medieval sense, in which the most heterogeneous elements are molten together by the fire and inspiration of the treatment. In one sense, too, it is an allegory. The little room, the scar on William Jordan's cheek, the *Book of the Ages*, even William Jordan himself and his father, are all symbols through which Snaith tried to express his philosophy of life. As to the interpretation, one may perhaps quote Tennyson's well-known aphorism: 'Poetry is like shot silk with many glancing colours, and every reader must find his own interpretation according to his ability and according to his sympathy with the poet.' To enjoy the book the reader has no need to trouble himself with attempts to analyse the inner meaning. When once he has adapted himself to the *new notation* the passion and humour of the story carry him breathlessly along.

William Jordan Junior gives the impression of having been written at a high speed and inadequately revised, and although nothing is known—and probably nothing can ever be known with any certainty—about the actual circumstances, it is probable that this is near the truth. One may surmise that Snaith began the book soon after the end of July at his father's cottage in Seaview Lane, Skegness, where he was staying (he may, of course, have been turning it over in his mind during the summer) and wrote in a growing exaltation and excitement for ten or twelve weeks, his mind becoming more and more detached from reality and more and more absorbed into the life of its creatures. Then the great misfortune of his life befell him and one that disastrously affected the whole of his subsequent career. As his excitement mounted he had bouts of sleeplessness. Then strange ideas began to form themselves in his mind. Sometimes he seemed actually to be the New Deliverer on whom he had so long been brooding. Sometimes he felt that he was on the point of discovering a sixth sense that would enable man to transcend time and communicate with the unseen, foreseeing the future and winning a strange kind of immortality. Sometimes he seemed on the brink of formulating a new science of rationalism which would comprehend the supra-rational.

On November 4th he told his father that he began to feel his mind slipping away from him. His father became alarmed and sent for the doctor. Two days later John was found shouting from the window that he had been sent down by God to save the world, the man previously sent down having proved a failure—no doubt a reference to Henry Northcote—and calling on the passers-by to help him. He resisted with violence the efforts of his father and the doctor to restrain him. His condition now grew rapidly worse, and by November 9th it had become necessary to certify him and remove him to an asylum with his mind completely overthrown.

But the attack though severe was relatively short. His strong

constitution and temperate life stood him in good stead, and at
the end of January he was discharged as fully cured.

How far he had proceeded with *William Jordan* before his seizure
and how much work he was able to put into it after his discharge,
it is impossible to say. He was well enough to play a good deal
of cricket during the summer, taking part in the Druids week at
Skegness in July, when he scored 241 for six innings, with a highest score of 110. But the book when published at the beginning
of October, showed too evident signs of the disaster which had
befallen its author. There were one or two flagrant inconsistencies;
some chapters were spoiled by clumsy writing; there were a good
many printers' errors and some grammatical mistakes, to which
Snaith was always rather prone. For example, in all his forty years
of authorship he never seemed to have realized that 'who' and
'which' and 'as' and 'like' are not always interchangeable. What
one infers, therefore, is that the first draft of *William Jordan Junior*
was completed very rapidly before the author's breakdown, for
this is most likely to have occurred when he was involved in the
intensely moving final scenes, and it is difficult to believe that
he would have been allowed to work on a book of such
emotional intensity while he was still under medical care. Nor is
it probable that even when he was discharged from the hospital,
he was in a fit state to tackle anything but a rather superficial
revision.

Whatever the exact succession of events, he did somehow manage to bring the book into a more or less fit state for publication;
and although he probably did not expect immediate success for
it—*Northcote*'s comparative failure would have prevented any
great optimism—he must have hoped for some recognition from
critics and public. But *Jordan*'s actual reception was calamitous.
The 'new notation' was altogether too much for the critics.
Neither the *Spectator*, the *Athenaeum*, the *Academy*, the *Speaker*, nor
the *Saturday Review* mentioned it, and *The Times Literary Supplement*, the only important literary periodical which reviewed it at
all, dismissed it as an altogether unworthy successor of *Broke* and
Northcote—'bizarre, grotesque, mysterious and incomprehensible.'

A few of his old admirers, particularly Augustine Birrell
(now President of the Board of Education and in the throes of
his Education Bill), recognized *Jordan*'s merits, and one young
novelist, whom he had never met, Hugh Walpole, wrote to him

enthusiastically; but, except for this, it was as though the book on which he had lavished such intense emotional effort, had never been written, and whether he realized it or not, his life from this point was destined to be a long-extended anti-climax.

Although he must have begun to write again very soon after the appearance of *Jordan*, and his most financially successful book, a stylistic Edwardian social comedy called *Araminta*, appeared in 1908, he was never again able to put forth his full powers. He published twenty-five more books, covering a very wide range of subjects—Ruritanian, Foreign Legion, political, historical, picaresque, social comedy (*Love Lane*, published in 1920, was a really finished and delightful picture of life in a provincial town during the First World War), crime (though never of the plain 'Whodunit' type), Wellsian scientific: now and then he even approximated to the methods of Mr. P. G. Wodehouse. But, although in many of these books there were scenes or descriptions in which his genius flashed out for a few pages, he knew only too well that he had reverted to his old 'potboiler' days.

Probably he never quite gave up hope of being able to undertake some book which might prove a worthy successor to *Broke*, *Northcote* and *Jordan*, and the outbreak of war in 1914 found him working on a subject which was calculated to call forth all his powers. This, inspired by Masefield's *Dauber*, was the life-story of a slum boy, a sensitive, delicate child with the education of the gutter and the imagination of a poet, who escapes from a brutal guardian and is sent to sea under an equally brutal skipper. The first half of this book (*The Sailor*, published 1916) is brilliantly and movingly carried out; but then once more there were threats of disaster—the strain of such tense spiritual effort, accentuated by the overpowering emotions raised by the outbreak of war, proved too much for Snaith's mental stability. He awoke in the small hours of a summer morning to find himself wandering about a distant London suburb, without any idea how he had come there, and had to finish off the book in a perfunctorily romantic vein quite unworthy of its beginning. But even this did not break his spirit. Within a few weeks he had started upon an extremely ambitious subject, which, had he been able to put into it all that he had put into *Jordan*, might have proved an even greater achievement. It was called *The Coming* (1917) and tells of a Christ-like youth who appears in a Sussex village in the middle of the war and is hounded

H

into an asylum by the well-meaning, efficient, unimaginative vicar, who regards him as a dangerous pacifist. A point of peculiar interest about this book, which appeared two years before Rutherford published in the *Philosophical Magazine* his evidence for the first artificial transmutation of matter, is that in it Snaith described an American scientist who has made discoveries which if pushed to their logical conclusion are likely to result in the destruction of organic life on our planet. The contrasts between the Christ-like central figure, the naïve, lovable, irresponsible Yankee, and the stupid, self-confident, well-intentioned clergyman, provided a splendid theme for a work of tragic irony. But the author dared not project the full force of his imagination into the delineation of the central figure of the parable, who never comes alive, with the result that the book fails to achieve greatness.

During the long anti-climax of his life Snaith must have known that he had shot his bolt. This never soured him or made him resentful. He had terrible memories of his mental suffering during the first months of his collapse. He remembered the anguish of being condemned to dig his way through the centre of the earth to the Antipodes with his jawbone. He remembered identifying himself with Jesus Christ and enduring the agonies of crucifixion. Yet he never allowed such thoughts to dominate him or deter him from carrying on his chosen profession within the limits which Nature had so tragically imposed on him. His mind was always teeming with ideas, and he enjoyed the mechanical job of constructing a story, in which he became very proficient. In certain moods he came to believe, as he would shyly confide to his very few intimates, that he was in some sense a reincarnation of the Greek poet Menander. Such dreams, no doubt, helped him to preserve his equilibrium, as did the cricket which he continued to play with undiminished keenness until the onset of diabetes in the early 1920s made this impossible. His bowling never came back to him, but he played many notable innings'. In 1914 he helped to put on 340 for the first wicket for Skegness and District, his own share being 156 not out; and in 1921 he scored his last and one of his most brilliant centuries for Clifford Bax's Old Broughtonians, blocking a fast yorker to the boundary for four runs in the course of it.

It was inevitable that he should show some traces of his spiritual tragedy.

'We nicknamed him "The Gloomy Scribe",' wrote Clifford Bax after his death. '"No," he said on the eve of a cricket tour, "you will be a happier party without me." But we were not. We came to be deeply fond of "The Gloomy Scribe", and all those of us who played cricket with him as our star batsman will remember him with affection as long as we live.'

After the death of his wife in 1931 he published nothing for nearly four years, but his last book, *One of the Ones*, issued in 1937 after his death, was the most buoyant and genial of his later comedies, and during the last year of his life he spoke more than once of the possibility that he might yet again be able to tackle a big subject. Perhaps he never really believed this and what buoyed him up through those solitary years, as he stalked to and fro between the Hampstead Garden Suburb and the Garrick Club, was the half-acknowledged hope that one day, after all, the world might recognize that it had been granted him to dip the stylus in his blood and add one paragraph, however brief, to *The Book of the Ages*.

ROY FRANCIS TRUSCOTT

Roy Francis Truscott

EVERY NOW and then a man, whose name never appears in *The Dictionary of National Biography*, or even in *Who's Who*, achieves through the intensity of his effort for others, the influence which he radiates and the affection which he arouses, a masterpiece of living. This essay endeavours to catalogue one such masterpiece in the life of Roy Francis Truscott.

Roy was born on 4th September 1881, of a family well known in the City of London. His grandfather, Sir Francis Truscott, had been Lord Mayor in 1879–80 and his uncle, Sir George Wyatt Truscott, was to hold the same office in 1908–9. The family fortunes were based on the printing house of James W. Truscott & Sons, founded in 1824 by James Truscott, father of Sir Francis, who had come from Cornwall to London soon after the birth of his son.

Roy was the third of four sons (of whom Ralph was the eldest and Cyril the youngest, while one died in infancy) and was brought up in the comfortable, conventional atmosphere of an established City family.

His childhood was a happy one. The brothers and their sister Doris were devoted to one another and Roy was adored by his mother, a woman of great vitality, humour and good nature, and he adored her in turn. His father died when he was only twelve years old.

As a child he was remarkable for his neatness and orderliness, for the openness of his nature, for his tremendous ringing laugh and for a vivacity which made him the leader in all nursery mischief and nursery enjoyments.

It was a home in which the world and the future were taken for granted, and a public-school education followed as a necessary part of the convention.

Clifton was the school chosen for Roy and he was admitted to Laxton's House in 1893, his elder brother being then at Brown's in the Upper School.

Roy came to Clifton at a fortunate time. The school had only been in existence just over thirty years. During that short time it had been built up to a splendid position by two great headmasters, John Perceval and James Maurice Wilson, aided by assistant masters who included the poet T. E. Brown, and that remarkable scholar and athlete H. G. Dakyns, two of the most striking personalities who ever ministered to youth. Both these men had left the school a year or two before Roy joined it, but there were other remarkable figures among the masters who were to influence him profoundly—notably W. W. Asquith, a brother of the future Lord Oxford, and Sidney T. Irwin. 'Pup' Asquith who, owing to an accident in childhood, was almost a dwarf, was a profound scholar and fiery Radical, who made up in spirit and Yorkshire toughness what he lacked in stature. Irwin was of a very different type, an Irishman, with a wide knowledge of the literatures of Greece, Rome and England, whose enthusiasm was guided, but not subdued, by an unerring taste.

Roy made no mark at Clifton either in work or play. Athletics he always found repugnant and he was too independent to allow his mind to be absorbed by the ordinary school studies. But he probably read by himself more widely (both in Literature and History) than any other boy in the school. More important even than his reading was his extraordinary genius for friendship. Though he was neither athlete nor scholar and never became a prefect, his study had, before he left the school, become the focal point to which everyone in the House, from the VIth Form downwards, seemed to drift in their leisure moments.

That Roy did, in fact, derive great benefit from his years at Clifton subsequent events clearly showed. At the time, however, he does not seem to have realized the extent to which school had developed him. Indeed, so little was this impressed on himself or his family that it was only at the very last minute that the idea arose of sending him to the University.

An Old Cliftonian and King's man, a friend of his elder brother Ralph, dining with the family one night in London, was struck with his conversation and said to him: 'Why don't you go up to King's?' The suggestion was greeted with amazement by Roy, who replied: 'I'm not clever enough for the University.' However, to King's, Cambridge, he went in October, 1899, when just over eighteen.

He went up without any reputation to pick him out from the herd, and had rooms over what was then Beale's firework-and-toy shop in the Market Square. The little old house has now made way for the tall new Corporation buildings. There were several other Cliftonian freshmen at Cambridge and these soon resumed the old school habit of drifting into his rooms when they felt companionable. After a time they began to bring others with them, and thus the foundation was laid for what in Roy's second and later years became an institution so important as to be the real hub of the College life.

Every King's man of Roy's time will remember his unique position in the social life of the College; one might call it his unquestioned 'reign'. There was never any man who occupied a position remotely comparable to his in that very complete little world, except perhaps the now almost legendary J. K. Stephen. And Stephen was much more the kind of man whom one would expect to achieve dominance among his fellow-undergraduates: a great, burly, full-blooded athlete, a paragon of all the talents—fully equipped, one would say, to take popularity by storm.

Roy was none of these things; he had none of the obvious qualifications; but he did possess the most obvious and usually decisive of all disqualifications, in being defiantly and ostentatiously the reverse of an athlete. The name by which he was known—and delighted to be known—was 'The Sloth'. He made a positive virtue of abstinence from any form of exercise whatever. He would rise somewhere in the neighbourhood of noon, and proceed in due course to take his solitary constitutional, from his rooms in the Market Square to the shop on the opposite side where he used to get shaved. Once a week an organized concourse of his friends would compel him, much against his will, to don flannels and would convey him to the tennis or fives court. Roy had no energy to waste in opposing them; he came, and he stayed for the duration of the game, striking at any ball that happened to come within reach, but refusing, on principle, to budge an inch in pursuit of those that did not.

It was even his humour to adorn the walls of his room with

wise maxims of Benjamin Franklin and others in praise of industry or dispraise of sloth.

That such a defiant slacker could ever have been tolerated, let alone lionized, in a society obsessed even more than now by a cult of strenuous athletics, was something like a miracle. And yet the miracle happened. Roy's sloth was accepted as one feature of his popularity; the term of direct abuse, applied to him, became an affectionate tribute.

It was not until he got rooms in College, on the ground floor of the first staircase in Bodley's Buildings, that he fully established this position. His rooms were ideally situated to become the meeting ground of the College, since they were immediately on the corner which everyone must pass on their way between the front court and Bodley's Buildings. They were seldom empty before three in the morning, and, however late the hour, it was always in spite of strong protests from the host that the last of his guests departed. Many will remember the almost feminine note of pleading in his voice, as he laid a persuasive hand on the coat-sleeve of his reluctant visitor:

'Now, my dear fellow—it isn't really late—just another cigarette. I can't possibly go to bed for an hour yet.'

A remarkable feature of his rooms was that they had a personality as strong as that of their owner. They were always beautifully tidy. Books all arranged in neat rows in detached glazed cases. Walls, shelves and mantelpiece decorated with prints, busts and medallions of his great hero, Napoleon. Piano and pianola neatly stacked with music and music rolls. Even when crowded with noisy visitors and hazy with tobacco smoke they never seemed anything but neatly and indelibly his own. And the host was always as neat and emphatic as his surroundings. There was something irresistibly attractive about his trim figure and strongly marked face, which seemed a happy blend between the features of Napoleon Bonaparte and Mr. Punch. There he sat, evening after evening, in his easy chair, with his black hair parted precisely in the middle, a perfectly fitting blue suit, stiff white double collar, shiny pumps and a 'Diamond Straightcut' cigarette between his lips. For all his alleged sluggishness, his hands, which were beautifully shaped, were seldom still. His dark eyes were always bright and lively and his face full of changing expression. Now and then he would smack his lips in almost physical enjoyment of a shrewd argument or repartee, or throw back his head, arching his body in his chair, to emit that tremendous ringing laugh, which could be heard across the river or the market place. Proof of his mental energy was to be found in two curious habits which he retained through life. Whenever he was sitting at table or lying in bed he would take tablecloth, napkin or sheet and, using both hands and considerable muscular force, press it into a series of concertina pleats. No host's or hostess's linen was safe from this treatment, which would sometimes affect a breadth of two or three feet of cloth. The other habit was that of drawing, with great economy of line, endless little heads, all exactly the same, representing an astute-looking little man, clean-shaven, with bald cranium and hair brushed back behind the ears. His lecture notebooks were full of these and he would often cover the tablecloth with them, either using a pencil or, if this was impossible, the point of his fork.

Neither of these activities appeared in any way to absorb his conscious attention, yet both were performed with extraordinary precision and industry.

Another very characteristic habit, which stuck to him from school days until the end of his life, was his conscious and half-humorous enjoyment of the rotund phrase. A porter's tip became in his mouth 'a suitable honorarium'—and when helping a child to jam he would ask with all gravity if he might 'assist her to a little preserve'. He seemed to enjoy a fine long word as he enjoyed a good port or an apt quotation.

But the extraordinary sway which Roy exercised over his fellows was due to something more than his unusual personality. A well-known historian and philosopher, who, coming up to King's as a rather shy and farouche freshman in Roy's third year, was immediately admitted to his circle, has described his power very aptly. In Roy's presence everybody felt at his best, and felt that he was getting the best out of everybody else. There was an urbanity about these gatherings, a good temper and good fellowship that was especially remarkable, considering the bitter exclusions and rivalries of undergraduate society even in the best regulated of colleges. To Roy's room all cliques and individuals resorted on a footing of perfect equality.

It was one of his chief pleasures to encourage and draw out what was best in everyone, and more than one man who has since made a considerable figure in the world, owed Roy a debt of gratitude infinitely great for the patience and sympathy with which he helped him to overcome difficulties of temperament that might have effectually prevented him from ever deriving full benefit from the rough and tumble of social life at Cambridge.

He found me a very awkward, shy, and defiant undergraduate, [writes one of these] with what I think would be known at the present day as an inferiority complex. And I shall never forget the wonderful tact and kindness with which he took me up, and gave me confidence in myself. My meeting him, I feel sure, was a turning point in my life, and his friendship was a joyous and lovely experience from which I must have derived untold good.

There was surely something of conscious art in the way in which Roy succeeded in breaking down every barrier and uniting all these otherwise discordant elements. He used to speak of his rooms as 'the horns of the altar', and in nothing did he take greater pleasure than in bringing together men who were notoriously uncongenial, and compelling them to fraternize in his presence.

Some of his devices were of extraordinary ingenuity. Once, for example, he healed what looked like being an irreconcilable feud between two fourth-year men, by staging a trial of their case in his rooms, with judge, counsel and witnesses all complete. The affair ended, precisely as Roy intended it to end, with everybody in the best of humours, and all bitterness laughed out of court.

But the influence he wielded was most of all due to the sheer goodness and sweetness of his nature. He desired nothing but the happiness of his friends, and his friendship embraced the whole circle of his acquaintance. Never, if he could help it, should anyone feel snubbed or humiliated in his presence. Never did he attempt to score off anybody, or allow anyone, however richly he may have deserved it, to lose face under his auspices. He could suffer fools gladly and lend an interested ear to bores, and often they would respond to his treatment in a way that no one would have imagined possible.

Every man at King's had to read for an honours degree, and Roy was entered for the History Tripos. He had the advantage of two very remarkable teachers, Lowes Dickinson and Oscar Browning, the famous 'O.B.'; but he cannot have done much work during his first three years and he certainly spent a good deal too much money on tobacco and refreshments for his *salon*, since he delighted to provide for his guests not only cigarettes and drinks, but such recondite delicacies as dessert biscuits, Chinese figs and Pei-wong ginger, the consumption of which must have been most heartening to the suppliers. The effect on his trustees was less favourable, and it is pleasant to recall the twinkling and deferential humour with which he would refer to their occasional remonstrances.

And his trustees were not his only embarrassment.

It was a standing joke about him in his undergraduate days that his path was strewn with the broken hearts of female admirers. It seemed impossible for any of Roy's lady acquaintances to refrain from falling hopelessly in love with him, and as it was not his way to hurt anybody's feelings with a stern negative, he was often hard put to it to make a final getaway from some determined huntress.

But in spite of more temptations than come to most men he was, and remained, in the deepest sense moral; and this, not so much as a matter of conscious principle, as because he was perfectly incapable of doing bodily or spiritual injury to anyone.

It was during this time that he first began to sing, taking lessons from Jos. Reid, a teacher in Cambridge. He had a baritone voice of quite remarkable range and brilliance, though a little metallic in tone. His ear and sense of rhythm were excellent, and a friend who often accompanied him put his finger on what was the main reason for his unfailing success. 'Roy Truscott,' he said, 'sang for the enjoyment of others and for his own'. He did not excel at classical songs. His highest flights were *Myself When Young* (Liza Lehmann) and Schumann's *Two Grenadiers*, of which he would give a rousing performance. But for the most part his repertoire consisted of songs like *Off to Philadelphia*, *Little Grey Fox* and, most popular of all, *Chorus, Gentlemen, Just Once More*. His holding of the last note in the refrain of this had to be heard to be believed. A thing which added not a little to the pleasure of Roy's audience was Jos. Reid's theory that by smiling on one's top notes one could add to their brightness—Roy's top-note smile, added to his natural geniality, was irresistible. He had little musical education and could only accompany himself in two songs—'*A tall stalwart lancer lay dying*, rendered with rigid and meticulous accuracy, and

Samson's song from *Samson and Delilah*, which he played excruciatingly and with conscious and even exaggerated inaccuracy, singing the while with an incredible gusto which never failed to bring down the house. But he had plenty of feeling in addition to his musical sense, and sang all his songs with insight not only for the melody but for the words, and made the audience go with him. Sometimes he sang well, sometimes indifferently, but always with abandon and with the idea fixed in his mind that he wished to give pleasure.

When in his fourth year he returned to his old rooms at Beale's, the other inhabitants of the Market Place and neighbouring streets would throw open their windows in the evening when he began to sing, and the close of every song was greeted with shouts and clapping of hands and loud calls for other favourites.

Roy's Cambridge career was unusually protracted. In his third year he had a serious attack of appendicitis which prevented him from taking his Tripos. This was probably fortunate for him as it gave him another year (out of College) in circumstances more favourable to sustained effort. Of course he had done a certain amount of work during his time in College and had profited greatly by spending the long vacation of 1900 with Canon J. F. Kendall, a well-known King's man and distinguished scholar who took pupils at his Norfolk vicarage. His gain from this visit was much more than scholastic, for he there met for the first time Ruth Kendall, then a child of eleven, who later became his wife.

One Easter vacation he spent with two friends on a so-called 'reading party' in Obersroth, a small village of about two hundred inhabitants in the Black Forest. Before many days had elapsed Roy was the accepted '*englischer Onkel*' of all the children in the village. Whenever he emerged from his *Gasthaus* the whole village was made aware of the fact by the shrieks of delight which arose, and there was an immediate stampede of twenty or more children to greet him. His German vocabulary was negligible and they, of course, had no English; but he knew them all by name and seemed to engage in quite intelligible conversations with them.

It so happened that one of the party came of age during their stay at Obersroth and Roy insisted that this event must be celebrated in proper fashion by a 'twenty-firster' dinner-party. Somehow he secured the attendance of the village policeman and postman with their wives, the local forester, the owner of the only shop in Obersroth, with wife and mother-in-law, and two or three others, together with the landlord of the inn and the whole of his staff. Fifteen sat down to dinner, which began at six and ended at about ten o'clock and was one of the most hilarious affairs ever remembered in the village. The effect of his speech (delivered in German) was indescribable.

During his last year, without seriously altering his mode of life, he managed to do a reasonable amount of reading. His notebooks of this period are models of neatness and precise method, and show clearly how it was that he succeeded in absorbing so much information with (apparently) so little expenditure of effort. Finally he came out with a very good Second Class—a feat which surprised most of his contemporaries, but not, I fancy, Lowes Dickinson or O.B., to whom he always felt he owed as much as to Irwin and Asquith. In O.B.'s happy phrase, he had shown that 'he could afford his bad habits'.

INTERLUDE

The years between Cambridge and his marriage were uneventful for Roy. It was decided that he should not enter the family business, as both his brothers were already working there, and he prepared to be called to the Bar, a feat which he accomplished at the Inner Temple in January, 1909, after a very leisurely preparation, during which he found the qualifying examinations rather an embarrassment.

During this period his great devotion to his mother, known universally as the 'R.P.' or 'Revered Parent', and the amenities of life at her home in Avenue Road, Regent's Park, rather absorbed his energies, though he continued all the time to read voraciously, and was always eager to talk and to encourage others to talk. He led a social existence and must have screwed up many acres of tablecloth and napkin, and driven many hostesses crazy by another of his idiosyncrasies.

He simply could not be punctual. If he arranged to meet one at, say, seven o'clock, it was probably nearer to half-past eight before he put in an appearance. If dinner was at eight, he rarely appeared before a quarter to nine. Many people must have recollections of anxious-looking hostesses and openly chafing hosts desperately trying to entertain their hungry guests while waiting for Roy to complete the party. When he did arrive, perhaps an hour late, his explanations and apologies would be so disarming that annoyance seemed to evaporate in the sunshine of his presence.

He was at first uncertain whether to practise on the Common Law or the Equity side. There was, however, no need to decide this forthwith, for there is no better preparation for a Common Law practice than a period spent in Chancery Chambers. Accordingly he went first as a pupil to chambers in Lincoln's Inn, where he acquired a knowledge of Conveyancing and Company Law, which many Common Law men find themselves constantly regretting that they do not possess. When after the war the family business claimed him, this experience was of the greatest value to him.

His original intention was to practise in London. This was natural for a member of a family which has for so many years taken a leading part in the affairs of the City. It was, however, at that time almost inevitable for a member of the Common Law Bar to join one or other of the circuits and to attend Assizes and Quarter Sessions for some years after his call, whatever his ultimate ambition might be. Several of Roy's friends at King's had joined the North-Eastern Circuit and were already beginning slowly and painfully to acquire practices there, and no doubt Roy was largely influenced by this fact when he chose the North-Eastern. Certainly his old friends welcomed his arrival there for the Winter Assizes of 1909.

Meanwhile only occasional briefs of very small importance came his way and, though he never complained, there can be no doubt that he was disappointed that his hopes of getting work from his connexion with the City were not fulfilled. It may well be that this would only have been a matter of time. His apprenticeship on circuit was not yet finished when war broke out, and London solicitors have an objection to delivering briefs to barristers whose practice takes them frequently out of London. In due course Roy would have given up circuit, but for the time being he was wisely gaining experience there.

During the first six months of 1911 he held the office of 'Junior'. To those who have never been on circuit this may seem a small matter. But in fact it is not so. Practically the whole of the

Roy Francis Truscott

arrangements necessary for circuit and for the circuit mess are under the Junior's control. He has to get in all subscriptions and has a very wide control over expenditure. In matters of professional discipline he is, so to speak, the executive officer, and his voice carries great weight. In addition, and by no means of least importance, he is the supreme head of all circuit festivities. From his decisions on these occasions there is no appeal and it is not expected that justice will have any bearing on the matter. In such a capacity Roy, of course, excelled and his period in the Junior's chair was long remembered.

To many it may have seemed that during these first years in London Roy was marking time and even wasting his abilities. But his spiritual development was continuing and his power of sympathy growing wider and deeper—perhaps his refusal to concentrate too severely on the practical side of life was essential to this development. The following account, written by Sir Hugh Walpole shortly after Roy's death, throws a clear light on his inner life and links Roy, the undergraduate of careless pre-war Cambridge, with Roy, the Happy Warrior of 1914–18:

In this brief sketch of Roy Truscott, as I knew him, I must seems I fear, egoistic. But anyone who remembers a friendship with Roy will remember himself, because that was what Roy always did— lived *for* you, encouraged you to feel that *your* problems were the only ones that mattered.

My small contribution to this book goes back a long way, and it is with a shock of surprise that I realize how seldom I saw him during the last thirty years—once or twice in the Athenaeum, once at dinner at his house. That is all. And yet I feel as though we had been often together.

For he was, as things so queerly happen, one of the most important people in my life, and I can imagine how many others have in this last year been saying the same and been surprised to find that it was so. There are people scattered here and there about the world who seem to exist chiefly to be friends to others at the exact moment when they are needed. Roy was like that. I don't mean that he was a self-abnegating saint, nor that he hadn't a perfectly good full happy life of his own, or that he wasn't practical and successful in it. But he was, I suspect, again and again the best sort of counsellor to people who had been driven by some stress or storm to see life askew and to feel some sort of terror because of that. I had better quote my own case.

I

I cannot remember where my own first meeting with Roy was. I can't remember him at all at Cambridge. He was my senior there. I arrived at Emmanuel very naïve, very self-conscious and very apprehensive. I was apprehensive because I had been a great failure both at school and at home. I shall never forget my realization that first night at dinner in Hall, of my beginning life entirely anew. As I looked round at the men sitting there, I thought: 'No one knows what a failure I am. What an ass I've been. They all take me for one of themselves.' I had been accustomed so long for everyone to think me a fool that this was an immense relief.

I was naïve and inexperienced because I had kept to myself for so long. I was intended for the Church but in my heart I didn't want to be a clergyman. I wanted to be a novelist and everyone thought that ambition not only ridiculous, but even criminal. I was bothered about religion. I was bothered about sex. And I had never talked to anyone about either of these problems.

But I did not meet Roy at first and as I have said, I am not sure that I met Roy at Cambridge at all. After a year there I was in complete confusion. A year's missioning in Cambridge had done my religion no good at all; but, worst of all, I did not know how to work. No one attempted to show me. Even my writing ambitions were frustrated, for when I wrote an essay on Meredith's poetry for the *Emmanuel College Magazine*, the editor of the same informed me that I was unhappily not up to their standard.

It was in this state of confusion and bewilderment that I met Roy. We must have become friends very quickly for my first actual picture of him is in his bedroom at his family's London house. I was a guest and a very happy one. That was the happiest family conceivable, and I can see now that all its happiness radiated round Roy. When he laughed—it was a queer, unique, rather shrill laugh—you had to laugh too, however serious or even miserable you might be.

I remember that the very first thing he tried to teach me was to be tidy in my clothes. He was himself immaculate and I can see him now examining his perfect finger-nails and sitting down with care, so that his clothes should not be spoiled. Not that he was a self-conscious dandy. Far from it! It was simply his innate determined sense of the perfect order of things.

From this came, I think, his then passion for Napoleon. Whether that lasted or no I can't be sure, but in those days his rooms were full of Napoleon portraits, busts, death-masks, snuff-boxes, letters. I was then, as always, a magpie collector, but I hated Napoleon and I will always remember Roy's calm, quiet good-humoured chuckle (he chuckled superbly) after one of my tirades. 'Quite, quite. But he was *single*-minded, the best thing to be.'

He said that perhaps because it was the very last thing he himself was. He was considered in those days, I remember, to be incorrigibly lazy. When we were reading history in the Vacation with Kendall—the Kendalls were an extraordinary family and Mrs. Kendall was so unique a personality that she demands a whole book to herself—Roy was always down very late in the morning. The Kendall boys were very athletic—Locke Kendall I cared for deeply—and Roy's horror at any sort of athletic accomplishment was a charming thing. He would walk, most perfectly dressed, smoking cigarettes, a little way down the road, and then would come that shrill cackle of laughter and instantly the country and country animals and running and racing and tennis and cricket would become slightly absurd.

And so it was, whether in London or at the Kendalls', that I received what I needed then more than anything else on earth—guidance and direction.

Roy was not only broad-minded; he was unshockable. He had the absolute legal mind that weighed always dispassionately every side of the question. But with the legal mind he had also the loving and humorous heart. I must have seemed to him a queer kind of being. He was already so truly sophisticated. He had been born, I think, with a deep knowledge of real life. I had none—only a panicky sense that I was heading for some sort of ruin.

When I saw that whatever I told him he would not laugh at me nor regard me with horror, I told him everything. He was the first human being in the whole world to whom I completely opened my heart. They were not, I suspect now, very terrible confessions but they seemed to me then quite terrible. It was one of the turning points of my life when Roy showed me that there were so many others like myself. He told me too, God forgive him the lie, that I had a fine future as a writer. He had, of course, nothing to go on at all, but I suppose that he saw that some sort of persuasion of that sort was what I badly needed. He must have seen too that I was badly suited to be a clergyman!

But the really wonderful thing about Roy was that in these little kindnesses to me, as in all his kindnesses all his life through, he forgot himself entirely. He was Christ-like in this. There are many people who, for policy or whatever, try to persuade you when you are with them that you are the only person who matters. With Roy it was always actually so. His unselfishness was a miracle and after he married Ruth Kendall even the natural slightly fussy pre-occupations with the daily order of his life left him.

He had, I think, exactly the right sense of proportion about life—never taking it too tragically, never allowing his heart to be deadened—and in his last long illness how that wise common sense and humorous chuckle and rock-bottom courage must have helped him!

The great debt I owe to him is that in my youth he took away my *horror* of life. He taught me a little to laugh at myself. And he showed me how a man, without priggishness and pomposity, can constantly give his life for others.

I have never myself learned that lesson. But I know that it can be done.

THE GREAT WAR, 1914–18

It may be that the Bar was not the ideal career for Roy—not because he lacked the requisite ability, but because it was too egotistic a profession for him. To bring out his full powers, he needed the feeling that he was working for others.

The spur came to him from two sources: first, his marriage in 1913—a perfect union of hearts and minds to which his debt in after years was incalculable and always most feelingly acknowledged; and secondly, the Great War.

It was the war which first fully revealed his essential greatness. One would have thought, judging by his habits and interests, that no one could have been less fitted to endure the restrictions of military discipline, the trivialities of military routine, and the appalling horrors and discomforts of life in the trenches; and indeed, these things were anathema to him.

Yet he endured them all with a cheerfulness and hardihood that could scarcely be excelled.

All discomforts and all suffering were compensated by his devotion to duty, his sense of comradeship and his delight in the magnificent qualities and the abounding humours of the British soldier.

Roy Truscott was certainly one of the most remarkable soldiers in the British Army in the First World War, remarkable for his apparent unsuitability ('as utterly unfitted for war as Mr. Pickwick' was the description of one who met him in France); for the originality of his methods; for his efficiency in every kind of situation, and for his amazing power of getting on with men of every rank, character and nationality.

The war brought to light capacities in him which none but his most intimate friends realized that he possessed, and perhaps no one had realized their full extent. It is small wonder that stories about him circulated by scores through all ranks, and are still remembered and recounted.

One of these related to his selection for the 16th Battalion of the Sherwood Foresters. At the conclusion of his six-months' training at Berkhamsted he found himself gazetted as subaltern in some battalion in which he had no personal interest. As many of his friends from the O.T.C. had already been picked for the Sherwood Foresters, he made a sudden Napoleonic decision to try a direct assault. The Colonel of the 16th Battalion was, he knew, selecting officers at Buxton and interviewing seven or eight candidates by appointment in a hotel. When all the men had been seen, the waiter came in to say that Lance-Corporal Truscott wished to see the Colonel. Roy had come from London on his own initiative, hoping for a vacancy, and the twinkle in his eye, combined with his complete disregard of convention, were irresistible—a vacancy was earmarked for him immediately.

He very soon settled down in his Battalion, and in September was promoted to Captain.

His first year showed him at his miraculous best. Paul Coleridge, who was his second-in-command in 'A' Company, has described it delightfully:

> My first impression of him was that he had somehow slipped off the cover of *Punch* and this was not belied by his behaviour, for he took everything as a joke and by always looking on the bright side had the same tonic effect on the spirits of his company as is claimed by that journal for its readers.

> It was amusing and also instructive to watch the effect of his method of dealing with the men compared with that of our Company Commander, a fire-eater of the old school, who used to curse and literally grind his teeth at the men on parade, with astonishingly little result, except perhaps a few hardly suppressed smiles; whereas Roy had only to indicate mildly what he wanted and even the old soldiers did it to the best of their ability.

> The private soldier is very quick in summing up his officers and by the time we got to Witley Ridge, Roy had become a kind of Father Confessor and friend to the men in his company and also to many others.

> He was incredibly industrious and painstaking and I can see him now in the lodgings which we shared with him and his wife,

surrounded with piles of conduct sheets and chits and bits of blotting-paper on which he had drawn countless strange-looking heads.

Just before we were due to go out a mule had the temerity to kick our Company Commander on the shin and, to the delight of everyone, Roy took over.

It would be difficult to imagine anyone less suited by nature for the life of an officer in the front line. He loathed mud with a bitter hatred only equalled by his horror of being cold and wet, and the thought of gas gave him the shivers. He could not bear the sight of blood and it seemed as if it would need an earthquake to keep him to time!

On the morning that we entrained for France he drove his wife—and mine—nearly frantic and it took their combined efforts and that of his batman to get him down to the station at all.

He got there at the last minute, arriving in the nick of time completely unruffled and as if he had all day to spare.

The same thing happened at Havre where he had a brother who suggested that it might be pleasant to sleep one more night in a decent bed. Naturally he went, and in the morning the company packed up and fell in ready to move off. No Roy! Time slipped by and there was his valise still open in his tent with his batman dancing round like a cat on hot bricks. The Transport Officer was yelling at him that if he didn't pack up that —— valise and put it on the —— transport straight away he would —— well leave it behind.

Presently two figures appeared at the far end of the parade ground strolling quietly along and obviously enjoying a joke. Of course, his kit got on to the transport all right but it must have taken a year off the life of his batman.

Being now a Company Officer it was his privilege to ride at the head of it. Poor Roy! One of his major attainments was certainly not horsemanship. The Transport Officer was approached and told to provide his best imitation of an animated armchair. The result was a small grey animal incredibly wide in the beam which looked as if it had come straight from pulling Queen Victoria in her old age.

The weather was cold and when riding Roy used to put on his trench coat over his British warm. By the time he had got on his equipment, water-bottle, revolver, map case and so forth, he was distinctly top heavy. In this kit mounting presented some difficulties, and sure enough his worst forebodings were fulfilled one very wet and windy day when, as he heaved himself up to the saddle, his horse, which had apparently been dozing before, suddenly came to life, with the result that Roy completed a semicircle and landed in a large and muddy pool on the offside. Most officers would be annoyed to say the least of it at taking a mud-bath in front of their men, but not Roy. That great laugh, which could be recognized a mile away, rang out and he came up smiling as usual thereby weaving one more strand in the skein which bound him to the hearts of his company.

And then the front line—with Roy, still surrounded with chits, calling for his batman to produce hot water in the most impossible places so that he could at least *try* to be clean. No bombardment would ever stop him from shaving and it appeared that he would rather be sniped than have his hands dirty.

At Richebourg where we were in the line for five weeks on end, he had a canvas bath brought and fixed up under some corrugated-iron sheets.

His extremely irreverent junior subaltern used to amuse us all—and him—by bombing the bath dugout with lumps of mud when Roy was attempting his ablutions. Unfortunately the German batteries joined in the fun—but not with mud—so the bathroom was reluctantly abandoned.

Back in rest billets no concert was complete unless he sang some of the old favourites with that deep baritone voice that nearly took the roof off and seemed so much too big for his body.

And so it went on, into trenches and out again, round the Salient and down on to the Somme.

Few companies can have been looked after with the fatherly care that Roy bestowed on us and he was continually crossing swords with higher authority over it.

One day when we were digging trenches in a back area, orders were issued that any new potatoes which were unearthed were to be set aside for the French inhabitants.

The Brigadier who was watching noticed that the men's pockets were getting very bulgy and presently he called 'Captain Truscott, what are your men doing with those potatoes?' Roy's prompt answer, 'That is what I'm trying not to see, sir', was not perhaps what he expected but it had the desired result, for the Brigadier turned his horse with suspicious haste and departed.

'A' Company was to all intents and purposes a happy family party, but this was too good to last. The Brigadier perceived what we had known all along, that here was a bright blade which was too keen to be dulled by the ordinary routine of trenches—and so we lost him. As each successive staff noted what the Brigadier had seen, they took him too, until he arrived at G.H.Q. Luckily for G.H.Q. he could not go any further, except perhaps to Buckingham Palace, which may be the reason—who knows?—why they never lost heart at G.H.Q., even in the blackest days.

Many stories filtered through to us from G.H.Q.

Most officers have a certain awe of the real 'Brass Hat' but to Roy they were simply fair game.

When the women drivers went out to Wimereux, an order was circulated that they must not be taken to lunch in restaurants by the staff officer they were driving.

To Roy it seemed the height of discourtesy to leave his fair driver in the car while he fed, so he used to take her in. One day they spied one of the G.H.Q. generals lunching with a very alluring French Countess. Next day the General had Roy on the mat and asked him why he had disobeyed the order, and I think his face must have gone as red as his tabs when Roy replied, 'Well, I didn't peach about you, sir!'

War is a grim business but at least it shows what is in a man.

For nine months we shared the same dugout, stood together through countless bombardments with our hearts in our mouths, wondering where the next shell would drop, kept each other awake in the chilly dawn at stand-to or basked together in the sun on quiet days.

Never once did he appear rattled or afraid. He was always his usual serene self, cheerful, confident and with that happy understanding of the man's point of view which is one of the rare gifts of leadership.

Few officers can win the hearts of an entire company in so short a time, but when they do they are beyond price.

Equally delightful is it to see him through the eyes of the men he commanded. It must be rare indeed that an officer has earned such accounts as some of them have written of him.

No doubt he was fortunate in his comrades. The Sherwood Foresters are recruited chiefly from the Notts and Derbyshire miners—a hardy, intelligent and loyal people.

From the first moment these men realized Roy's wonderful character. A. Alvey, who was his orderly from 15th June 1915, and then his batman in France, recalls a typical incident. Alvey was a miner and had been brought in (a very raw hand indeed) to wait at the officers' mess. He found himself completely out of his depth; not even knowing when a course was finished, or on which side of a diner to serve. He was on the point of giving up in despair, when a young lieutenant at the table hastily scribbled a note and covertly passed it to him:

"Drink right — Food left — Knives and Forks together first."

This gave the man fresh hope and enabled him to continue the evening's work without serious blunder. The lieutenant was, of course, Roy.

It was no wonder that his men kept his memory alive in their hearts long after the coming of peace had parted them from him, and that when Death took him in the prime of his years it seemed a blow struck at their own firesides, calling forth tributes worth more than all the honours in the Army List.

Enclosed please find my attempt [wrote Sergeant Wiggett, No. 1 Platoon A Company] to tell a few incidents of Colonel Truscott's life as I knew him. All the incidents are related by one or other of the following:

> Sergeant Hildreth
> Pte. A. Alvey
> Pte. J. Watts
> Pte. Hutchinson
> Pte. Richardson
> Sgt. Pegg
> Sgt. Trower
> Pte. B. Fletcher
> Myself,

but all I have mentioned are incidents that I can remember as far as I can remember in correct detail.

*　　*　　*

A public-house in a mining village just outside Nottingham.
'Hello, Alf., what brings you here?'
'Some very sad news, mate—the Colonel has passed away.'
'What, "Father", do you mean?'
'Yes, I am sorry to say.'
Placing his half-empty pint pot of beer on the counter, sits down on a form as though stunned.
'You don't mean it—is it true?'
'Yes.'
'Well, I am sorry; we old miners of old 'A' Company have lost the best pal anyone ever had. Right from Buxton 1915 to now, he has always thought of us, yes and helped us many a time when things have been bad with us.'
Enter three other members of his old Company. They are each

given a pint of beer before breaking the sad news. The effect of the news on these men, I shall never forget, men used to a hard life in France and in the mines, all were speechless, and without a word, hats were taken off, glasses raised and not a word spoken.

After a time the conversation turned to Colonel Truscott.

'Do you remember him at Buxton?'

'Don't I just! when he first went on parade with No. 1 Platoon, how small he looked in front of all those fine Derbyshire policemen —you remember No. 1 Platoon was made up of nearly all policemen at the start, but they was soon moved to other Platoons and Companies as N.C.O.s, and No. 1 Platoon was made up of miners; we soon found out he was a Toff and understood the miners almost at once.'

'What about when we marched to Sheffield, how he started us to sing as we marched along. I can see him now beating time with his cane, while we tried to sing "Tipperary". Yes and when we got to Hope, how he looked after us, seeing that we all had plenty to eat, yes, and subbed one or two of you old Blighters to get a pint.'

'He did that. I was one of them.'

'At Sheffield he soon made himself felt, what about that first Concert in the Y.M.C.A.? How the boys cheered and clapped after he had sung "Up From Somerset" and "Glorious Devon" and after that he was always top of the bill at our Concerts.'

'What about when he took us in rifle drill for the first time at Sheffield, do you remember the command 'Sloop!' how he hung on to it so long, that not only himself, but the whole Company had to burst out laughing; how the boys enjoyed it.'

'That was the time when the news came that we had to go to Aldershot, how he sent round to the Company, and said if anyone wanted to go on leave and had not the money, to go and see him; what a parade at Company Orderly Room: how much did he lend, did you say? about £70, but what he took back was another matter. I can assure you he was a poor moneylender.'

'Do you remember when he paid out the Sergeant at Witley, the one that had borrowed money from the Privates, and made him pay them all back, how the men liked him for that action, and how many weeks that Sergeant had to go without pay.'

'How did the Old Man wangle all those extra tins of salmon after that very long test march at Witley? You remember the march when he was giving a hand to carry men's rifles, etc., so that they did not drop out and not a man in his Company did.'

'Do you remember him standing by the Medical Officer on our final inspection before going to France? What a risk he ran: several members of his Company wanted to go to France with him, but was not fit. Their names was not called, but all was marked fit.'

During the period of training in England he had very little crime in his Company, and any man that had to be brought before him was treated as a man. During the evidence Capt. Truscott would sit quite unconcerned drawing faces on the blotter (some say a horse's, others, ladies').

When the evidence was finished, his usual question:

'Did you do it?'

'What did you do it for?'

'Don't do it again, please,' and very few did.

Never was a man punished if there was a possible way of getting round *King's Rules and Regulations*; if there was, you could rely on Capt. Truscott's knowing it.

By this method every man in his Company was put on his honour, and very seldom was he let down. If he was, Capt. Truscott would say: 'My boy, he has done as well as he knew how to do.'

How we wondered what he would be like in France, whether he would keep that smile and wonderful spirit, but we had not long to wait to find out that the smile would not come off. When we set out to march up to the line, how it snowed when we started, and about mid-day the sun came out and nearly boiled us all; do you remember how he started us singing and never let our spirits drop; he was wonderful for I consider it was the most trying march we ever did.

Our first trip in the line at Laventie surprised most of us; do you remember the first night those mines going up on our right, and how Jerry started to shell us. I can see the Old Man now going round the line as if nothing was happening; when the strafe had finished and all was well, how particular he was to see that the N.C.O.s had made out their duty sheets, so that every man had a fair share of duty, and not only did he see that the N.C.O.s did their share, but he did his part, and invariably his turn was between midnight and 4.0 a.m. On many occasions it was my privilege to accompany him, and unfortunately he got me into one of his habits, chain-smoking, for Capt. Truscott always had a large box or tin of 'Gold Flake', and during our turn of duty it was all smoke. He did like a 'Gold Flake'.

'Do you remember that man of another Company that got Field Punishment and was tied to a wagon wheel when we came out of the line, in full view of the battalion. As soon as Capt. Truscott saw him, by some means he had him moved to another part of the camp out of view and advised the man to volunteer to do his sentence in the line, which he did; he was not tied up again.'

'How we laughed at the way he got over the Brass Hats that got into the habit of coming round the line about 10.0 a.m., fetching the Company Officer out to go round with them. Captain Truscott had a sentry on duty with instructions to say that he was just taking a rest and was not to be disturbed, as he had had a very strenuous night; it always worked, and many a time he has been sitting doing his office work, writing to wives and mothers in England of men that had been killed or wounded, just as if he was sitting in Company Headquarters at camp in England—yes, and always that smile on his face.'

'Do you remember how upset he was when the Colonel found the man asleep on Gas Guard, after he had only been on duty about ten minutes. Of course that man had to go before the Commanding Officer, but Captain Truscott pleaded that the man must be unwell, got him sent before the Medical Officer; the last I heard of that man was that he was sent home and died of consumption. Before the man was found asleep he appeared to be in the best of health, but Captain Truscott insisted that he would not have gone to sleep had he been well. He was right.'

'Captain Truscott always seemed to be helping someone to get out of trouble. You remember the man that was court-martialled for being asleep on duty on the islands, how he placed all the N.C.O.s' duty sheets before the court and proved what long hours he had done, but it did not save him, it was two years' sentence he got if I remember rightly, but I can see Captain Truscott now standing with one hand on the boy's shoulder (for he was but a boy not much more than nineteen) saying, "Ask to be transferred to the Trench-Mortar Battery and do your sentence in the line"; inside three months his sentence was wiped out, and later on he received a decoration I believe.'

'You was on working party up the line, when the Company Head-quarters at Festubert was shelled and set on fire just as Captain Truscott was in the middle of a bath, you should have seen him running about in his birthday suit directing salvage operations, in his same old smiling way, not in the least perturbed, more interested in the cooker than his clothes.'

'How we missed him when he joined the Brass Hats. He used to visit us whenever possible; on one occasion when we was behind the line, a party of us was sitting on the floor of our shed playing cards, "brag" was the game, when a knock came at the door and in walked Major Truscott. Of course we started to get up, he soon stopped us, made us finish our game, then sat down on a blanket and talked of old times whilst we all ate his chocolates and smoked his "Gold Flakes".'

'The next time I saw Captain Truscott in France was the barracks at Ypres, you remember when he came to defend that Sergeant that was court-martialled.'

'Oh yes, the Sergeant that was transferred from some other regiment and had only been with us a short time when he was charged with being drunk in the line.'

'My word, it was smart how he got him off. You know what a slow job those court martials was, after taking all the evidence and writing it down, the Chairman called on Major Truscott for the defence. He looked at 'is watch and said: "Gentlemen, it is nearly one o'clock, and as my defence will take a long time, I propose we adjourn for lunch." The Court agree and into our Officers' Mess they go for lunch, Major Truscott leads the way. When he gets inside he calls "H——" (that was the head waiter) "I am very cold, bring me a tot of rum." All the officers did the same, a good lunch, what they had to drink with it I do not know, but just before it was time to go and carry on with the Court, Major Truscott calls out: "H——, I have a very long job on this afternoon and it is very cold, bring me a tot of rum to keep me warm." All officers had same.'

'When Court commenced again, all evidence read over in which it stated that this Sergeant had his rum issue with 'B' Company then had another with 'A' Company, Major Truscott got up with that confident smile on his face, pulled his British warm into position, and said: "Gentlemen, after hearing the evidence, I am afraid my defence will not take as long as I anticipated, for if this N.C.O., a time-serving N.C.O. at that, was drunk on two tots of rum, I must ask you to draw the Court to a close for we are all drunk." The Sergeant walked out a free man.'

Here is another soldier's reminiscence (from Sergeant Trower):

I remember once, when we came off the Somme, and we were resting in billets at Volkerinhove, one morning I was acting C.S.M. I had a working party to parade and as I had them on parade (in line) how he gave them a lecture, about borrowing money from him. He said that they were borrowing all the time till pay day, when (some) would pay back on pay day, and start borrowing again next morning. He said this must cease. And after this talk I moved them to the right in fours. 'Form fours—right,' and just as if prearranged, about on the third or fourth step they struck up singing 'Working, working, working, always b——y working, from Reveille to Lights Out, we are working all the time.' To the tune in *Ancient and Modern* 'Holy, Holy, Holy'. Well—how I recall the incident. How he stood and laughed, he about cracked his sides.

And one from Sergeant Barkes, which I think sums up what his men felt and those that are left still feel for Roy:

Now, Alf, I must relate one little incident that always sticks in my memory. 'Stand to' in the front line trench, day-break, everybody including myself fed up and not caring what happens next. Along comes that smiling face of Captain Truscott, parcel under his arm, might be walking down the Strand, certainly not troubling much about Jerry. After the usual 'Good morning' the following is what he said to me. 'Well Barkes, I do exceedingly well as a money-lender. I am now going to try cigarette selling.' With that out comes the parcel and we are all given three packets each. They were not army issue either. My word, the change that came over the faces of those boys. How they loved that gentleman, could anyone help but do? Never happy unless he was doing something for the comfort of others. Those Notts and Derby miners worshipped him, and Lord have mercy on anyone who hurt him! They would have followed him to the bitter end.

The Rev. A. P. Daniels, the Chaplain of the Battalion, explained admirably the secret and value of his indomitable cheerfulness:

One could always feel that there was a sense of proportion in his philosophy. There were probably 'blind spots' and points of view he was unable to share, though he treated them with respect, but his whole outlook was firmly established on a broad and liberal basis. It was this sense of proportion that justified the ringing laughter often heard far down a trench and bringing a lightening of heart to those who heard it. It betokened not the vacant mind but the balanced mind, able to give human things their proper place and to see life in its true proportions, death too, if need be: yet this was not because it was removed from human things but because there was love in it, love for all dear human things, for their very humanity and weakness. So he was able to invest trifles with their own relative importance precisely because his sense of proportion enabled him to see that they *were* trifles. A memory comes of him clad in furlined British warm (how he hated the cold) finishing a late breakfast in a dugout on the bank of the Yser Canal after an active night. The urbanity of the temper overcame, as it frequently did, the incongruity of the surroundings. 'What does a gentleman do every morning first thing after breakfast?', and after a pause of wild conjecture, 'He shakes out *The Times*.'

The laughter could turn inwards. He was fond of comparing himself with Napoleon, 'that great Commander' on the strength of two characteristics, that he could go to sleep anywhere and that he could not ride, though he was a comfortable sight on 'Tagalie' at the head of his company during training.

The brave gaiety which was so imperturbable was no superficial gaiety of manner, but a gaiety of soul, founded on a philosophy in which both mind and soul had found themselves. Perhaps that was the explanation of his unconquerable spirit and of the love he inspired in us all. We found in him reality of soul. At the bottom of it was a spiritual power. He fulfilled the Clifton motto *Spiritus intus alit*. His presence could be felt after we had left his actual company, can still be felt now that he has left us. One who knew him well said —'to have known Truscott was the one good thing that came out of the war'. To know him was certainly a gift of God.

Brigade Headquarters and General Headquarters

Amongst his many activities during his year with the Sherwood Foresters was one, mentioned by Sergeant Wiggett for which his practice at the Bar had been an excellent preparation—that of acting as prisoner's friend at courts-martial. A letter written by him at Christmas, 1916, contains an amusing reference to this:

The next day I gave a concert in the Church Army Hut, one of the best I have ever got up and one of the best they have had in the Hut they say. It was crammed. There were some very good items on the programme. I sang 'Land of Hope and Glory' with a piccolo *obligato*, 'Glorious Devon' and 'Stone-cracker John'.

You know that I told you I defended one of my corporals at a court martial—and got him off. I think I told you that it was a case the General said he wanted to make an example of.·

Two days ago two corporals were court martialled by order of the General. He was very annoyed about their offence.

They asked me to help them and I got them both off.

I wanted to see what the General would say.

Yesterday I gave another concert. It was even better than the first and went with a terrific swing. I asked the General to come and he did with the Colonel and a good many other officers. I sang two songs—and after about an hour the General had to go so I escorted him to the door. As he hurried off he turned on me with this parting shot. 'Thank you very much Truscott for your songs. I like you very much better as a singer than as a prisoner's friend!'

This, however, was only one of the many ways in which Roy's natural ability showed itself. In spite of his peculiar ideas about discipline and his unpunctuality and other military eccentricities, he soon grasped the essentials of a military career and set himself methodically and conscientiously to master its details. He made a close study of trench warfare in all its aspects, and condensed his conclusions on the subject of taking over trenches into a small pamphlet which was subsequently issued as standard practice throughout the Army, and many other suggestions of his were from time to time embodied in official orders and instructions.

Further proof of his thoroughness is to be found in the *History of the 16th Battalion of the Sherwood Foresters*, which he wrote after the war, and which is a model of what such a book should be.

It is not surprising, therefore, that he very soon attracted the attention of the Brigade Staff, to which he was removed in March, 1917.

The work of Brigade H.Q. gave Roy opportunities of showing what he could do in the way of large-scale organization. He specialized in omnibus transport and claimed to have added to the English language some new words—*embuss*, *debuss* and their appropriate substantives *embussment* and *debussment*.

He writes in August, 1917, an admirable description of a feat of 'bus transportation from behind the line to the forward area:

In due course, we were officially informed that the Brigade would move to the forward area by bus on a certain date. That set the ball rolling. Every dispatch rider brought letters containing instructions on embussing. Divisional, Corps and Army Gen. H.Qs. all had their views on it. The Staff Capt. went away a day before to see to billets in the new area and I saw that I was in for a thick time, as on me descended the duty of arranging this move.

The day before we started, a car was sent for me and I was taken miles away to Omnibus H.Qs. where a Colonel further instructed me on Embussing. I felt the war was really on my shoulders now and that there must be some obscure and hidden snare about getting in and out of buses that I had missed in Piccadilly and at Marlborough Road Station. The Colonel practically said that the efficiency of a Brigade was judged by its embussing. He said it had taken one Brigade two hours to embus. I asked what the shortest time taken to date had been. He said seven minutes. I said I would guarantee my Brigade to do six. He thought I was flippant and I was duly returned to my own H.Qs. by the car that had fetched me.

Then I explained to the General the importance of 'bussing'—and the seriousness of the operation before us on the morrow. I then went privately to the Brigade Major and told him that as the General was being lent a car he must take him to lunch at St. Omer so that he would be out of the way if anything went wrong. I further settled this by letting it be known that there would be no lunch at H.Qs. as we should be packed up—sandwiches would be issued to those desiring them. That settled it. I repaired to my office to write a mighty work on embussing, collected from all the pamphlets I had received and the information gathered in the morning. Other pamphlets arrived too late to be embodied in my work—they kept coming in up to the last moment. My work was finished at 1.0 a.m. and was duly typed and sent to Battalions by the early dispatch rider. I went to bed. Ralph's car arrived at 10.0 a.m. the next morning and I went in it to the embussing point where I met all the Adjutants. Then we paced our road. Every Battalion had sent me its exact numbers; also the two Machine Gun Companies, the Trench-Mortar Batteries and H.Qs. itself. These units had to be split up in parties of twenty-five for each busload—each party numbered and ten yards between each party—a very careful calculation was necessary and in the end each Adjutant knew the exact point in the road at which he had to station the head of his column.

Then we repaired to H.Qs. to pack up and send the General off to lunch, and at 2.30 p.m. returned to the Embussment, where was the whole brigade, some 5,000 men, ready in little parties by the side of the road. It took nearly two miles of roadway and I shot up and down in Ralph's car admiring my handiwork.

The buses were late and in the interval the General slipped his leash and returned to see the embussment. He came prepared to be entertained—I explained to him that an embussment was really rather serious. Soon afterwards the Great Armada began to arrive with a vanguard and flankguard of dust. They lumbered on, snorting, hissing and making all the awful noises motors can make. Still they came on—after twenty minutes only seventy had passed and there were 179 altogether. On they came and each one I had numbered in chalk as it passed, so that each party being also numbered should know its own bus—on they came—it took fifty minutes for the Great Armada to get into position. The bugle sounded ADVANCE—then we embussed—in four minutes—never was there such an Embussment. The General was very pleased and went off. The Armada turned its handles and the whole rumbling, clanging, snorting cavalcade got into motion. I got into Ralph's car, fled down a side road to avoid the dust and took a quiet tea with my select companions in St. Omer.

We caught up the Armada just before the rest halt. Fields had been arranged for our brave troops to rest in—the Armada stopped, stretching away far into the distance. Everybody disembarked—or debussed—and went to his own properly labelled field. Fires were soon going and tea provided. The regimental band played selections and everyone wore a thickish veneer of dust on his face, his clothes and his equipment.

The General turned up having had his dinner and was vastly pleased because the Omnibus Colonel blew in at this point and told me he had heard I had topped the record and that my idea of chalking numbers on the buses and numbering the parties was so excellent a one that he would embody it in his next pamphlet of instructions. So succeeding Divisional Brigades will have yet another pamphlet on embussing to read.

Well, about 8.0 p.m. we re-embussed. Having started the old thing on its way again, I fled like Cleopatra from Actium with my boon companions.

After six months with the Brigade Staff, Roy was again transferred to a wider sphere—the Xth Corps Staff. This brought him to the Headquarters of the Second Army, then in charge of the Ypres front. After a short period of work there he was, in June, 1918, transferred again, this time to General Headquarters, where he was appointed Staff Captain to deal with billeting, claims, hirings, requisitions, accommodation at ports and on the lines of communication, and a host of similar subjects. Here his energy, loyalty, tact and clear-sighted common sense proved of great value. He left nothing over for the morrow which could be done today. Unless he had completed, to his own satisfaction—and he was a strict judge—all outstanding matters, he would not go to his billet to sleep. Even more valuable were his cheerful optimism and constant sympathy with the men in the front line—the latter a quality which was apt to be lost by officers isolated at H.Q. In all his arrangements he kept foremost in his mind the needs and trials of the man in the trenches, and he missed no opportunity of personal help or service where cases of need came to his notice. The same qualities were invaluable when differences of opinion arose with Allied commanders, civil officials, or French civilian claimants. It soon became the accepted practice to send Captain Truscott to settle such differences on the spot. When once the matter was put into his charge, it was regarded by his C.O. as settled, and it always was—amicably, sometimes even uproariously.

The final phase of his military service was concerned with demobilization and the disposal of war material in France after the end of hostilities. He was placed with the British troops in France and Flanders serving as a D.A.Q.M.G. at General Headquarters, which was moved from Montreuil to a hutted camp at Wimereux.

The number of troops and others in this Command was 30,000 officers and 1,000,000 other ranks, together with 75,000 animals. Of these numbers about 100,000 were Native labour—(Chinese, Indians, West Indians, Fijians) and nearly 200,000 prisoners of war —Germans, Austrians, Russians, Rumanians and Poles.

There were over 5,000 units.

The process of demobilization with the continuous dispersal of personnel, and more especially the constant change of responsible officers, interfered seriously with the process of 'clearing up , and it became necessary to develop a new organization, with some semblance of permanency, to carry out the sorting, collection, protection and disposal of the gigantic stocks scattered over a large part of France and Belgium.

The question of ownership was often difficult, and particularly so in the areas from which the German armies had been driven.

Huge factories had been utilized as German installations and were full of machinery, electrical plant, stores and material of all sorts and description. Some of these things had been in the factories originally; others had been collected from parts of Belgium and France in enemy occupation; others had been obtained from Germany, and yet others had been captured from the Allies.

Again, there were thousands of railway trucks and hundreds of barges laden with equipment, machinery, and so forth, which the Germans had collected and were unable to move away during the retreat of their armies.

Dumps and depots, lighting installations, animals, guns, munitions of innumerable types and kinds, hutments, vehicles, apparatus of all sorts—British, Belgian, French and German— were scattered in their thousands over these large tracts of country.

Simultaneously there was not only the demobilization of the British troops in France and Flanders to carry on, but attention had to be given to the passage of troops from Italy, Salonika, the Black Sea, Egypt and the Rhine, including sick and wounded, who passed through France on their way home. Further, there was the evacuation of the Native labour contingents—Chinese,

Egyptians, South Africans, Indians, Fijians, West Indians, as well as about a quarter of a million prisoners of war.

The agreements made with the French and Belgian authorities gave rise to many complex problems and lengthy investigations. The branch of the 'Q' staff (Q.4) of which Roy was a member and of which he ultimately had charge, was responsible for such matters as the transfer of hutments with their component stores to the *Regions Libérées* and *Reconstruction Industrielle*, stores sold to the Morocco Forestry Service, stores issued to communal authorities, railway material transferred to the Belgian State Railways, the allocation and disposal of *prix de guerre*, losses, demurrage, rates of pay of civilians employed, allowances, payments for land occupied, commitments in respect of municipal roads, hiring of premises, port dues, and outstanding bills for and against the French Government—complex subjects involving much meticulous investigation and careful sifting. The sense of oppression which might be expected in offices engaged in delving daily into vast files and in constantly referring to lengthy and highly technical agreements, was never to be found in Q.4. The staff officers in that branch, led by Roy, had the faculty of discovering humour in every one of the many hundreds of files they handled, and their gaiety and cheerfulness became major assets when the negotiations for settling claims with our Allies took place. But it was not only in creating and maintaining a bright and cheerful working atmosphere amongst his staff that he excelled: his flair in successfully handling complicated financial problems encouraged his staff, who might well have been excused if, after having just passed through the trials and tribulations of the war, they had shown weariness at what must have been to most of them singularly dreary tasks.

Roy revelled in overcoming difficulties and ensuring complete thoroughness in the solution of the problems that came his way, and there was nothing half-hearted in his rejoicings when he had proved his case, rejoicings in which all his staff had to participate and which sometimes involved other branches of the Headquarters Staff in the huts surrounding those occupied by Q.4.

His relations with other sections of the military community were always of the happiest and he was *persona grata* with the representatives of the Allies, who were charmed by his tact, *bonhomie* and comradeship.

How high his reputation was at G.H.Q. is shown by the following report written by the General Officer Commanding in his Record of Service:

> Lieut.-Colonel R. F. Truscott is a most able and talented 'Q' Staff Officer.
>
> He has all the qualities necessary for securing successful work. His cheerful temperament, keenness and enthusiasm are transmitted by his personality to his subordinates.
>
> At General Headquarters, as an A.Q.M.G., he had charge of a branch of 'Q' which was entrusted principally with the solution of financial problems of every sort and description. Many of these varied problems, especially those which were legacies of the war, have been of a most complex and complicated nature. Colonel Truscott has tackled them with tremendous energy and industry and with great business acumen and thoroughness. His memoranda setting forth the salient points of any question for the consideration of higher authority have been most clear and lucid and skilfully prepared, and the excellence of his judgment is indicated by the fact that his recommendations have invariably been accepted by the Army Council.
>
> He co-operates harmoniously and well with all branches of the Staff, and with the various Services and Departments.
>
> His dealings with the French and Belgians have been marked with the success which is characteristic of all his work.
>
> A most valuable officer of outstanding merit.

Many legends sprang up regarding this closing period of Roy's military career. It was said, for instance, that he once kept the late Lord Birkenhead waiting half an hour for an interview, owing to the inability of his very incompetent orderly to repeat the name of the visitor, Roy having given strict orders that he would see no one without knowing their name in advance.

Another story relates to the Portuguese army, which became attached to G.H.Q. after the Armistice and could not be dislodged. The G.O.C., like an English King on an historic occasion, sighed audibly for someone to rid him of this incubus, and Roy undertook to see what could be done. A few days later he reported to the General that the Portuguese had gone, and when pressed as to the means adopted to secure this desirable end, calmly explained that having discovered that they were attached to the British Headquarters for rations, he had adopted the brilliantly simple expedient of posting an order that after the following week they would be detached for rations. The unfortunate Portuguese finding themselves thus deprived of sustenance, had no alternative but to disappear, and, it was said, were compelled, in the absence of any nearer means of transport, to march all the way to Le Havre.

This story is undoubtedly true, for Roy himself once told it in the course of an address to an audience of young printers, as an example of the kind of circumstances in which it is desirable to ignore regulations and to take decisions on one's own responsibility. He pointed out that the Portuguese wanted to be gone as much as the British wanted to be rid of them, but that to await for official authority would have involved weeks of delay while complicated negotiations proceeded between the Foreign Offices and War Departments of the two nations. That his action was not resented by our oldest Allies is shown by the fact that Roy, in due course, received the Order of Aviz of Portugal.

This was only one of very many occasions during the complex and exacting work of demobilization when Roy gave proof of his ability, energy and resource, and it was due to this that he remained on the Headquarters Staff of the rapidly dwindling British Armies until 1920, when he was finally demobilized with the rank of Lieut.-Colonel and the O.B.E.

There is no doubt that the war helped Roy to find himself. It revealed to him not only his own latent powers but the unsuspected capacities and virtues of the man in the street, the field, the mine and the factory. It opened his eyes and his heart to the need for comradeship between all classes, and to the urgent duty which our common humanity lays upon every man to give the utmost service to his fellows.

Roy himself summed up the experiences and lessons of these war years in the Armistice Day addresses which he gave from time to time in the parish church of Hartshead, in Yorkshire, at the invitation of his friend and war comrade, Brig.-General Sir George Armytage, who had been G.O.C. of the 117th Infantry Brigade.

I think I cannot more fitly close my story of his war service than by quoting the address which he gave in 1934, only a few days before the onset of his last illness:

> Let us go back for a few minutes to the war—to the real war—not
> the war of profiteers, of exploiters of the nation, of intriguers for

place and power—but the war of the soldiers in the trenches—let us see what we may learn from them and where we may have gone wrong. By putting the clock back let us try and visualize the ideals we had then.

War is a terrible, a tragic thing—it always has been—but it became a horrible thing in the late war with its accompaniment of the slaughter of non-combatants, of women and children. It promises in the future to be more horrible still. We may well pray God that we may be spared another.

But fire purges. War is not all loss. Let me give a quotation which explains what I mean much better than I could. It is from a book called *Adventure*, by a very gallant gentleman, General Seeley, now Lord Mottistone.

'They say that war is sordid and brutalizing to the men who fight. It is no such thing. The greatest heights of unselfishness and devotion are brought out in war, "Greater love hath no man than this, that he lay down his life for his friend". To rush forward to counter or receive the bayonet thrust directed at your comrade, to throw yourself on his prostrate body as the bomb explodes, above all fearlessly to lead the last desperate attack, so that thus you may give heart and courage to your followers in that supreme moment—these things which I have seen again and again with my own eyes, are the very pith of our Christian faith. Let no man who values his soul depreciate them. War is ennobling to the combatants.'

Friendship, comradeship, unselfishness, courage, cheerfulness—these are the lessons war teaches; and they are not ignoble ones. The war begat a wonderful freemasonry. All those who served feel they are a great brotherhood. You have only to listen to any of them talking, meeting for the first time perhaps some other who served. They are comrades at once, freely exchanging adventures, often finding out they had similar experiences in the same parts of the line, and for the time being they live those days over again, oblivious of the realities of the present. The war was the greatest experience of their lives. They know that nothing can rob them of it. They know that those who were not privileged to serve are the poorer for it. They know that the onlookers missed something that nothing else in life can quite give.

In the last two or three months, I have received some twenty or thirty letters from members of my battalion, though they live in Derbyshire and Nottinghamshire and I in London—so that we seldom meet. The same feeling animates them. They are, as someone said to me only a fortnight ago, very beautiful letters, perhaps more beautiful because they are simple and direct.

One writes: 'My mind travelled back to the old war days—days I know we do not wish to see again—but in spite of all, I must say this, both as a private and N.C.O., the spirit and good feeling that prevailed in the battalion was fine—the comradeship—the sharing out of parcels—the sharing of rations—the hardships which the officers understood and shared—all this I think of to-day—what fine principles to live up to in the face of death—*if we could only get that same feeling to-day, I am sure we all should be much better.*'

Another says: 'Now Sir, I oftimes think about . . . the times of long ago as they seem to be now—while no man wants to see those days, memory never fades and sometimes when I'm left to myself for a time, *my mind goes whirling back to those days when comradeship was much more than it is to-day. For in these days there seems very little of comradeship.*'

Yet another: 'Your letter brings sad memories back to us—but we also had our good and humorous times as well. . . . I could not finish your letter without a kind of mist before my eyes or a little moisture if you like, as it brings so many things looming up again—that makes us feel proud in rubbing shoulders with one another—the rough outward appearance of most of us miners and then the frail-looking chaps out of the big towns and factories, all jumbled together in one common cause—but what a shedding of that stubborn appearance and rough exterior of the miner and the frailness of the factory and townspeople when it came to helping one another—*what a game to show the world* what lay beneath the rough and the frail exterior. *Humanity* to man. Comradeship!'

EAST AFRICA

Roy was demobilized in June, 1920, and came back to England. He did not return to the Bar, as his services were sorely needed in the family business, his brother Cyril and his first cousin Francis having both fallen in the war, so that he and Ralph were the only members of the Truscott family in their generation available to carry on the work. He immediately moved into the Suffolk Lane office, but it was characteristic of him and indicative of the esteem in which he was held by the military authorities, that he continued for some time to give assistance to the Q.M.G. department of G.H.Q. This went on for several months, both by telephone between Suffolk Lane and France and by special messengers from G.H.Q. to London.

He threw himself with tremendous energy into his new career, and rapidly mastered the complicated mechanism of the printing trade, becoming a Director of the Company in 1921. He also found time to join in the formation of a small 'reconstruction' group under his own Chairmanship. The objects of this are outlined in the following extract from an introductory statement in the minute-book:

In the months following the Armistice much was talked of Utopian Reconstruction Schemes, whereby this land of ours was to be made, not only 'Safe for Democracy' (whatever that might mean!) but also 'A Land Fit for Heroes to Live In'. Pamphlets on social problems were issued, Ministries formed or proposed, and the masses were once more taught to hope that the Promised Land about which they had heard so much but of which they had seen so little, was at long last at hand. Month, however, succeeded month, and no material progress was made. On the other hand a mad orgy of reckless expenditure ran riot throughout the country. So the spirit of hope changed, slowly, to a spirit of discontent.

In the labouring classes this spark of discontent was fanned by skilful agitators into 'labour troubles', strikes for higher wages, shorter hours, better homes, for a chance to raise their condition above that of mere animals; for, in short, all that had been promised them by their so-called governors and elected representatives.

In the middle classes who, by their education and environment, had achieved much of that for which the others strove, this spirit of discontent showed itself, in some cases, by an outcry against high rates and increased taxation, without any endeavour to ascertain whether such increases were justified or not; in others by a vague dissatisfaction with things as they found them; by a latent feeling that they, who, in comparison with the others had greatly received, were not greatly giving too. Many of them realized that whatever else the war had brought, it had brought them two great lessons: first, the need for leadership and the capacity for leadership in the individual— that leadership which, where it cannot drive a man to heaven, may often lead him even to hell—second, the realization of the truth of '*tout comprendre c'est tout pardonner*', and third, the infinite value of comradeship.

It was the realization of the existence of this feeling of good fellowship combined with a sense of dissatisfaction that led us to meet together, in the first place to consider whether or not six or seven of us could formulate some scheme whereby this realization of what, for want of a better term, we call *noblesse oblige*, might not be turned to some practical use in remedying, or in attempting to

remedy, the rottenness in what we are pleased to call civilization
to-day; and so to safeguard the community from the dangers that
are resulting, and that, in the future, must result therefrom. In other
words, to consider the possibility of forming some co-ordinating
centre, controlling and advising, not only ourselves but other
workers in some field or fields of social reform to be decided on.

But before Roy had been engaged for a full twelve months in
these new activities, there came another upheaval.

Early in 1921 J. Truscott & Sons obtained the right to a controlling interest in the *East African Standard*, the most influential
newspaper in that part of the Empire, and decided to send Roy out
to the colony as Managing Director and Editor-in-Chief. The
decision delighted him, for it seemed to offer the chance of
constructive work in a young and vital community at a critical
stage of its development. East Africa was still in the first generation
of European settlement and the war had made the world realize
how vast were its undeveloped resources, while the acceptance by
Britain of the Mandate for the former German colony had inspired
enthusiasts with the vision of a great East African Dominion with
Kenya as its dominant partner. But there were serious problems to
be faced. Chief among these was the mixture of three widely
diverse racial elements, none of them well educated politically and
each too apt to be actuated by naked self-interest—about 10,000
Europeans (including a large group of untried settlers under the
Soldier Settlement Scheme and a large proportion of Civil Servants
with practically no stake in the country), the Indian immigrants and
the native population. Closely linked with this fundamental problem were the two more limited but exceedingly important ones of
taxation and the stabilization of the currency, which it was clear,
must be divorced from the Indian rupee. The currency problem
inevitably aroused suspicion that the settlers would try to benefit
themselves at the expense of the native standard of living, and the
Home Government had definitely laid down that the very necessary
increase in taxation would not be sanctioned until non-native
taxation approximated more closely to the burden which the
natives were already carrying. The official view that a direct tax
on incomes would be the best way of achieving this, aroused violent opposition from the European community.

It was obvious that the local Press, if wisely managed, could
contribute much to the solution of these problems, which were

made more acute by the slump of 1921; but a less courageous man than Roy might well have shrunk from attempting such a task with the existing staff of the *East African Standard*. The editor was a young reporter who, though able and idealistic, had spent the whole of his working life in the Home and East African Civil Service. Neither he nor his staff had any journalistic or political experience, while Roy himself had never had any contact with the Press, and his knowledge of administration had been almost entirely acquired in the Army. But life had given him an instinctive understanding of men and affairs, and a political sense based on sound historical knowledge, and he was incurably optimistic. Shortly after his arrival, his young editor expressed doubts whether the existing organization was capable of dealing with the grave problems which had to be faced, and suggested that a new and more experienced editor-in-chief should be sent for from London. Roy replied cheerfully: 'Since when has anything real been done in Africa except by amateurs? I don't despair of either of us yet. If later on you do, speak to me again and I will think about it.'

His first task was to win the confidence of the staff, which was, like the population as a whole, a blend of European, Indian and native. This was soon accomplished, for no one could long withstand Roy's unforced geniality and charm. It was not so easy to give them confidence in themselves. This he achieved by leaving them in entire control of administrative detail and showing on every possible occasion his own confidence in their (very slightly) superior journalistic experience. Before long he had made them feel that he and they were engaged together in an exhilarating adventure and that he was relying on them to pull him through. Sometimes his detachment had unfortunate results, as when an article violently attacking the policy of the Government appeared on the morning of his first luncheon engagement at Government House. Fortunately he had not had time to read the issue and his obvious surprise and the great laugh with which he greeted the discovery, saved the situation.

He pursued the same policy with regard to improvements and new features. These were always talked over with the staff in advance and, so far as possible, made to appear of their initiation. Before long there was an excellent literary section with reviews by Roy and Ruth, articles by important authorities from overseas;

sketches, essays and poems by local amateurs; an agricultural essay competition, and other special features.

Over the policy of the paper he maintained a strict control. The Government having established an income tax were reluctant to give it up, even when the commercial development of the Colony had reached a point which made the building up of a scientific Customs Tariff possible. European interests strongly attacked the tax. Some even challenged the basic principle of higher non-native taxation. Roy had small sympathy with the flood of rich people who were pouring into Kenya to avoid the British income tax, and he realized clearly that the African had a future of his own which no one could foresee, and could not be regarded merely as a source of labour and taxes. But he felt strongly that a direct income tax was *inappropriate at that stage of the Colony's development* when local enterprise was so badly in need of imported capital. In taking this line he had to fight not only the Government, but also those who were always ready to find an anti-native bias in the local British Press. But he enjoyed the fight, for he was sure of his case, and he made the staff enjoy it, too. There is no doubt that the lead which he gave, not only through almost daily articles in the paper but by personal work at committees, public meetings and deputations, had a considerable influence on the result. Within twelve months of his arrival he had the satisfaction of seeing Government sanction given to the replacement of income tax by Customs duties on articles of non-native consumption. The entirely gratuitous promise in the Government's Bill that income tax would not be levied for the year ended December 31st, 1922, or *any subsequent year* he welcomed with a roar of delighted incredulity, and the promise has, of course, long since been broken.

The much more complex Indian issue could not be so easily settled. It touched the very heart of Africa's well-being and a false step might be impossible to retrieve.

Its revival during Roy's year with the *Standard* sprang from the pronouncement of a Joint Parliamentary Committee that the treatment of Indians in Kenya must be not less favourable than that of any other class of His Majesty's subjects there. This became known just at the moment when elected representatives of the European community were being sent to the Legislative Council, and the result was an immediate Indian demand for equality of representation and for equal rights to hold land in the much coveted highlands. A deputation from the European Convention of Associations was sent to South Africa to secure help for resisting Indian domination and the Rev. C. F. Andrews, an intimate friend of Mahatma Gandhi, came to Kenya to help the Indian cause. Just before Roy arrived, Sir Edward Northey had been called to London to discuss matters with Mr. Churchill, then Secretary of State for the Colonies. The storm had now become a hurricane. Suggestions for boycott and black-list were in the air and people were talking freely of resort to violence. Roy of course would give no countenance to such extravagances.

His position, based on a sound knowledge of African and Indian history, was quite simple, and it aimed at simplification for the future. He could never think of East Africa as a hybrid state, and he found immeasurably dangerous the idea put forward by some of his Liberal colleagues that in young Kenya a practical test might, for the benefit of a distracted world, be made of the capacity of the three great branches of the human race to live together in political equality. He fought against the educational or economic penalization of the Indians, but he opposed with equal force the further considerable concessions that the Indian Party demanded, because he felt they would be gravely detrimental to the realization of Great Britain's primary function in Central Africa—the gradual civilizing of the African on *Western* lines. Such a policy of course pleased the extremists of neither Party, but he confronted with equal serenity a settler who threatened to horsewhip him and his Editor into more blatant headlines, and the lofty humanitarianism of visiting Indian delegates.

This great controversy had not reached the stage of detailed solution before he left the country, but he had the consolation of knowing that the Imperial Government had unalterably adopted as its basic and overriding policy the development of Native Africa.

Roy could not have made his influence so strongly felt during the few months of his stay in Africa if he had confined his activities to the pages of the *Standard*. His trim figure, rather stouter now, and sleek black head, slightly greying at the temples, became familiar at the meetings of the chief commercial and political Committees and Associations, where even his opponents welcomed the little joke or great burst of laughter which always seemed able to bring the gloomiest controversy out into the sunlight.

He was active in the establishment of a City club for business men, in the formation of a Produce Exchange, and in fighting for the improvement of the freights and services of the Uganda Railway. He was closely associated with the organization formed for relieving unemployment among Europeans, caused in part by the hasty application of the Soldier Settlement Scheme. He was a generous, if candid, supporter of the East African Women's League, then a very young body of great promise, and of the S.P.C.A., making one of his earliest public appearances in a Nairobi police court as chief witness in a charge which he had brought of cruelty to mules.

He contributed to the *Standard* a series of articles on the native question which embodied a most concise and complete analysis of the problem and of the solutions proposed for it. He compiled and printed a short history of East Africa from prehistoric times down to the end of the war. He made a close study of the complicated Zanzibar clove question—one of vital importance to Zanzibar but of little interest to the outside world—and he continued his active work on this right up to 1926, thus rendering a real service to the Arab community of the Protectorate.

It was a formidable list of activities for a newcomer whose stay in Kenya lasted less than twelve months and whose constant and overriding preoccupation was the business management and editorial control of a daily newspaper; nor was it easy for a newcomer to steer his way through the jungle of self-interest and ill-informed idealisms which surrounded him. He was never wholly free from the fear that he might unwittingly lend himself to exploitation, and his friends and colleagues could see that he was sometimes bitterly hurt by treatment which a less sensitive nature would hardly have felt.

As important as all this political activity was the social influence that radiated from Roy's house in Nairobi. Ruth was a charming musician, whose sweet and expressive soprano formed an admirable contrast to his uproarious baritone. No one ever accompanied him so well, for she could adapt herself to his irregularities with an affectionate indulgence which made their appeal irresistible. Before long, all who appreciated good music, good talk and good fellowship began to find a focal point in the Truscotts' home.

It was not surprising that, as the months passed, his position in the political and social life of the community grew daily stronger. Then, before he had been a full year in Africa, came what for him was a tragic disappointment. Truscotts' directors, alarmed by the growing menace of the slump, and perhaps also by the atmosphere of controversy in which they could see that the *Standard* was becoming involved under Roy's courageous leadership, decided not to take up their option and he was recalled to London. His heart was in the work which he was doing in and for Africa, and it was hard to believe that the surrender of it would be compensated by work of equal importance elsewhere; but he would not allow those with whom he was working to see his disappointment. He remained cheerful, helpful and considerate to the end; only a very few signs escaped, but these were eloquent to those who knew him.

A notable farewell dinner was organized for him at the New Stanley Hotel, under the Chairmanship of Lord Delamere. All sections of the European community were represented—commercial, financial, political, ecclesiastical, social and sporting— and a 'composite toast' was spoken to by the Chairman, the Colonial Secretary, the President of the Association of Chambers, the managing director of the opposition paper, and the Editor of the *Standard*. References to his work came in messages from the political and commercial Associations and the other societies with which he had worked.

It was a moving tribute to one who had been in the country for less than a year; equally moving were the tributes in the Press. Even the rival paper, *The Critic*, while strongly opposing the policy of the *Standard* and of many of those who organized the farewell dinner to its editor-in-chief, added:

There is no man living for whom, in the personal sense, the *Critic* entertains a higher regard. His departure from Kenya Colony will mark the extinction, so far as this country is concerned, of a most lovable, courteous, kindly, humane, genial and gentlemanly figure. That is admitted on all hands, and the pleasant function on Tuesday night at which Colonel Truscott was the guest of the evening, was the natural climax to a high appreciation by all parts of the community of one who has consistently advocated the public good as far as lay in his power and according to his own ideals.

Not less plesasant to Roy himself was the memory of the

Africans crowding round him the night before he left Nairobi, with cries of '*Kwa Heri Bwana, Kwa Heri!*' (Go in peace).

THE PRINTING INDUSTRY

On his return to London, Roy was immediately absorbed into the Truscott business, and very soon made a name and position for himself in the printing industry.

His work as a printer falls into two divisions: first, as a member of the family business; and secondly, through membership of the various federations and associations which look after the affairs of the industry as a whole.

It must have been a difficult task for him to begin an entirely new job in middle life, especially as the printing industry is a very complicated one, both technically and commercially. Moreover, he had to face very great responsibilities before he had been two full years in the City, for his brother Ralph died suddenly in 1924 and he was immediately appointed managing director of the Company.

He faced these responsibilities with his usual thoroughness, taking especial interest in the artistic and human sides of the industry. He made a close study of typography and of the history of the craft and devoted much thought to the question of apprenticeship. He took the utmost care in selecting the boys for Truscott's, giving preference to the sons and grandsons of members of the staff, but also closely scrutinizing school records and personal character. The eternal problem of the office boy evoked his special sympathy, and he always tried to make the boys' work as educative as possible by varying their jobs and interests. One who was often with him recalls, as an illustration of his sympathy and understanding of the young, that when he took parties of young master printers round his works for educative purposes, if there was something unusual to be noticed he would ask the works manager to explain it to him as if he knew nothing about it. His 'Oh, I see,' made the younger generation feel that he was one of themselves.

He himself was always accessible to all, and the staff loved to see the managing director sitting in his room with the door open so that anyone could come in. And, indeed, it seemed that everyone took advantage of the invitation, for the stream of visitors was often continuous and so interfered with other business that he had to work through the luncheon interval, when potential callers were otherwise engaged. At such times he would dispose of accumulated correspondence with amazing rapidity.

The methods which he adopted in management were characteristic. He would spare no pains to get to the bottom of a problem, and he showed all his old genius for dealing with men. Consequently, even if a decision which he gave was contrary to a person's own ideas, there was never any question of 'Is that right?' If 'Colonel Roy' had made the decision it was accepted without question and there were no ill feelings.

His resource in handling awkward situations was infinite. He once patiently endured for some time the annoying behaviour of the heads of two departments who were not on speaking terms, which resulted in all kinds of petty questions finding their way to and through his office. At last he decided that he wouldn't be a post-office any longer, sent for the two people concerned and said to one: 'Mr. A., I would like to introduce you to our Mr. B.', and to the other: 'Mr. B., I want you to meet our Mr. A. You have both been here for many years, but do not appear to have been properly introduced before. I am sure you will find a lot in common with each other.' He was not troubled again.

But though so considerate of others he had a very high sense of duty, which evoked a ready response from the staff. He expected people to give their best, and though he did not mind an occasional mistake, the same mistake must not be made twice; and he objected very strongly when he thought people were not using their brains.

The success of his methods could be judged by the affection felt for him by the whole staff.

His success in the wider sphere of trade politics was equally great, although it was some time before his fellow-printers realized his great ability. This was perhaps not surprising as he was so unlike the general conception of the director of a large business, and his methods of dealing with business problems were so unconventional. He himself realized something of this attitude, for he used to say that he thought his fellow master printers had considered him rather a joke at the beginning. But they soon came to realize how valuable were his power of impersonal judgment, his wisdom and his happy temperament. After that his progress

L

was rapid. In 1927 he was President of the London Master Printers' Association and he also became, in 1930, President of the Home Counties Master Printers' Alliance and a member of the Council of the British Federation of Master Printers. He was, in 1931, asked to offer himself for the Vice-Presidency of this body, which would have led ultimately to the Presidency—the highest position in the printing industry—but just at that moment he was beginning to think of a career in the City which his friends hoped would have carried him ultimately to the Mansion House, so he was forced to decline. This, however, did not diminish his interest in the work of the various trade organizations, and he paid particular attention to their labour and costing activities, sitting on the appropriate committees and giving much thought to the intricate questions involved.

Here, again, the rapidity with which he was able to master complicated problems was remarkable, and a pamphlet which he wrote on *Handling Charges* became a printing-trade classic.

Of course he brought to the council tables of the printing trade an unexpected and very welcome atmosphere.

R. A. Austen Leigh wrote of his work on trade committees:

> Forceful in debate, humorous in argument, with a quick grasp of the main points of discussion, and with a natural ease in expressing himself, he was a tower of strength to whatever cause he supported. His very idiosyncrasies endeared him to his colleagues, such as his frequently belated appearances and equally early departures from the various committees of which he was a member, when once the important matter in which he was interested had been discussed; such, too, as the concentrated intentness with which he spent the duller moments of debate in tracing his name on paper in Old English characters; and above all, his hearty and infectious laughter at any points which struck him as humorous.

In spite of the heavy demands of his new career as master printer, Roy maintained unabated the breadth of his interests. For instance, he joined in the work of the Council of Christianity and War, and I find the following interesting letter addressed by him, in 1923, to the Secretary of a Conference which the Council was organizing at Birmingham:

> . . . The statement of the pacifist position [in a memorandum for the Conference] is, to my mind, unconvincing. I should make it clear

at the outset, however, that I am not in agreement with that position, though, as an advocate, I can conceive it as arguable. The pacifist position undoubtedly must be put forward if the ultimate report of your Commission is to reflect the opinion of every important section of the public, but in order to have any value it must frankly face the difficulties. It is no use Christian pacifists running away from their troubles like Christian teetotallers, who either, as the extremists in America, definitely state that Christ was morally wrong in turning water into wine, or, as some sections in England, deny that the wine was fermented; with all the evidence against them.

The alternative to Section 3 which you have sent me is based entirely on the principle which I may for brevity conveniently label 'Turning the other cheek'.

(*a*) Violence in language is in principle the same as violence in action, and we must keep to principle. The degree may be different, but in a sensitive age many will tell you words hurt more than blows. If I am right so far, the advocate of non-violence has to meet the difficulties raised by Christ's invectives against the Pharisees and such phrases as 'It were better that a millstone were hanged about his neck', etc. I do not wish to press unduly what may be merely said rhetorically, but when every allowance is made on these lines, such phrases must present difficulties to the pacifist as they amount to an incentive to violent action.

(*b*) In your alternative section, para. 2 states that reason and suffering are the only redemptive influences, and 'if the Master would not, surely the Church cannot, contemplate any other method of overcoming evil'. The turning of the money-changer out of the Temple was not done by turning the other cheek, and it is quite clear a considerable amount of violence was exercised in order to cause men to leave not only their merchandise but their money behind.

Surely the trend of the teaching of all art, books, drama, pictures in the last twenty years has been to show that many principles in the ethical world which were regarded as absolute are really relative. We can now begin to appreciate that Christ took up the position in regard to morals that Einstein has with regard to physics. The teachings of Christ on any given subject are surely not absolute but relative. Are not laws but guides? Our judgment has a part to play in fusing law and equity in our dealings with difficulties.

I do not wish to trouble you by labouring the point, but you will see that I regard the turning of the money-changers out of the Temple with a scourge, not as a contradiction, but as the complement of turning the other cheek. I will cite another instance to illustrate what I mean: They are the two phrases which begin 'Let your light so shine before men', etc., and its complement 'Let not your right hand know what your left hand doeth'. Literally taken these are contradictory, though in my view they are complementary. It is for us to decide, then, say whether to head a subscription list is setting a good example or mere vulgar ostentation.

All through these years his advice was widely sought by friends and acquaintances on all kinds of subjects. It was always readily given and with a humane common sense that commended it immediately to the recipient.

Very characteristic is the following letter written to a young friend who had consulted him on the choice of a career:

My Dear Henry,

You have been good enough to repose such confidence in me, as to consult me from time to time on your future, and I have given much thought to it.

As a result I feel that you are working from the wrong end—I said something of the sort in a hurried way on Thursday last week, but have thought the matter over more seriously since.

In the hope that my consideration of the question may be of some trifling assistance to you in solving the most difficult problem—i.e., deciding a career—which any of us has put to him in life, I am enclosing a note of my reflections.

With the best wishes of
Yours
Roy.

Memorandum

Henry is an individualist—who does not wish to be in a subordinate position. In an endeavour to meet this characteristic, he is trying to buy himself into a position at the top of some business, irrespective of whether he is by qualification or temperament fitted for the position or not.

The result is, he answers advertisements, the inserters of all of which want his money as additional capital. They don't want Henry. They hardly trouble to inquire his qualifications, so little are they interested. They are business men feeling the draught, who need capital and are willing to have an extra so-called director as the price they pay for it.

The work they generally suggest to occupy the new director is

'clerical'—(positions in their office which they can fill for £150 a
year) or 'representative' i.e. a traveller—or salesman—glorified by
a directorate—the most difficult job in business unless one has the
flair; travellers are 'born and not made' like poets and cooks. The
born traveller knows he can do it and loves the job. He has confidence
in his powers in that direction. Henry has not indicated such confidence or desire. With his particular characteristics the following
would appear to be the openings for Henry i.e. To:

1. Go in for one of the professions.

2. Do something on the land either at home or in the Empire.

3. Look out for a position in a business where his particular qualifications are required, e.g., a gentleman, good appearance, public
school, 'Varsity Honours Degree, languages, general culture,
accountancy—and where they take *him* and not his money—but
where they say later on *if they like him and he likes them*, they will
allow him to have an interest in the business by putting some
capital into it.

4. Definitely decide *what* he wants to do—*some one thing*—(say publishing) and go for it all out solidly, and determinedly, by application, advertisement, introduction, etc.

5. Definitely decide to subordinate his characteristics and join some
sound business—learn it and work his way up by those merits and
abilities with which a generous Providence has lavishly endowed
him.

Equally characteristic was the brevity of the following reply to
one of the many people for whom he was trustee:

> 24, Palace Court, W.2.
> 1.20 a.m.   31.10.33

My dear———
    Thank you for your letter. As a fact—you may as well know it—
financially you are one of the most difficult conundrums anyone may
have to deal with—but personally you are the most charming of
men. God bless you.

> Love,
> ROY.

His interest in the Army and in his old comrades went on
unabated. For a time he took over the control of the Housing
Branch of the Officers' Association, and he played the principal
part in the formation of the London Branch of the Sherwood

Foresters' Old Comrades' Association. Through this and Sergeant Wiggett he kept in touch with his old friends in the Regiment. During the General Strike of 1926 he begged old clothes from his friends and sold them, sending the proceeds to help men who were in need. Out of his own pocket he paid the rates for a member of the Association who, owing to the Strike, could not find the necessary cash. Another member he helped to emigrate to Australia, and whenever he heard that one of his old friends was ill, he was always ready to send brandy or any special delicacy or remedy which might be beyond the invalid's capacity to buy. When there was difficulty in getting a badly shell-shocked man to sign a form which was needed to enable him to benefit from a certain charity, Roy made a journey of one and a half hours into the country, spent two hours with the man and came back in triumph with the form duly signed. More than once, when passing through the Midlands by car, he arranged for all the men from the Battalion who could, to meet him at a fish-and-chips saloon for a meal.

Another interest which his return from Africa revived was in his old school, Clifton. When, in 1923, a new Headmaster, Mr. Whatley, was appointed, he soon established relations with him and with the Old Cliftonian Society, of which he had previously been an active member. From that time the work which he did for the Society and the School continually increased. One form which this took was the very practical one of urging, and not seldom helping, his friends and relations to send their sons to the School. Sometimes there would be four or five of his *protégés* in Brown's House at the same time, and he would come to Clifton every term to see them and discuss their progress with the Head-master. He also made a most valuable collection of books and cuttings relating to the history of the School and its members. In 1931, a characteristically generous action gave him a still closer interest in the School. Lieut.-Col. H. T. Cunningham, whom he had known at G.H.Q. in 1918 and afterwards as a settler in Kenya, had come over to England to arrange about the education of his son Peter. Roy and Ruth offered to act as guardians to the boy so long as he remained in England, and they promised to absorb him into their home life while he went first of all to a preparatory school and then, in due course, as Roy had done, to Clifton and King's. Peter Cunningham supplied to Roy what had been the one great gap in his life—the want of a child. He loved children and had at least twelve god-children, to each one of whom he more than fulfilled a god-father's obligations. Peter soon became like his own son—or in the language of one of their favourite books, Kipling's *Kim*, he became Roy's Chela in whose upbringing and education he took an absorbing interest. One of his chief educational techniques was the collector's. He had the collector's spirit to the full and his scope was unlimited. Stamps, stones, crests, trees, wildflowers, Cliftoniana, press-cuttings and press photographs on a score of subjects, all arranged with incredible neatness, gave the Chela a wide range of miscellaneous knowledge and interests and an excellent training in craftsmanship.

For holidays, Roy's favourite haunt had, since his return from Africa, been Exmoor. It was in 1923 that he and Ruth visited Brendon for the first time, and from then onwards the Staghunters Inn became their regular holiday resort. Roy was never happier than when rambling over the moor or fishing in the moorland streams, and he quickly became a notable and well-loved figure throughout the district. His exploration of Exmoor was the cause of a very characteristic act on his part. He came across an inn belonging to a most admirable married couple who were an ideal host and hostess, but owing to lack of capital and the onset of the slump of 1931, found themselves, as did many others at that time, in a very difficult position. He discovered this quite accidentally and immediately took the matter in hand. With the help of a few friends he formed a small private company which took over the enterprise, of course under the same management. The scheme proved a complete success; the inn was put on a sound basis and soon became a flourishing enterprise.

With Peter's holidays to provide for and the ever-increasing strain of business responsibilities, Exmoor came to play every year a more important part in Roy's life. There, after the strange closing scene of his pilgrimage, he was destined to find rest at the last.

The Last Phase

In 1934, in the midst of this life of intense activity and widely varied interests and usefulness, Roy was laid low by a sudden and severe illness which entirely deprived him of the power of speech and the use of his right side. No doubt the war and the strenuous months in Africa had left their mark on him, and the years of his management at Suffolk Street had not been altogether easy. Latterly, with increasing knowledge and self-confidence, he had felt justified in proposing radical changes of policy, and when these did not meet with the sympathy and support of the proprietors, he felt the disappointment grievously. This, coupled with ten years of unsparing work, had seriously weakened him. After a short period of complete prostration he began to mend, but his disabilities only showed very slow and gradual improvement.

Now began the most astonishing phase of his career. Deep as was the impression that he made at Cambridge, in the war, in Africa, and in the printing industry, no one can really have known the full greatness and vital force of his character who did not see him during these closing years.

He never recovered the power of speech, though he became able to say 'Yes' and 'No', to count up to *eight*, and now and then to use some other simple word. Nor did he ever recover the use of his right side, though for a time he was able to hobble a short distance with a stick. His brain, however, remained perfectly clear, and, with the devoted help of his wife, he was able to retain undiminished his many-sided interest in life; indeed, one is tempted to believe that he retained undiminished his enjoyment of it and his power to communicate this to others.

The following account, written by one of his many godchildren, Hallam Tennyson, shows the impression which his amazing courage and cheerfulness made on a boy of fifteen:

I had hardly met my godfather Roy Truscott before he was taken ill and it was with some trepidation that I rang the front-door bell of his flat one wintry afternoon. My nervousness increased as I laid my hat and coat neatly on a chair in the hall, and I remember taking great care with its fold and creases, so as to give me more time to think of an opening sentence suitable to an invalid, afflicted as my godfather was. But little need I have worried, for no sooner had I opened the door than the tremulous words of greeting I had rehearsed were stilled on my lips by a loud and vociferous bellow of welcome, followed by a long peal of laughter which lasted well over thirty seconds by the mantelpiece clock.

At first I was rather stunned and could only force an embarrassed grin, but then quite suddenly all my nervousness vanished and I found myself laughing too and felt myself no longer a shy boy, but a real and intimate acquaintance. There was such whole-hearted

joie de vivre in that remarkable laugh of my godfather's, something
so redolent of goodwill and zest for life in that chuckle which ended
in a crescendo of mirth, that he must have been hard-hearted and
insensitive indeed, who could resist it and remain unmoved.

Soon I was plunged in a whirlpool of autobiography, recounting
all my adventures of the past few months, a visit to the theatre—
Hamlet at the Old Vic; my work at school, a proposed trip to Italy
in the following Easter; to all he listened intent. I felt somehow that
I had enlisted his sympathy and understanding, and this inspired me
with confidence, a feeling rare in a shy boy of fifteen engaged in a
conversation with his elders.

When after a while it was my godfather's turn to entertain me,
he intimated that there was something he wanted to show me.

Immediately all was confusion, questions were fired concerning the
species of article and, when it was discovered to be a book, shelves
were unloaded and brought for his inspection.

Volume after volume was peremptorily turned down but at last
it was found—a book of picture cuttings—and its discovery was
greeted with shouts of triumphant joy, in which we all joined.

Finding out what he meant, would have been with anyone else
treated as a rather embarrassing necessity, but here it was raised to
the level of a delightful guessing game, a sort of hunt the slipper, the
prize for which was one of those precious bursts of laughter. This
was a game in which his wife, with her unfailing knowledge of my
godfather, playing with consummate skill, rarely failed to carry off
the prize.

After this my visits became quite frequent. I no longer approached
the front door with nervousness or apprehension, but with feelings
of joyful expectation and delight.

Selfishness is the almost inevitable outcome of an illness in which
a man's mobility is affected and in which he is forced to rely entirely
on other people. But selfish my godfather never became; his thoughts
were not for himself but for his friends, whether they were young or
old. He never lost interest in anything they did.

To spend an hour with him was to spend an hour with someone
who was really 'great' in the best and highest meaning of that mis-
used word.

That plump jolly figure, with the sparkling humorous eyes, firm
nose and mouth, and silvered hair, had transcended fortune and risen
beyond and above the strokes of fate.

To every fresh blow he replied with an indomitable peal of laughter; he refused to relinquish his normal active life and he refused to
admit any change in the ordinary course of his existence. In anyone

else this might have appeared as an attempt to hide the facts, a brave and wonderful one, but nevertheless an attempt that was slightly forced, a gaiety squeezed from a care-laden heart. But in my godfather it seemed perfectly natural—there was no sympathetic and rather uncomfortable silence at his dinner parties, for he radiated a simple, child-like and unaffected good humour that dispelled all thoughts of his suffering. He possessed a flame that no misfortune could ever quench.

All through this time people continued to come to him as before for help and advice. Those in sorrow sought his sympathy, those in difficulty came for counsel, and those who loved him came—because they enjoyed coming, in spite of the pain which one could not but feel at his physical overthrow. Mentally and spiritually the old Roy was still there, and the fact that he could not speak seemed to hinder hardly at all his power to give himself to others.

He pursued his collections with all his old ardour. With Ruth's help he organized and held charity sales in his flat, framing prints and doing other craft work with his left hand. He entertained his friends of all ages and both sexes, and if he had moments of depression no one was allowed to know of them.

Nor did he permit his disabilities to keep him entirely out of public work. In March, 1937, he attended the dinner of the Old Comrades' (Sherwood Foresters) Association, of which he was chairman, though he had to allow someone else to officiate for him. He himself was wheeled to the table in his invalid chair, greeting old friends with complete freedom from embarrassment, and saluting with shouts of merriment the rather awkward attempts of his attendants to wedge him in between the other chairs and the table legs.

In June of the same year he went down by car to Clifton for Commemoration, and attended every function. The Headmaster wrote of this visit:

> It was a very great joy to us all when we heard that he felt able to undertake a visit to the School for the Commemoration of 1937. He not only carried out the visit, but he carried it out thoroughly. He attended the Chapel Service, he attended the Old Cliftonian Supper: anywhere that an invalid chair could be persuaded to go, Truscott went in it, and during the visit he supervised the taking of the film of the School which is so valuable a historical record and

will always be a great memorial of him. It was a very gallant visit.

I only saw him once after that. In July of the same year he showed the same courage and determination in attending the Old Cliftonian dinner in London. The film of Clifton whose preparation had been his concern at Commemoration was shown after the dinner to a delighted and grateful audience.

His last effort at public work was to attend a meeting of the Board of his favourite Exmoor Hotel Company, when he was able to propose to his fellow-directors a scheme of action for the coming year, which was adopted by them as the Company's policy.

In the autumn of 1937 he entered on the last phase, with Ruth's description of which I close this labour of love:

A few more months were left to us—it must have been a super-human effort to him, but, if it was, he never showed it. In spite of severe bouts of pain, he had no self-pity, no complaint, and he was infinitely gentle and tender to us all.

One night, after listening to a service on the wireless, something made me say to him 'The way of life is the Cross isn't it?' and some-thing in the quiet firm tone in which he said 'Yes' arrested my atten-tion—from that moment I understood the secret of his power, I realized how far beyond us all he had travelled, and I knew that nothing could touch him any more.

In September we went to Devonshire. We had learnt the tech-nique of travelling easily by then, and the faithful friends who saw us off at Paddington will not easily forget his gay laugh as he was wheeled up two boards into the guard's van. We had a hilarious journey; as usual he missed nothing and every step further west his spirits rose higher and higher. When we reached Exeter the authori-ties had forgotten to arrange, as they had promised, to have boards ready to wheel him down on to the platform. Although deprived of speech he made it clear to the guard that he was 'goods to be deliv-ered', and all of us, guard and porters included, were engulfed in helpless laughter while the Cornish express was held up. Eventually one of those high luggage trolleys was produced and he was wheeled on to it and the train steamed off with the guard waving a cheery farewell.

A fortnight on Dartmoor and then to his beloved Exmoor, to Millslade in Brendon where we got a warm welcome from our kind hosts and their children. Here we had happy weeks. Every evening after school the children of the house and others in the village would come in to play. First we made a model of the village. In the day he would go out in his chair and carefully scrutinize the contours of the river bank and meadows in order that the children might model it accurately. At this time, too, they had formed a little society of their own called 'Kindness to animals'. They asked him to become a member and there was a charming little ceremony when a scrap of a child pinned his badge of membership, made by herself, into the lapel of his coat. He next turned his attention to a model toy theatre. He sent for the village carpenter—the latter had never been inside a theatre, which didn't make matters easier, and Roy had no speech—but he got what he wanted built. From this point the children were to do everything themselves, and at Christmas we were to have a pantomime. This resulted in happy evenings, the boys hammering, and painting the theatre, the girls sewing or painting pictures, each bringing him their work at intervals to know if it passed the standard. It was astounding to watch him with no speech, always serene and smiling, controlling the different activities, and with his left hand shaping here, moulding there, or writing if required.

Then Exeter again, and the operation on his leg and our high hopes for the future. This delayed the pantomime, we did not get back to Brendon till March and we were to have the pantomime on Saturday, April 9th. Everything was planned; all the village was coming; on the evening of the 8th we were to have the dress rehearsal. In the morning he got up and breakfasted, gay and full of spirits, and planned his day. At 1 p.m. he finished writing with his left hand a beautiful card he had made for me for Easter—at 2 o'clock he had a heart attack.

The doctor said he must rest for a few days, that he had pulled himself through so much he might do it again—but we knew the risk of pneumonia was great. All Saturday and Sunday we held our breath and a hush fell over the village. On Sunday night I telephoned to Holland where his Chela was spending part of his holiday with a Clifton friend, and told him to catch the first plane in the morning.

On Monday our worst fears were realized, for pneumonia and pleurisy had set in.

At 6.30 a.m. on Tuesday he asked for something to drink, and with a sweet smile and infinite courtesy he thanked his nurse. Less than four hours after, still holding my hand, he slipped swiftly and quietly away. . . .

*   *   *

The village carpenter and his mate, who so recently had built us our toy theatre, were able to meet our simple needs now. Two days later they laid him on the little lawn outside.

Here he lay among the bird boxes which he had put up three weeks before, and in which the tits were nesting, surrounded by friends (every cottage in the village and the outlying hamlets had sent a representative), within sight and sound of the Lyn on whose banks he had spent such happy hours, still covered with the primroses, wood anemones, and wild violets which the village children had brought him.

So they carried him through the garden gate, and he went through the village of Brendon for the last time.

As I followed shortly afterwards, I saw one who had stood bareheaded in the garden, throwing a fly on the water, and further on the village blacksmith back in his leather apron hammering at his anvil. I thought how this would have pleased him. I thought too with profound thankfulness that though he loved life he had no fear of death and indeed said he thought it would be 'a great adventure'.

And for myself—as I went home that beautiful evening, I stood at a point on the Moor that he particularly loved, and with the sun a red ball dipping in the west, I looked over the great stretches, across which we had walked and talked and laughed a hundred times, over the valley of Brendon, across the Bristol Channel to the coast of Wales beyond, and I knew that the challenge of Life must be faced and that then and always, looking at the past, grappling with the present, dreaming of the future, I should be sustained by a constant inspiration, a clear and vital vision—ROY.

PENROSE AND JULIAN TENNYSON

Penrose and Julian Tennyson

CHILDHOOD

WAR HAS tragically annihilated many lives of brilliant promise. Some, through their early struggles with circumstance or temperament, the brightness of their young achievement and the readiness of their final sacrifice, leave, even with those who mourn their loss, a sense of fulfilment. Such were Penrose and Julian Tennyson, great-grandsons of Alfred, Lord Tennyson, and grandsons of his second son Lionel, who, like them, lost his life before he had completed his thirty-first year.

Penrose was born on 26th August, 1912, and Julian on 7th February, 1915. From the beginning their personalities and characters were strongly contrasted. The elder boy was deeply affectionate, pugnacious and adventurous, a fearless rider from the age of three and an omnivorous reader, with an imagination easily stirred by books. His large dark eyes and fair, almost silvery, hair gave his expression a remarkable intensity, and, as he grew up, he developed a striking resemblance to the well-known portrait of his great-grandfather by Samuel Laurence.

The younger brother, known from babyhood as 'Dooley', grew into an infant of mercurial energy and vivacity, an instinctive comedian, with grey eyes, which slanted a little upwards and outwards, and a round cherubic face, over which there flitted with amazing rapidity every shade of feeling from inexpressible merriment to agonized gloom—merriment, however, generally prevailing. In spite of his liveliness, however, he was shy, nervous and sensitive, and this made him very dependent on affection, which he himself lavished impartially on his parents, his brothers, his pets and his favourite toys.

Both boys early developed their powers of expression. At three Julian was composing little rhymes and singing them to tunes of his own making, and at six he would dash off, entirely unaided, letters like the following from the country, where he was visiting his godmother, Cordelia Curle, Charles Fisher's sister:

Darling Mummy. I am so glad you have errangd a way of taking all my toys up to London. I hope you are keeping all my letters and letting Daddy and Pen read them. Little Leonor bought a gun and I bought five little brass cats and Adam is ill and I promised to give him a Morehen and now I will tell you all about how I did it. First of all I got a pece of wood and then I got some nales and stuck one into the wood and then I got some illasstick and then I tied it to the nail that I stuck in the wood and then I went to the Hollends to ask them what more hens eat and they said the remains of what the chickens eat so thy gave me some mays and wen I went for the mays I brought my horne to be querd[1] and do you know how the more hens got koght. I made a little loop in the illasstick and then more hens wood come and get ther foot koght and now I am just going to see if ther is eny more hens koght and to get my horne. From Dooley.

★   ★   ★

Darling Mummy. Ther was an uther rabbit hunt and now I will tel you all about it. First of all we put the ferrits down the rabbit hole and all of a sudden I felt a riggle under my feet and I looked down and I could not see enything but wen I looked at the side of me I saw a rabbit and Redgy took up his gun and fird at it but he hit it and he hurt it, but it was to hurt to get away and Harry ran after it and fount it dead in the steau pond. And then I asked Harry if he thorght there was any more rabbits in the tree but Harry said no. We put the ferrit down the hole and its coller got stuck and Redgy started to take the pine down and suddenly Redgy said heres a rabbit and sprung on it and then he shot a more hen and then Harry said theres a stoat just here and he started to jump on the pine but the stoat got out while we wer gone and I forgot to tell you befor we killd the second rabbit I hurd a squeak and a frog came out with the ferrit after it and Redgy shot a cartridge. I found a bean in the cartridg he had shot and wen I was at rest I saw the hounds and Anty Cor calld me up and just as I looked out of the window the huntsman came galloping along and Lemend saw the fox and the huntsman said to him wers the hounds and he said the fox has just gone up here. Then the huntsman said oh I dont car about the fox I want to know

[1] An old cow's horn which Mrs. Holland, the farmer's wife, had promised to cure for him.

wer the hounds are and he said the hounds followed the fox. From
Dooley.

*　　*　　*

A few weeks later, lying on the hearthrug in front of the
drawing-room fire, he definitely 'commenced author'. In
laborious capitals and with his nose almost touching the paper, but
with hardly a moment's hesitation for a thought or a word, he
wrote out the following tale:

THE FIRST DEERES IN ENGLAND

CHAPTER (1)

ONCE UPON A TIME THER WAS A BABBY DEER WHO DIDNT CARE
MUCH FOR HIS MUMMY AND DADDY AND HIS NAME WAS FRANCIS

CHAPTER (2)

AND HE CALLD HIS MUMMY SLUG HEAD AND HE CALLED HIS DADDY
RUD GUTTER

CHAPTER (3)

AND HIS MUMMY HAD OFTEN TOLD FRANCIS NOT TO GO INTO THE
WOODS WITHOUT SOME ONE WITH HIM BUT HE WOULD NOT TAKE
ENY NOTISE AND ONE DAY HE DID GO INTO THE WOODS

CHAPTER (4)

AND HE WANDERED ABOUT TILL HE GOT HUNGRY AND TRIED TO FIND
SOMETHING TO EAT AND HE SURCHED AND HE SURCHED UNTIL HE WAS
SPRUNG ON BY A MAN

CHAPTER (5)

NOW THE MAN THAT HAD CAUGHT FRANCIS WAS A HIGHWAMAN AND
HE TRIED TO KILL FRANCIS FOR THE SAKE OF HIS SKIN

CHAPTER (6)

BUT FRANCIS KICKED NOW FRANCIS WAS ABOUT SIX AND THE HIGH-
WAMAN WAS THINKING HOW TO BULD A SHED TO PUT FRANCIS IN
FRANCIS RAN AWAY AND STAYED IN THE WOODS FOR 4 YEARS UNTILL
HE WAS QUIT OLD AND HE SURCHED AND HE SURCHED UNTILL HE FOUND
A WIFE AND THE NAME OF HIS WIFE WAS RUDEN AND THEY MARRED AT
WHAT FRANCIS CALLD RUFLY HILL AND THE CLERGYMANS NAME WAS
MR RUSTENG

CHAPTER (7)

AND FRANCIS AND RUDEN TRIED TO FINDE A HOME AND WHILE THEY
WER TRIEING TO FINDE A HOME THEY SAW A LION AND RUDEN SED SHE
THOUGHT IT MIGHT BE VISHES AND FRANCIS SAID WELL THEN YOU STAY
THER WHILE I GO AND FIGHT IT WITH MY HORNES AND WITH A SUDEN
GALLOP HE BUTTED IT AND THE LION WITH A SUDEN RAW OF ANGER
WENT FOR FRANCIS AND FRANCIS PUT OUT HIS HORNES AND THE LION
PUT OUT HIS TEETH AND THEY BOTH FOGHT UNTILL FRANCISS THINKING
HE WAS BEEING BEATEN GAVE THE LION 7 SHARP BUTS ON WICH THE
LION FLED FROM FRANCIS

CHAPTER (8)

NOW WHILE ALL THIS FIGHTING HAD BEEN GOING ON RUDEN HAD
CETELD DOWN IN A SPOT AND HAD SOME BABBYS AND FRANCIS HAD
COME BACK TO HER AND BEFOR FRANCIS DID ANY THING ELSE HE
TURND ALL THE BABBYS OVER TO SEE THAT THEY WER ALL RIGHT AND
NICE AND PLUMP

CHAPTER (9)

HE FOUND THEM AS HE WISHD TO FIND THEM THER DEN WAS WARM
AND WIDE BY THIS TIME FRANCIS WAS TEN NOW THE BABBYS OF RUDEN
THER NAMES WER RUTH AND RODNICK AND THER ADGES WER RODNICK
WAS A WEEK OLD AND RUTH WAS HALF A WEEK OLD AND BOTH THE
BABBYS LOOKED JUST LIK A BALL OF WOOL BUT WEN THEY GOT OLD
THEY GOT IN THE HABBIT OF FIGHTING

CHAPTER (10)

FRANCIS WAS 13 AND IN THREE WEEK OF TIME HE DIAD AND SO DID
RUDEN

CHAPTER (11)

AND BY THIS TIME THE BABBYS WER 6 YEARS OLD AND RUTH SAID SHE
THORGHT THEY HAD BETTER START MAKING A LIVING FOR THEMSELVES

CHAPTER (12)

AND THEY DID SO AND THEY TRIED TO FINDE SOMETHING TO EAT
AND THEY DID FINDE SOMETHING TO EAT AND THEY CETELD DOWN IN
A HOME

CHAPTER (13)

BOTH THE THE BABBYS WERE 9 YEARS OLD AND WER PLANING OUT
HOW THEY THORGHT WAS THE BEST WAY TO MAKE A LIVING

CHAPTER (14)

THE FIRST THING THEY DID WAS TO GO INTO A SMALL COPPICE WER
THEY PULD UP ROOTS TO EAT AND THEN CHANGED OUT INTO THE NEW
FOREST WER THEY HAD SOME BABYS

CHAPTER (15)

AND ONE DAY INTO THE WOODS CAME WILLEM RUPHES AND HUNTED
RUTH AND SO HE SHOT AN ARROW AT HER BUT IT STRUCK A TREE AND
THEN BONCED BACK ONTO WILLEM RUPHES AND HE FELL DEAD AND
WILLEM RUPHES FRIEN FLED LIKE THE DEER ONLY IN ANUTHER DIRESHN

CHAPTER (16)

NOW RUTH WEN SHE GOT HOME SHE TOLD RODNICK THE STORY BY
THIS TIME THE DEER WER 12 YEARS OLD AND THER COATS WAS GETTING
GRAY AND THER EYES WER TURNING WEEK AND THEM SELVES WER
GETTING THIN AND THEY COULD NO MORE TRED ON SNALES AND THINGS
LIKE THEY YOST TO DO WEN THEY WER YUNG AND STRONG SO THEY SAT
DOWN AND HELD A CONVESHEN ABOUT WHAT A HAPPY LIFE THEY HAD
HAD BY THIS TIME THEY WER NEARLY 13 YEARS OLD AND FELT VERRY
WEEK AND WEN THEY PUT THER MOUTH TO DRINK THEY NEARLY FELL
OVER ON THER SIDES BECUSE THEY FELT SO WEEK AND IN 6 WEEK THEY
DIAD AND WER PUT IN THE MUSERM AND IF YOU GO TO THE MUSERM
ON THE LEFT HAND SIDE YOU WILL SEE THEM.

★   ★   ★

At their preparatory school the careers of the two boys were
very different. Pen never made any mark either at work or games,
chiefly, I think, because there was always a streak of the rebel in
him and he reacted against school conventions and school discipline; but he was remembered as a happy, independent boy who
seemed older than the others because of his self-reliance, and not
only took the Scott and Thackeray novels out of the library for
his own reading (the first boy who had done so for many years),
but also persuaded other boys to read them. Julian made a very
different impression, as his school nicknames—'Squib', 'Microbe',
'Baggage' and so on, testify. He was as irrepressible at school as
at home and soon became a general favourite. He got into the
school football and cricket elevens in due course (becoming captain of the latter), and in spite of his wayward and erratic methods

of thought, it was hoped that he might win a scholarship at Eton. These responsibilities, however, and a bad attack of influenza in May, proved rather too much for his mercurial temperament. He failed to do himself justice in the scholarship examination and was only placed in the Middle Fourth at Eton, where in September, 1928, he joined Pen, who had already been there for three years.

But it was home rather than school which showed the development of the two boys during these early years. In the spring of 1922 the family settled at Shiplake Rise, Binfield Heath, a mile or so from the Thames and about three hundred feet above sea level. The house was only half a mile from the Old Shiplake Vicarage from which Alfred Tennyson had been married to Emily Selwood in 1850, and next to Holmwood, where Emily had slept the night before the wedding. Nor was this the only poetic association of the village, for Holmwood had at one time belonged to Admiral Swinburne, and it was there that Algernon had retired to recuperate after his first collapse in London.

Shiplake Rise was a plain, old-fashioned house which had once been a small farm. The little property included a simple farmhouse garden, a large orchard, pigsties, cowsheds, an old granary on staddles, and twelve acres of pasture. The house stood on the southern slope of the hills, with a wide view over the Thames valley, including a gleam of the river in the foreground and distant glimpses of the Hog's Back and Windsor Castle. There were beautiful beech-woods, carpeted with bluebells in spring, and disused chalk-pits, the most delightful of playgrounds. Crowsley Park, with its teeming rabbits and noble chestnut-trees, was only a mile away.

Julian felt the influence of Shiplake Rise particularly, for he had two clear years there, while Pen had already begun his career at a boarding-school before it became the family home. But Pen, when he came for the holidays, threw himself wholeheartedly into the spirit of the home life and Julian ungrudgingly followed his leadership. Hallam, the youngest brother, who was just one and a quarter when the family life at Shiplake began, grew up a placid, serious infant, with a quiet sense of humour, who never minded however much his brothers made fun of him, and had enough imagination to appreciate and fall in with all Dooley's extravagances.

Dooley did not follow up the achievement of '*The First Deeres in England*'. He exercised his imagination chiefly by creating an elaborate nonsense world of which Hallam, under his nickname of 'Darmin', was centre and king. This saga grew in volume and complexity year by year, and Dooley delighted to invent the most fantastic names for its places and people. Its warring races inhabited provinces with names like 'Nakeland', 'Chickerub' and 'Bluskabib', while King Darmin's chief opponent was the sinister 'Mickabob', lesser heroes bearing such titles as 'Skate', 'Bellyband', 'Toogoocrack' and 'Galumphagloo'. The inhabitants of these strange lands lived entirely on chocolate biscuits and ginger-beer (Hallam's favourite delicacies), and the commonest cause of death was explosion due to excess or the attack of hostile 'paunch prickers'. The addition to the family when Hallam was about six years old, of the boys' cousins, Harold and Mark Tennyson, added substantially to the gaiety of the household and the scope of Dooley's saga.

Most important of all for Dooley was the great love of the country and of country things, creatures and people, which during these years more and more absorbed him. The garden was soon filled with his bird baths, feeding tables and nesting boxes, and immediately he was allowed an air-gun he set about forming a collection of stuffed birds, enlisting the help of a retired brick-layer in Henley, who was a skilled taxidermist. His reading was (with the exception of some child classics like the *Doolittle* Series) confined to books about birds and beasts, from *Black Beauty* to the works of Cherry Kearton, and a succession of dogs engaged his passionate affection, chief of these being Nobby, a black-and-white springer spaniel, with whom he would scour the garden *ventre à terre*, for he early developed an amazing faculty for running on all fours.

As Pen grew up he began to develop the sporting possibilities of Shiplake Rise. The twelve-acre meadow contained two thickly-grown clumps of trees into which the rabbits used to run from the hedgerows in the morning, staying there to feed during the day. The two boys spent many hours watching these clumps, gun in hand, while Nobby rushed madly round and round inside, trying to make the rabbits bolt, which in the end he generally succeeded in doing.

Then Dooley became more ambitious and devised a scheme for getting partridges. He built himself a hide of hurdles and boughs in the middle of the meadow, and would crouch in this with his gun for hours together, waiting until a covey moved slowly across the field, feeding as it came. When (as happened surprisingly often) the birds came within range, he would jump and fire through the boughs. It was remarkable how many birds he got by this very unconventional procedure, which was altogether too protracted for his more impetuous elder brother.

The year 1925 marked a new era in the life of the two boys with their introduction to Suffolk. A visit to Aldeburgh in August proved so successful that it was repeated year after year, until the grim little town, where George Crabbe was so unhappy and 'Fitz' used to come and muse by the grey North Sea, became a second home.

Aldeburgh meant a great deal to Pen and Dooley during the next five years. They learned to sail and row on the shallow meres at Thorpe, a mile to the north, where they could fish for roach, when sailing and rowing palled. They bathed from the long shingly Aldeburgh beach, with its pleasantly irregular row of houses behind and the two curious watch-towers, below which the fishermen congregate and gaze towards the sea. Most fascinating of all was Slaughden Quay, on the river Alde to the south. There the tidal river curves by on its twenty-mile course from Snape Mills, past Iken Cliffs, shadowed by tall oaks and backed by great stretches of heath and forest, and 'the Mansion', embowered in woods, where the herons build in spring, and the hens sit on the nests in the treetops with their long legs dangling comically over the side, while the cocks sail in and out over the wood like giant rooks in a rookery. The river here is a mile wide, or more, at high tide, and the view over the marshes from Little Japan, the high clump of pines to the east, is worth walking many a mile to see, especially in the breeding season when the broad stretch of water is sprinkled thickly with shell-duck, mallard, teal and widgeon. Opposite is Stanny's Creek, the centre of the wild-fowling country, and the Alde flows on past the brick dock and town marsh to Slaughden. There it turns abruptly to the south and runs parallel to the sea (from which it is separated only by a high and often narrow shingle bank), past the little medieval town of Orford, with its Norman keep and church, past Havergate Island and Butley marshes, till it flows into the German Ocean at Shingle Street twelve miles away.

In summer Slaughden Reach is always full of craft—schooners, dinghies, cruising yachts and rowboats; one can trawl for sole and flounder, or fish with a line or pritch for eels, and the Quay and its environs are covered with sheds and shacks in which the fishermen and boat-owners keep their gear and ply their trade, among them Jerry Woods, fisherman, fowler and yachtsman, the greatest character on the river, to whom Pen and Dooley owed their first instruction in the arts of which he is so great a master.

In 1927 Pen and his mother, as senior and junior partners, purchased an old converted beach boat, the *Laura*. She was not very smart, for she had been knocking about sea and river for fifty or sixty years, but she was safe and roomy and being about twenty feet long, with cabin accommodation for two, was to Pen a veritable *Golden Hind*.

That was the beginning of wonderful experiences for Pen; river picnics at Iken, Orford and Havergate Island; all-night trawling expeditions with his mother, the 'senior partner', when supper and breakfast were cooked on the boat; racing, both in the *Laura* and as crew in other craft; wild-fowling with Jerry, and later on Dooley. Sometimes the boys would take the *Laura* to a quiet spot on the Butley river and lie up there for a day or two, shooting at dusk and dawn and sleeping and idling by day. The beauty and excitement and humours of those days sank deep into the hearts of both the brothers. They grew to love not only the river, but the sailors, fowlers and fishermen who make their living from it. With their first instructor in the arts of sailing and fowling, the bond was particularly close, forged through many hours of waiting for the flight in the morning and evening stillness, or yarning in the *Laura*'s little cabin or on her half-deck under the stars. And Jerry was the best of teachers, for he taught the boys to work and think for themselves. He laughed when they drifted on the mud or missed their moorings, and never saved his time or their trouble at the expense of their education. When they had passed on into the fiercer excitements of the battle of life, they always rejoiced in the chance of a sail to Iken moorings or Orford or a flight on the marsh, and the mention of 'little old Pen' or 'little old Dooley' never failed to evoke on Jerry's mobile face a grin of affectionate reminiscence.

ETON

Nineteen-twenty-five saw Pen's introduction to both Aldeburgh and Eton. His entry to Eton was a challenge. For the first
time he seemed to realize that there were worlds for him to
conquer, and he was fortunate to begin his career under Cyril
Mowbray Wells, a famous scholar and athlete and a tutor of
genius, who could encourage without being sentimental and
discourage without austerity. Even the smallest urchin felt that he
was a friend and companion, yet he maintained excellent discipline, always in some original way which made the delinquent
realize its justice and his own stupidity. He immediately saw Pen's
possibilities and in his very first half made him enter for the
Rosebery History Prize which is open to the whole of the
Lower School. Pen won the Prize with papers on which the exam-
iner wrote, 'Marvellous for any boy, and incredible for a Lower
boy'. His success was so startling that he became something of a
hero among the Lower boys at his tutor's, who, unaccustomed
as small boys are to value intellectual achievement, could not help
feeling that a new lustre had been shed upon their species.

He also took enthusiastically to Eton football, the individualism
of which strongly appealed to him, and was speedily promoted to
the House second eleven in spite of his small and frail physique.
Thereafter his career at Eton was chequered and exciting, marred
by repeated ill-health and diversified by a growing disinclination
to concentrate on normal school studies or respect conventional
school discipline. Had 'C.M.W.' continued his tutor, no doubt
much of this trouble would have been avoided; but he retired at
the end of Pen's first year and Pen did not find his successor—a
most high-minded and conscientious housemaster, but lacking
Wells's peculiar genius and geniality—so much to his liking.

Looking at the record of his five years at Eton, one is struck by
the amount he achieved, the amount of trouble he got into, and
the amount of enjoyment he extracted from life in spite of serious
ill-health, which included an emergency operation for appendicitis in March, 1926, repeated and extensive absence from school
during the next twelve months, and, later, a long spell of digestive
trouble.

This weakness of health was, however, not without compensations. It gave him some relief from school routine, which he was

apt to find irksome, and enabled him to pursue his own lines of development. During convalescence he was allowed to fish instead of playing games, and took eagerly to the sport, teaching himself to use a dry fly for chub, to spin for pike, and to bottle small bleak for bait. Before long he had accumulated a useful angling library, beginning, of course, with Isaak Walton.

He continued to read voraciously and whenever there was a literature prize available he entered for it and generally won it. He even began writing a novel, the plot of which he outlined in one of his letters:

> Robert and Louis, two stepbrothers, make love to the same female; Robert gets engaged to the said female but one night, returning from her house, he is arrested for highway robbery and hanged. Louis marries said female about 6 or 7 years after. They get on badly. Louis takes to drink and on the strength of some tale he tells while almost drunk, he is arrested, tried and hung. He makes a full confession of the robbery; the unfortunate girl goes mad. Is it not a melancholy and morbid tale? Still it gives one's literary powers pretty good scope and some parts should be pretty juicy. The girl will not be very beautiful. The hero by no means perfect and the villain in spite of his failings will in reality be quite decent. The hero is arrested and hung on account of the likeness. Would it be better to make them twins and the hero perfect and the other foul?

But all this in no way weakened his passion for Eton football and he quickly made himself a reputation as 'Post', the toughest position on the field, for 'Post' is the central man in the scrum or bully, who has to hold the ball between his feet against the concentrated attack of the whole of the opposing bully. He early showed the gift of leadership. Even his austere House tutor smiled when he saw his tiny figure standing plastered with mud in the middle of the field during some Lower Boy match, and shouting to his larger but less strenuous colleagues:

'By God, you fellows! you MUST back me up!'

Although he had not great speed or finesse as a player, and in his own words 'seemed generally to be the person backing up or who stops the ball with his stomach for someone else to get a run with', he was from the beginning marked as an ultimate captain of the House football, and this position he achieved early in his seventeenth year.

In the summer he took things less strenuously. After the romance and beauty of the Alde, the idea of paddling up and down the Thames in a sculling boat or sweating in an eight with an irascible coach, did not appeal to him, and he preferred a little desultory cricket, making it his object to stay in as long as he could, and, if possible, without adding a run to the score. He was particularly gratified when he could see entered in the score book:

'Tennyson. Hit wickets by request—o'.

Unfortunately his interest in school work began to evaporate after a year or two. At first his ambition to excel in whatever he undertook had made him industrious, even in ordinary school subjects which did not naturally appeal to him. Then came a change. He gave up Greek after rather a languid struggle, nor did he attain sufficient knowledge of Latin to derive any enjoyment from reading it. It soon became plain that he would never devote to mathematics or science more than the minimum of attention needed to get him through the Certificate Examination. From now onward every half brought the same kind of reports from his masters. He was clearly the ablest boy in the Division, but would not take the trouble to grapple with uncongenial subjects or give the time to preparation which real progress demanded. This, of course, by no means applied to English subjects. He would take any amount of trouble over these, and, whatever his place in the school, would generally carry off the prizes for essay writing and English literature. Both in the House and in school his high spirits and sense of humour made him prone to 'mob' on the slightest provocation. This became a constant source of trouble both with his House tutor and his Division masters. Moreover, his mind was becoming increasingly restless and critical and he did not hesitate to give very free expression to his opinions, which were often of a kind to conflict sharply with the accepted doctrines of the school. His essays and answers to Sunday Questions were criticized as interesting but wild, once even provoking the comment that he was not a Christian, and he began to find the compulsory Chapel services irksome.

He had looked forward to his transfer from Lower to Upper Chapel as he thought he would hear better sermons there, but alas! the preachers in Upper Chapel came in for some very rough handling in his letters: 'Today's sermon pitiful,' he wrote one

Sunday at the end of March, 'inaudible to the majority, dull to the minority.' Another Sunday the victim was: 'the world's most massive prelate. He must have scaled 14 stone out of garments! Enormous! However, he was slightly disappointing in action, as he bellowed out disconnected platitudes for twenty-two minutes'. He complained that so many of the preachers 'seem to be pessimists or fanatics. They never realize that life is a fairly cheerful affair for a boy and either talk about our trials or our troubles. Thank God at present I haven't any and the average Etonian hasn't either.'

A sermon from a venerable visiting canon was characterized as 'sepulchral and mouldy', a Church dignitary who succeeded him was dismissed as 'dirty, pallid and incoherent', and another as 'evasive'. Of one very spruce and complacent ecclesiastic he wrote, 'When I look at him I can always understand why people enjoyed pulling down monasteries so much'. Finally, came a reference to one of his favourite preachers who quite unexpectedly produced 'a perfectly frightful sermon, hollow as an empty barrell'.

His attitude was, of course, not wholly frivolous, as his school essays showed. These, whatever their subject, seemed during these years increasingly to take a social or political trend. He was becoming more and more alive to the realities of life, and like most eager and imaginative boys, the more he thought about them the more inadequate seemed the efforts of humanity to cope with them. This feeling embraced the institutions with which he was at that time in closest contact, the educational and ecclesiastical, and as he expressed his views with considerable force and complete candour, the effect on those responsible for his education was often unfortunate. One of his 'Sunday Questions' on the 'Value of Lent' proved too much for his Divinity master's equanimity:

Lent has not started yet. The purple altar-cloth has not yet been substituted for its red brother. The preachers have not yet pulled their Lenten faces or introduced the Lenten strain into their discourses. The suggestions concerning 'tuck', the 'Eton Mission' and various other equally interesting subjects which are showered upon us, have not yet been heard. We are still allowed to enjoy ourselves. That is one of the things I object to about the Church; faces long or short have to be pulled so regularly. I am reminded of the preacher last Sunday who asked in chapel:

'Why are you all here, boys?'

Well, of course the answer is quite obvious. 'Because we get 250 lines if we don't come.' But the preacher hastily answers his own question with some well-known tag. That is the chief trouble with Christianity; so many questions are asked and answered in the same breath. It is done in Chapel and out (*vide* the Headmaster's new book). Lent is one of the most obvious of these little tricks. That parsons think Lent an excellent institution is clear. But in the modern industrial world in which we must all become units one day, there is absolutely no room for Lent. The whole system is so entirely and completely ruthless as to eliminate the possibility of cutting any pleasure out of a man's life without making his existence intolerable. What is a working-man on the wages of 30s. a week to cut out of his life or to give to the church? What is any business man whose holidays are often not more than a week *in toto* during the whole year and whose pleasures are as scanty as his holidays, to eliminate from his life? Life is quite intolerable enough for most men without dragging abnegation into it. That is the value of Lent to the ordinary man who earns his own bread and butter; but to us who do nothing but waste that well-earned money in various pursuits, the value of Lent is much greater. Of course we take no notice of Lent; but the value of self-abnegation to us cannot be over-estimated. Nothing can be better for the character of the idle or the wealthy than self-denial. Anything which is difficult to accomplish is worth accomplishing and nothing is more difficult to achieve than the deliberate putting away of some pleasure. Such an act, apart from its religious value, crystallizes and forms the character. Why do we not all do it?

More apparently serious was an essay on 'A Religious Revival.' Its general thesis was unexceptionable, but the comments on the Church were not likely to be very welcome:

The Church at present is the most out-of-date machine in the world. It has taken no steps whatever to meet modern exigencies. It has just started to reform the Prayer Book which has been in use for three hundred years and over. It is squabbling and bickering miserably in the process. Its servants are wretchedly paid and overworked. Its services are frequently dull. It is in a rut. And it makes no attempt to leave the rut; apparently believing that when it is necessary some divine power will move it from its rut. There is an old saying that 'the gods help those who help themselves'. It is a very true saying. All great movements have been started by some man. Jesus and Luther both in their turn have set in motion the two greatest forces of good ever released. But the age of the individual is to some extent

passed. It is to the representative bodies that we look for decisions
and deeds. And it should be to the Church, the representative body
of God on earth, that we should look for the next great movement
in the world's history.

Let the Church first be at unity in itself and then let it prepare to
help and renovate society.

Even less acceptable would have been a comparison between
the Film and the Church in a letter which he wrote to his mother,
describing a visit to a film called 'Broadway Melody':

Nothing has annoyed me so much [he wrote] since my last Sunday
Chapel. The extraordinary thing is that they are both as Jerry would
say 'similar in many respects'. The one professes to appeal to your
so-called better side through the conventionalities of song and sentiment, the other appeals to your worst side through the conventionalities of chorus girls and chemises. But the really infuriating thing
about them is that their methods are not necessary—what everybody
really enjoyed last night was a fat man who stuttered. If the only
way you could get people to a cinema was by showing them pictures
of a lot of harlots walking about in their underclothes, well the public would be to blame, not the producers. But this is not so.

Sometimes he would tilt against conventional education, as in
the following fable—'The Gates of Heaven':

'Spirit,' said the Chief Justice, 'you are accused of immorality and
idleness. Have you anything to say in your defence?'
'Yes,' said the spirit. 'I was a Peer and educated at a Public
School.'
'Oh well,' interposed the Chief Justice to the waiting angel, 'open
the gates.'

In another fable he had a dig at the opposite extreme—excessive
asceticism:

'Happiness,' said the Brahmin, as he seated himself firmly on a
large spike, 'is to be found only in the next world.'

Pen, no doubt, got plenty of fun out of these gibes and tirades,
though he meant them seriously, too. Complacency and
inertia he detested. Discontent seemed, by contrast, a positive
virtue.

If a Fairy Godmother happened to appear at one of my offsprings' christening, supposing I was ever so foolish as to beget any, and asked me what qualities I wished him or her to be endowed with, I should say 'Make it a discontented little swine'. . . . Discontent and humour are the very salt of life. Forty-five may find me with a pot-belly and a passion for golf or with a handcart and an interest in rags and bones, but I hope that, whatever the Fates may unroll, I shall still be discontented with myself and all about me.

Characteristic, too, was his reaction to a performance of *Othello* in the School Hall. 'It pretty well bowled me over. I am still picking up mental fragments here and there.' How deep the impression was is shown by an essay which he wrote some months afterwards on 'The Function of Tragedy'. In this he combated the theory of Aristotle that the function of tragedy is to purge the soul of the emotions of pity and terror, and maintained that it was rather to purge the soul of petty emotions and restore it to a true sense of proportion.

> I saw *Othello* on a Saturday night at Eton. The only external result was that I did not do my Sunday Questions on the following day— what was the authorship of the Book of Proverbs to me when I had just seen *Othello*? But the greater result was that for the first time in my life I realized the exact amount of my own importance. The chief effect of a great tragic presentation should be to make us realize our own insignificance in proportion to the Universe, in proportion even to the figures and figments represented.

One of the most remarkable features about Eton is its tolerance, and, irritating as Pen's attitude to school discipline and conventions must have been, the authorities did not take it too seriously and were able to give due weight to the unusual ability and sincerity which lay behind. In 1929, as Captain of Games for his House, he became jointly responsible with the Captain of the House for its management, and whatever his irresponsibility in other spheres, he took the position with becoming seriousness. He also became editor of an ephemeral magazine called *The Burning Bush*, which came out once a term,. He threw himself with enthusiasm into this undertaking, secured literary contributions from famous Old Etonians like Desmond MacCarthy, Bernard Darwin and Gilbert Frankau, and canvassed strenuously

CHARLES JULIAN TENNYSON

FREDERICK PENROSE TENNYSON

for advertisements. The result was such a substantial profit to himself and his co-editor that the Headmaster issued an edict that no future editor should be allowed to retain more than five pounds of the profits, the balance being diverted to the Eton Mission in East London.

There was much discussion about his future during these months. He himself had made up his mind some years before—when he was not more than twelve—to seek a career in the film industry and he wanted to get to grips with life as soon as possible. His tutor, however, wanted him to try for a scholarship at Balliol, and as one of his closest friends was going up for this, he at last, though with some reluctance, agreed to do the same. It was hoped that he would spend a last year steadily reading for Balliol, bringing out further numbers of *The Burning Bush*, and in the autumn lead the House football team again and perhaps get his School colours. He made an ecstatic plunge into English literature, revelling in Byron's *Don Juan* and Keats's *Endymion*, the incredible verbiage of which, he said, made his head spin. Then in May, 1930, his digestion completely broke down and he had to go into a nursing home for treatment. It was clear now that if he stayed on at Eton, with his responsibilities in his House and the work for Balliol, there would be a serious danger of further breakdown, and, with great regret, it was decided that he should leave school at the end of the summer half and work at home for his scholarship.

$$\star \quad \star \quad \star$$

When Pen left Eton in July, 1930, Julian had been there two years. The two brothers had kept closely in touch after Pen had left his preparatory school, corresponding regularly and sending each other presents. Pen would generally arrange for a tin of sweets to be waiting for Julian on his arrival at school and he plied him regularly with 'Bonzo' cards, that canine hero being a great favourite of Dooley's.

> I got an awfully nice letter from Pen, [writes Dooley in June 1927]. He is the nicest brother that I could possibly have. He keeps sending me presents. On Monday I sent him my three monkeys.

N

When Dooley came to Eton Pen, in spite of the inconvenience of having a much younger boy suddenly projected into the intimate circle of his school life, insisted that he should share his room, as he feared that Dooley, who was extremely sensitive, would otherwise find his introduction to Eton rather trying. With his elder brother's help Dooley made a good start, showing promise at football and finding the work in the comparatively low position in which he had entered the School, unexpectedly easy. His greatest pleasure was to go with Pen on Sunday afternoons into Luxmoore's Garden, a beautiful corner on a backwater of the Thames, which had been left to the School by a former master and was reserved for Upper boys. There he would loiter as long as he was allowed, watching the birds and water rats, and it was a bitter disappointment if a Sunday came when Pen could not take him. Pen watched over him carefully; rejoiced when he performed the unusual feat of taking a double remove two terms running and so got himself a place in the School more worthy of his abilities; coached him in football and wrote copious reports on his progress to his mother. After a time, however, Julian began to find this position rather oppressive. He could not bring his own friends to Pen's room and it was awkward for him to be there when Pen's friends came, since they were all much older and higher up in the School than himself. It was a relief to both brothers when a small room, looking out on the Chapel graveyard, became available. Julian moved into it with high hopes, and set about furnishing it with a touching delight. His large collection of carved birds and animals were crowded precariously on to the tiny mantelpiece, backed by a goodly row of family photographs. On the walls hung pictures which he had chosen with the greatest care—a photograph of Nobby—two setters on a moor—a wild duck rising from the reedbeds—a covey of partridges—a grouse drive —lastly, a jay in a fir-tree. 'This,' he wrote, 'is really rather a good picture, though the jay's head looks more like an errand boy with his hair brushed back and parted in the middle than what it is meant to be.' Then arose the question of a window-box, and he spent hours in Windsor market haggling over plants which he thought his mother would like when she came for the Fourth of June. Small as the room was, he decided to keep it as long as he remained at Eton, and wrote of the pleasure which he had in looking out on the rough old graveyard, backed by the grey bulk of Chapel, about which the pigeons and jackdaws darted and circled, and of his longing for the day when the trees would be in full leaf and shut out the view of the noisy roadway.

Then immediately after the Fourth he went down with an attack of measles, which was succeeded by pneumonia. For some days there was serious anxiety about him, and although he rallied quickly when once the crisis was over, he had to leave Eton for the rest of the half, which meant a serious interruption of his work and the loss of any chance of distinction at cricket.

Pen left Eton in July, 1930, and Dooley went back to school completely on his own. He was chosen to play football for the House, made an excellent start in his Division work and began to prepare eagerly for the Literature Prize, the subject for which was his favourite *Reynard the Fox*—a poem he already knew almost by heart, for his taste in literature was maturing and Masefield's poems had, for some months, especially delighted him. But at the end of November came another blow. He was laid up with a bad attack of boils, which made him miss the literature examination and robbed him of his place in the House side. This misfortune, following his serious illness in the summer, meant that a vital year of his Eton life was practically wasted. Worse than this was the sense of frustration and disappointment, just when his diffident and sensitive nature was beginning to face the bewildering trials of adolescence. A few months of good health and some success at work and games might have saved him much suffering during the years which followed.

The beginning of 1931 saw a great change in the family life, for Shiplake Rise was given up and a permanent home rented at Aldeburgh. The days of 'long leave' in the Easter half were the last that Julian spent at Shiplake, and he felt intensely parting from the country and friends that had meant so much to him. But Aldeburgh had already become a second home and offered a romance and opportunity for adventure which Shiplake could not afford. From this time there was never any doubt that Suffolk held the first place in his affections. The change came at a moment when his emotions and sensibilities were rapidly developing, and in the spring he sent us home a poem which was a more serious attempt at self-expression than anything he had attempted since 'The First Deeres in England'.

Next to the College Chapel lies
The graveyard, open to the skies,
And here in May, as the cars go by,
The Starlings and the Jackdaws fly.
And every night when the lights are low,
The white owls hoot as they come and go,
Swooping swiftly from some dark hole
To snatch at a mouse or a poor blind mole.
When morning breaks and the Jackdaws chatter,
The owls retire from the traffic's clatter,
And lifting his head from his tiny wing
The red cock linnet begins to sing:
Sings to his mate in the sun's warm glow
Songs that are beautiful, swift and slow.
The grass is so high and the bushes so gay
That the tombs are all shrouded in summer's array.
And sometimes the dead, those that lie there below,
Must think of the Spring that enlivens us so.

He himself took a very humble view of his achievement, and was extremely flattered when his Division master asked if he had written it all himself. In fact, this poem marked the beginning of a new stage in his development, for he now began to experience in full severity the difficult passage from boyhood to manhood. He wrote no more, and steadily fell behind in his work at Eton. But he was developing his capacities all the time. The river and the marshes were the chief factors in this development. He and Pen now owned a double duck-punt as well as the *Laura*. This they could row up to the nearer shooting grounds when it was not worth while to take the larger boat. Julian also loved to go shooting on the town marsh, which was accessible on foot though not so good for birds, with Walter Cracknell, a retired gamekeeper turned gardener, and the two spent many hours together talking of gamekeeping and poaching and the wild life of field and woodland. All the time his poetic imagination was steadily developing and he came strongly under the spell of *In Memoriam*. From now until the day of his death he always carried a manuscript copy of the introductory stanzas ('Strong Son of God, Immortal Love') in his pocket-book.

Thus nearly two years of his school life passed uneasily away. All hope that he might achieve any distinction at Eton was dashed by a football accident in the autumn of 1931, which necessitated an operation on his leg, kept him away from school for several weeks and robbed him once more of his place in the House side. This misfortune, following his illnesses of 1930 and 1931, made it more than ever difficult for him to settle down, and during 1932 it became increasingly obvious, both to him and to his parents, that he would not get any advantage from staying at Eton after passing the Certificate Examination. There was much talk about his future, and as he showed no marked inclination to any particular kind of career, it was agreed that he should aim at becoming a schoolmaster, and with this in view leave Eton in July, 1932, go abroad until the following summer and then to Trinity, Cambridge, to take the Modern Language Tripos.

'Prentice Years

As Julian was, in many ways, young for his age, it seemed desirable that he should keep up his general education while learning French. He was therefore sent to Versailles, where he lived in a charming French family and attended the Lycée, which he found extremely cosmopolitan.

The work at the Lycée gave him great amusement and he wrote Pen a vivid description of a class, which was presided over by an exceedingly irascible master.

This is the sort of scene you get in the French class.

Beak: Vous supposerez que vous êtes en Afrique: vous allez m'ecrire une composition sur le chef de la tribu noire. . . .

Voices: 'Hafi, monsieur, Hafi.' (Hafi is the boy who comes from Algiers.)

Beak: (hitting nearest boy on head with a pencil): 'Voyons! qu'est que c'est que cette attitude? Hafi, faut-il que je vous mette a la porte pour faire du bruit? Allons! Pambourkdgian me fera douze pages pour bavarder.' (Writes in note book.)

Pambourk: 'Oh, monsieur, oh! . . .'

Beak: 'Silence ! ! ! Faut-il que je mette une retenu? Silence!!! Pambourkdgian me fera quinze pages pour me repondre . . . Leon!! qu'est-ce que vous faites la? ? Leon! Non, ne parlez pas. Vous me

ferez quatres heures de plus pour mauvaise volonté. . Leon!!
Faut-il que je fasse un rapport? ? Leon, me fera six heures de plus.
. . . Silence! ! Leon! Voulez-vous etre mis a la porte?? Qu-est-ce
que c'est cette attitude? ? Leon! Ne parlez pas! Non! Non! Leon me
fera dix heures de plus. . . . Vous êtes hypocrite! Vous mentez!
Vous faites du bruit! Non, ne parlez pas. . . .'

By this time the noise is terrific, but above all the din can be heard
Leon swearing in Egyptian and receiving 'douze heures de plus;
non! ne parlez pas . . .'

The beak can only talk French so when the foreigners get poenas
they say what they like; this is the sort of thing—

Pambourkdgian: (Armenian): Habblehoovahumphapankerum . . .'

Leon (Egyptian): Swears in hieroglyphics, so it can't be written
down, but it sounds awfully good.

Wilbur Woolf (Canadian): 'Say you wump-headed plug-ugly . . .
you big flat-headed skate, you yellow-bellied shrimp, you pie-faced
gazooni. . . .'

Hafi (Algerian): 'Hallelujah, gastroporoogi baas!'

Sadovsky (Russian): 'Damnski, I'l bustski yourblanovitch, would
you punishovitch the great Sadovsky?'

Abraham-ian (Persian): x.y.z. p.q.r.! ! ? ? ! !—! x.y! !—

Unfortunately, when he had been at Versailles barely three
weeks he fell ill with bronchial influenza, which turned into slight
pneumonia and kept him out of action, on a very low diet, for the
best part of a month, during which he solaced himself by making
up and sending home menus of what he would like to eat if he
were 'in good old England'—as, for example:

BREAKFAST

1. *Grapenuts and Devonshire cream*
2. *Scrambled egg*
   Fried bread (very brown)
   Bacon
   Mushrooms
3. *Toast*
   Marmalade (thin, jellied sort)
4. *Coffee.*

LUNCH

1. *Cold beef (not too well done)*
   Baked potatoes
   Pickallilli
2. *Trifle (Devonshire cream)*
3. *Digestive biscuits*
   Stilton cheese
4. *Chrystallized fruits*
5. *Coffee.*

TEA

1. *Toast (hot and very buttered)*
   Honey
2. *Tea (China)*
3. *Cakes (like the ones you get in Paris—winners)*

DINNER

1. *Ox-tail soup*
2. *Fresh plaice*
3. *Roast wild duck*
   Roast potatoes
   French beans
   Bread sauce
4. *Ice-pudding with chocolate sauce*
5. *See lunch 3, 4 and 5.*

FADE-OUT

Me going into the kitchen to eat the remains of the ice-pudding.

This enforced inactivity, however, had one excellent result: it stimulated him for the first time to make a sustained attempt at writing. The creative mood was started by some nonsense verses which he wrote for his father (then Secretary of the Dunlop Rubber Company):

To My Father, on his Fifty-third Birthday

Who is it makes directors quail?
However gorged with food and ale
Under his eyes their faces pale,
They shrivel into something frail,
They draw their horns in like a snail,
And e'en hand in their dinner-pail.
When great C.T. is on the trail
They know that they are doomed to fail,
And soon he'll have 'em by the tail:
So off across the seas they sail.

Some go to seek the Holy Grail
Others as pilgrims chant and wail.
But they may hide them where they will
The great C.T. will find them still
And make them pay full many a time,
These poor directors for their crime.

The great financier 'makes a deal',
(For he's as slippery as an eel),
In china, glass, or iron or steel.
But when he comes to deal in rubber,
Well may he yodel, scream and blubber.
What chance has such a man as he
Against that king of men, C.T.?

Directors aye shall sing his praise
And emulate his business ways,
Striving their infant sons to teach
To deal in pebbles on the beach.
And when the great man comes in sight,
They hide cigars in mortal fright,
And grovel, whining, at his feet,
Trying in vain his eye to meet.

But erring clerks must live in fear;
With trembling lips they drink their beer,
With furtive steps they creep to bed,
Their false teeth rattling in their head,
Thinking with every step to see
Old Dunlop's pride, the great C.T.
(His age, my dears, is fifty-three).

Then he plunged into a long poem, in the manner of Masefield, describing a duck-shooting expedition at Aldeburgh. He was astonished at the speed with which he wrote, and the whole poem, which was deeply felt and full of vivid observation, was finished very quickly.

Meanwhile he had written some lines, which he called 'The Full Moon', describing his favourite Little Japan, and one or two short lyrics. These, though sometimes crude and unequal, showed a considerable advance on anything he had done before.

The Full-moon

The moon rose clear above the trees,
Which rustled in the fitful breeze,
Sweet sounds of night disturbed the air,
Those sounds which always turn the hair
Of people bred in town and slum,
But which to every rustic come
As natural as the sounds of day.

I saw the owl swoop for his prey,
I heard his talons rend the beast,
His bloody lips clacked o'er the feast.
I heard the nightjar's rattling whirr,
That ghostly sound, so made to stir
The blood of those who fear the night,
I heard a rabbit squeal in fright,
Caught by some weasel unaware,
Or in the slowly tightening snare,
That cruellest and most lingering death;
With starting eyes and gasping breath,
The victim strains and fights for life,
While biting wire cuts like a knife.

All these I heard . . . and then I ran
To where the scented marsh began,
I passed the bull-frog in the dyke,
The shining pond, where lurked the pike.
And so I reached the lofty bank,
Bordered by pines on either flank.
I gazed enraptured, and my eyes
Saw, like a flock of sleeping flies,
The myriad wildfowl, swans and coot,
Which lay on the water like specks of soot,
Save where the moon, with her powerful light,
Shone on the wings of a duck in flight.
Pochard and widgeon, mallard and teal
Making the best of their midnight meal—
I looked to Heaven and uttered thanks
That no punt-gunner had spoiled their ranks.
I sniffed the breeze and the scents of the marsh,
And the voice of a heron, croaking harsh,
Came to me, as he speared his eels,
And stored in his crop for future meals.

Then, as the moon through the heavens crept,
I dropped on the dewy grass and . . . slept.

The redshank piped on the gleaming flats,
And the dunlin chirped like a troop of bats.
A curlew rose with a bubbling note
And a bittern boomed in his long, deep throat,
And the moon went down, and the sun rose high,
And still I slept, while he swept the sky.

The Captive

Now the red sun sinks to rest,
Lingering, reluctant, slow,
Crimson radiance in the west
Bathes the fields with twilight glow;
In the dank and fetid cages,
Restless through the long night's stages,
Furtive shadows come and go.

Tranquil in the starry light
Lies the circus, white and chill;
Piercing through the summer night
Rings a cry with piercing thrill,
Deep, despairing, soft and sobbing,
Quick, vibrating, slow and throbbing,
Falling, fading, dying—still.

Phosphorescent eyes afire,
Blazing as the Northern Lights,
With the fierce but vain desire
For the whisp'ring jungle nights—
Who will free him, sad and pining,
Set those lustrous opals shining
With the joy of long-lost sights?

Julian's return from France at the end of 1932 coincided with a temporary severance of his tie with Suffolk, since it had become necessary, for family reasons, for his parents to make Farringford, the Tennyson house at the west end of the Isle of Wight, the holiday home. Julian felt acutely his parting from Jerry Woods, Walter Cracknell, Stanney's Creek and Little Japan. The *Laura*, in which he and Pen had passed so many winter and summer nights, had to be sold, though they kept the double duck-punt in the hope that Fate might now and then allow them a visit to the Alde. However, when once the parting was over, the new home offered many compensations. It was full of family associations; there were many friends to welcome them; the Island was a paradise for birds and there was an excellent rough shoot of five hundred acres of which Julian was immediately appointed keeper, an experience which was to prove of great benefit to him later on. In this task he was assisted by a new dog, Buster, a large liver-and-white spaniel, successor to Nobby, who had died shortly before, worn out by his own exuberance and zest for life. Buster had not Nobby's intelligence or vivacity, and as a gun dog he was too wild and headstrong to be very satisfactory. But he was an animal of noble appearance, with a magnificent head and drooping eyes, like those of a St. Bernard, and a sobriety and sagacity of manner which was never disturbed even by the violent attacks

of hiccoughs which often beset him. He at once became passionately attached to Dooley and, though he could never be to him all
that Nobby had been, he was destined to become a great source
of consolation and amusement during the difficult years that
followed.

By the time the family had settled at Farringford, Pen was
already launched on the career which was in less than eight years
of strenuous and brilliant effort to bring him to the front rank of
British film production. He had won an Exhibition at Balliol in
November. There had been considerable doubt among the
examiners whether he ought not to be given the scholarship, but
a grievous lapse in the Latin paper robbed him of this. The first
six months of the next year, 1931, he spent in Switzerland learning
French and reading a good deal more English than he should have
done (but coming home for Christmas at Aldeburgh); and then
in October he went up to Oxford. A boy coming from Eton with
an Exhibition in literature and the name of Tennyson was sure of
an interested reception at a college which remembered Alfred
Tennyson's friendship with its greatest master, and Pen with his
wide interests and quick brain, his flashing humour and warm
sympathies, quickly made his mark. He was to read History, but
the subject made little appeal to him, as appeared from a letter
which he wrote within a few days of his arrival: 'I find unfortunately, now, that my conscience no longer pricks me if I spend
the evening reading Flaubert instead of mugging up *Gesta
Francorum* with a crib—this is unfortunate, sinister and may even
be significant!'
However he seemed to be settling down happily enough,
sailing at Abingdon, occasionally getting a day's shooting with
friends, and becoming film critic to one of the Oxford periodicals.
Then something happened which put an end to all hope of his
staying up long enough to take a degree. He fell in love with a
delightful undergraduate from one of the women's colleges. The
result was that he failed in the examination which he had to take
at the end of the term, and, although the Dean, 'Sligger' Urquhart,
who had become his staunch friend, defended him strenuously to
the Master, he himself was convinced that he would not stay the
course. It happened that just at this time his parents were rather
pinched for money and it was agreed that he should leave the

University at Easter. The College authorities, when they heard that finance had something to do with his proposed departure, very generously offered to keep him without fees, but this he would not agree to, as he felt that to accept would mean that he would have to stay up for three or four years and take his degree, which he had no intention of doing. Fortunately his mother was able to secure him an opening with the Gaumont British Film Company, to whose studio in Shepherd's Bush he duly went in May, 1932.

His two terms at Oxford had not been wasted. He had made many friends. Contact with men like 'Sligger', Roger Mynors, Harold Hartley and Humphrey Sumner, who were all dons at the College, had broadened his outlook, improved his sense of proportion and helped him to realize and develop his own mental powers. As for the love affair into which he had entered so enthusiastically, this succumbed in due course to the force of circumstances, as it was bound to do, causing him much suffering in the process, and intensifying for a time a natural tendency to cynicism.

When he entered the Gaumont British studio at Shepherd's Bush early in May of 1932, a rather frail, sensitive-looking boy of nineteen, the studio, which had had some experience of failures from the universities, were convinced that he would not last more than two months.

He came to the industry at a very interesting moment. The British industry was just beginning to recover from the onset of the 'Talkies', which had entirely revolutionized the technique and objects of film production. There were very few experienced directors, those who had experience having for the most part been brought up in the technique of the silent film.

The Gaumont British Company had just completed an important scheme of reconstruction and amalgamation. It had a large studio and office building at Shepherd's Bush and, as it owned a big chain of theatres, the prospects of an ambitious production policy seemed to be favourable. There were, however, elements of danger. The dominant position of the American film industry in the world's markets meant that there was little hope of British pictures obtaining any substantial export sales, so that British producers would have to rely almost entirely on the British market, which could only yield a limited return. Economy in production was therefore essential, or even a first-rate picture might fail to cover expenses. Unfortunately it is very difficult to build up a large-scale organization on economical lines without a considerable period of trial and error, especially when there is a shortage of experienced staff.

Pen was first put in the scenario department, where he spent a few irritating weeks, reading third-rate novels and making recommendations to which he knew no one would ever pay any attention. Michael Balcon, who was producer at Shepherd's Bush, had, however, only put him on this work in order to give him a quick introduction to the business. In August he was brought down to the studio to act as third assistant director—a great day, for he felt that he was now fairly launched. The first picture on which he worked was Priestley's 'The Good Companions', and George Pearson was assistant producer.

It was very lucky for Pen that in this first venture he had to work under such sympathetic producers as Michael Balcon and George Pearson. 'Mick' was young, imaginative and with a mind plastic enough to adapt itself easily to the new conditions. Moreover, he had a natural refinement and sensibility to which Pen's personality made an immediate appeal. George had been a schoolmaster, and his gentle and idealistic nature never seemed really at home in the hurly-burly of the film industry. Yet he lived for picture-making and knew the technique as few others did. He became deeply attached to Pen, who grew to love and respect him in return.

It was a strenuous life, for it is inevitable that the production of a picture on the floor of the studio should involve a fight against time, carried through in an atmosphere of intense nervous strain. The assistant directors, of whom there may be three or four on an important picture, are the director's henchmen, who have to see that the actors, technicians, crowd artists, sets and properties are available from hour to hour—whether in the studio or 'on location'—according to schedule, and everything ready for the director when he wants it; they also have to be continually on hand to do odd jobs and cope with emergencies under his instructions. The better the studio organization and the more complete and methodical the preliminary preparations, the easier is the task of the director and his staff. But however good preparation and organization may be, there is always the risk of sickness or accident upsetting arrangements. When this occurs everyone's nerves are on edge and everyone in a responsible position is apt to look for an alibi. The director, nine times out of ten, looks for this in his assistants. The assistant director, therefore, learns his job in a hard school and it is so exacting and demands such a meticulous attention to detail that success in it is apt to kill creative ability, and relatively few of those who start as assistants ever emerge to become directors.

Pen was determined not to let himself be submerged in this way, for he meant to get to the top of the tree, and make his own pictures according to his own ideas while he was still young and vigorous.

It was a continuous source of amazement to his friends how he stood up to the long hours of harassing work, without holidays and often without a day off for weeks on end. This was the more remarkable as his digestion was still weak, and he soon began to suffer severely from varicose veins and haemorrhoids, and often, when hard pressed, had bouts of sleeplessness. Fortunately he took at once to the free-and-easy cosmopolitan life of the studios, where everyone is on Christian-name terms, social distinctions are unknown and the Anglo-American language is used with an Elizabethan freedom. But he was very glad of the relief when at the beginning of June, 1933, after the completion of the second picture on which he had been assistant director, he was sent to make two short films of York and Sandwich, for it was a sign of unusual confidence that the management entrusted him, after only twelve months' experience, with an independent job, even though it was not one of great importance. Pen was, of course, delighted at the opportunity and immediately determined that he would, if by any means possible, make something with more backbone and imaginative appeal than 'scenics' can usually boast.

As he wrote to his mother, he was hurtled up to York without a script, with four days to make the picture in and a camera-man of rigid ideas, who immediately he was left to himself went off and photographed:

1. The Boer War Memorial.
2. A public lavatory in the style of the Gothic revival.
3. A statue of the founder of the York and Darlington railway.

All day and every day Pen was out finding locations, 'shooting, touting, stealing'; up at the crack of dawn to shoot sunrise behind the Minster; tramping round the town after dinner to visit local bigwigs for permits and authorities of various kinds—the Archbishop, the Dean, the Mayor, all were pressed into the service. Then, when bigwigs had retired to bed, progress and continuity reports had to be written up. Moreover, as he had been given no time to prepare a scenario in advance, everything had to be done concurrently and it was almost impossible to work to any schedule. Nevertheless, although in the end he realized that the picture would, because of the lack of preparation, be no better than the ordinary short, he was able to write on his last day at York:

> This has been easily the most enjoyable week I've spent since I went into the business. The exercise makes such an enormous difference. You would not recognize the spotty-faced lad you saw at Whitsun! *And* I can do this job, such as it is, really well without strain. I've turned the town inside out.

Sandwich he turned inside out as thoroughly as he had done the City of York, even inducing the Mayor and Corporation to don their robes and display the ancient insignia of the Borough with appropriate gestures. One experience which particularly delighted him was an interview with an eighty-year-old cottager, who recited 'Crossing the Bar' to him from her bed. His first thought on getting back to London was to send her a copy of Tennyson's *Works*, with an autograph of the poet. A few days later he was at Farringford.

Oddly enough, although Pen found much at Farringford to delight and interest him, the atmosphere of the place seemed less congenial to him than to Julian. The green gloom of the copses which pressed about the old house, its vaguely ecclesiastical style of architecture, the crimson gloom of its interior, with its dim old paintings, faded photographs and marble busts glimmering grimly in dark corners, weighed upon him and he seemed to feel his individuality submerged by something stronger than itself. But he celebrated his twenty-first birthday there very happily, with fireworks and (on his insistence) plenty of beer for the tenants and staff. The next week he and Julian and Buster successfully inaugurated the shoot.

Early in September the brothers parted full of optimism. Yet, had they known, each of them was facing a period of frustration and disappointment, which for Julian was to be the most unhappy of his short life. Before the end of the holidays he had succumbed to the fate which had overtaken Pen at Oxford—he had fallen desperately in love. With his intense sensibility and imagination it was inevitable that he should taste to the full the joy and the agony of this experience. They were both under twenty and his mother, feeling that what seemed to them so beautiful and so eternal would almost certainly end in disappointment, made them both promise that if anything arose on either side which made a breach inevitable, it should be communicated to her first of all, so that she might do what she could to lessen the shock. When the holidays ended the dream was still unbroken, and Dooley set out for Cambridge in high spirits and looking forward with keen pleasure to the new chapter which was opening in his life.

He had been entered at Trinity, in the hope that the strong family tradition there would be helpful to him, and that the large and varied membership of the College would make it easy for him to find congenial friends; but Fate was against him. Before his first term was over, his poor little romance was pitifully broken. After this he found himself entirely unable to settle down at Trinity, and at the end of July, 1934, he left the University without taking a degree, which meant that all idea of a teaching career had to be given up. This did not trouble him, for he had for some time been feeling that he was very ill-suited to be a schoolmaster.

There followed some months of apprenticeship on a farm, supported by the faithful Buster, which unfortunately made it clear that his restless spirit would never settle down to the routine of an agricultural life.

Then he thought of music and the stage, for he had an excellent ear and an unusually fine baritone voice. But this was only a passing fancy. He had been writing verse steadily, and though this had not shown any noticeable improvement on what he had written at Versailles, it was evident that he felt a real need for self-expression, and that his thoughts were turning more and more towards literature for a profession.

o

By the spring of 1935 it had been arranged for him to go for a year as an apprentice in the office of a small firm which had had a distinguished history for twenty years as publishers of contemporary fiction, poetry and *belles lettres*.

This decision was to prove a turning-point in Julian's career. He took to the work with enthusiasm, and was touchingly pleased at the suggestion that if he passed through his apprenticeship successfully, he might be taken on permanently at three pounds a week. He proved an accurate, sensible and conscientious worker, and astonished everyone by the skill with which he handled the firm's accounts. Indeed, he claimed to be the first person who had ever succeeded in making these balance. He was soon entrusted with the task of advising on manuscripts submitted by aspiring authors, and, before the autumn, had acquired an excellent knowledge of the scope and method of a publisher's business. More important than all this was the incentive to read which the work gave him. The firm had an excellent list of copyrights and a fine stock of books under the charge of a little Cockney who had known every phase of London's literary life for the past fifty years. Dooley loved nothing better than a gossip with the 'Gnome' (as he called him) in the dark recesses of his underground warehouse, and spent every farthing he could lay hands on in the formation of a library with books bought from stock at trade prices. In this way he began to acquire a good knowledge of such writers as George Moore, D. H. Lawrence, Arthur Machen, Richard Jefferies and George Borrow. He also made three literary friendships, which were to mean much to him in the years to come—these were with Lord Alfred Douglas, Robert Nichols and his godfather, J. C. Snaith. The first of these friendships arose from Julian's own initiative, for he wrote to Lord Alfred to express his deep admiration for his poetry and his indignation at the poet's treatment by critics and public. The letter brought a friendly reply; Julian visited Lord Alfred several times at Brighton, and there was some talk of his helping him with the preparation of his autobiography. This, however, came to nothing.

Robert Nichols he met at a friend's house in Chelsea and was fascinated by his brilliant personality and conversation. The meeting led to a friendship, which ended only with the older man's death in 1944.

Snaith was now a sick man living a solitary, stoical life in

Hampstead. Thirty years before, he had struggled furiously to express his genius in three strange, crude novels of great emotional power—*Broke of Covenden*, *Henry Northcote*, and *William Jordan, Junior*—but the effort had been too much for him and, though he had, after a serious breakdown, recovered sufficiently to earn a living with his pen, he had never been able to realize his great abilities. The failure had not soured him. He was greatly attracted by Julian's simplicity and natural charm, and the two had many pleasant meetings together during 1935 and 1936.

Another event of vital importance to Julian was the family's return to Suffolk in 1935—this time to 'The Ancient House', at Peasenhall in the heart of East Suffolk, half-way between the Alde and the Waveney, a medium-sized house, part of which dated from 1500, and part had been panelled and decorated in about 1700. The greatest charm of the place was its delightful garden, with yew and beech hedges ten feet high, and an old orchard of apple, pear, mulberry, medlar, quince and walnut trees. Julian fell in love with the place directly he saw it and claimed as his own a little room at the extreme end of the house over the kitchen and back staircase, which had been fitted out with bookshelves and a wooden partition as a bed-sitting-room. Peasenhall lies in undulating and well-timbered country, intersected by small streams and dotted with unspoiled villages, in most of which stand noble square-towered parish churches. The variety of material with which these villages are built—brick, in a wide range of colour, flint, plaster, often coloured pink or pale-blue, half-timber and weather boarding, with roofs of tile or thatch (sometimes now, alas! of corrugated iron)—gives the whole land an extraordinary charm and richness; and there are magnificent mansions which recall the county's grandeur in former ages, and beautiful small manor houses and moated farms. Ten miles to the east is the sea coast, with its stretches of wild heath and marsh, and its estuaries teeming with wildfowl.

The Ancient House was only twelve miles from Aldeburgh, so Julian was able to renew his friendship with Jerry and Cracknell, and he made a new friend (the introduction was due to Buster) who was to be more important to him than either. This was Alec Bloomfield, the gamekeeper on a neighbouring estate, a man of tremendous physique and remarkable character, strong, sincere, conscientious, affectionate and open-hearted, with an unrivalled knowledge of English wild life and of the East Suffolk countryside. During the next four years Julian seldom came to Peasenhall without visiting his cottage, and many were the hours that he spent walking with Alec about the woods, fields and marshes and learning the intricacies of a gamekeeper's life.

He soon had an opportunity of putting this knowledge into practice on a small rough shoot, of which it was arranged that he should act as keeper, looking after the nests, campaigning against vermin, arranging for beaters when the shooting season began, and directing the small parties of six or seven guns which he collected to shoot the ground. In this way he began to make many friendships among the village folk, particularly with Harry Baylam, prince of beaters, and Walter Howe, ex-gamekeeper and landlord of 'The Swan', in whose bar he became a frequent and welcome guest.

It was not surprising that as the year progressed he grew more settled in spirit. He still suffered from the collapse of his love affair, but he was now able to think of this with more detachment. Ever since he left school he had been writing intermittently, but during the period of his most acute unsettlement the results had not justified the promise of his work at Versailles. Now, with mind more at ease, he produced some lyrics, such as the following, which seemed to show a real advance:

Second Birth

If you should die,
There'd be no beauty on the earth,
No splendour in the sky
For me, nor love, nor mirth:
The years gone by
Would dwindle to a dream,
To the pin-point gleam
Of a night-cat's eye.
Thus would it seem,
My life of second birth,
If you should die.

Twilight Song

O river that flows to the jubilant sea!
O river, so lithe, so fleet!
Speak low, speak low to my love for me
From the eddies that curl at her feet:
And my love shall hearken in glee,
And her soft little heart shall beat
To your murmurous music so tender and free,
And the lilt of your laughter sweet.
O river that flows to the jubilant sea!
O river so lithe, so fleet!

O bird with the sheen on your velvety wing!
O bird with the strong sure flight!
Fly swift, fly swift to my love and cling
To her casement eaves to-night:
And my love shall sleep as you sing
With notes so tuneful and slight,
And her face shall be fair as a blossom of Spring,
Till she wakes with the morning light.
O bird with the sheen on your velvety wing!
O bird with the strong, sure flight!

O marbled moon with the silvery stare!
O moon in the breathless skies!
Shine down, shine down on my love so fair,
As she smiles in her sleep and sighs:
And my love shall float on the air
Through a milk-white Paradise,
Till the sun showers gold on her gossamer hair,
And the soft lights dance in her eyes.
O marbled moon with the silvery stare!
O moon in the breathless skies!

The Music Ends

To-day when all the drowsy world lay still,
Upon the cool, mist-vapoured air I heard
One voice that thrilled aloft, nor slacked nor slurred,
But clear, sharp, quick—it rose, it soared, until
All joy, all life, all love welled up, sweet bird,
From your full throat—and soft the rushes stirred
Their dew-pearled plumes that glistened up the hill.

Alas! there was another heard your song,
And in his heart a fiercer fury burned:
Silent he came, he watched, he hovered high,
Braced his proud pinions, steeled his talons strong,
Soared as you soared, and turning as you turned—
He stooped, he fell, he hurtled from the sky!

But Julian was not yet out of his troubles. Before the end of 1935 his employer had decided to give up business, and he found himself once more without a job. It was clearly no good to look for any further opening in the publishing trade and he decided to try for a place on a daily newspaper. This proved almost as difficult. The London papers would take no one who had not had previous experience, at least on a provincial paper, and he was utterly unable to find any provincial paper with a vacancy. In May he succeeded in getting taken on by the *Evening Standard* as a reporter 'on space', that is to say without any salary, but on terms of liberal payment for any report of his which was accepted for publication. All through the summer he attended regularly at the office in Fleet Street, and was sent out daily to report on one or other of the myriad incidents, tragic or comical, which are the raw material of a popular London newspaper. He enjoyed the excitement and variety of the work, made many friends amongst members of the editorial and reporting staff and, while the season lasted, earned a substantial income. Then, as soon as the summer was over, he was abruptly told the paper had no further need for his services. But, meanwhile, something far more important had happened. In January he had met again and fallen in love with Yvonne Le Cornu, whose acquaintance he had first made in the Isle of Wight two years before.

There was no chance of any regular work for him during the rest of the year, but throughout the autumn and winter he wrote more continuously than he had ever done before. He was now establishing connexions with various periodicals. Lord Gorell was much impressed by his work and accepted two poems for *The Cornhill*, and he had both verse and prose contributions printed in *The Field*, of which Mr. Eric Parker was then the distinguished editor. Moreover, his verse was gaining in scope and technical skill, as will be seen from the following poems written during 1936:

The Moon-ghost

Fantastic moonlight floods the ghostly hall,
The clock ticks on with dim and hollow sound,
The midnight chimes ring out, and all around
Great silence spreads the shadow of its pall.

No sound within, no sound without—the air
Is coldly still; but, suddenly, close by,
The leaves about the lattice seem to sigh,
As if a something stirred the ivy there:

A breath that faintly flares and fades, no more,
A shy, slight motion, trembling tinily,
The murmur of a moment's mystery,
As if some presence, pausing at the door,

Sighed, and passed on; but yet nor beast nor bird
With startled voice betrays the secret night,
No rabbit flashes from the pathway bright,
No creature moves, and not a cry is heard.

Only Orion trembling in the sky,
Only the pine-tree lifting gaunt and tall
Above the starry pool, and over all
The moon in frosted fulness flowing by!

A glorious galleon with a glittering trail,
Streaming her fleece-foamed course above the wrack,
While some star-pinnace flying at her back
Flutters a pennant to her silver sail!

But stay! Who moved just now upon the path?
No footstep sounds, nor is there shadow dark
To show his way: the listener fans a spark
To kindle comfort from the dying hearth.

It is the moon-ghost: when the moon doth show
Her round, full face, about the countryside
The harmless spirit wanders far and wide,
Nor ever rests until her orb sinks low.

There is a knowledge that his presence brings—
A sense, a feeling when he passes near:
A far, faint sound that strikes the watchful ear
As of a breeze that wakens drowsy things:

A whisper that goes sighing through the trees,
A ripple running lightly on the grass,
A branch that bends as if to let him pass—
Thus is his spirit felt, in one of these.

Onward he goes now, roaming at his will
Along the highroad, down the shaded lane:
Stays but to watch, to hear, then on again
Across the field and up the high bright hill.

The splendid stallion on his bracken bed—
His great hide taut and twitching in a dream
Of chariots leaping to a phantom team—
Hears not without the moon-ghost's airy tread.

The silent cattle munching in their stall
Fix their slow thoughts with wide, reproachful stare
Of dark eyes deep and dreaming—unaware
Of reedy rustling faint beyond the wall.

The mongrel sleeps with light, uneasy snore,
Chained to his kennel in a curled cocoon,
Who howled a welcome to the waking moon
From that same kennel scarce an hour before.

The moon-ghost passes on his noiseless way
And starts no babbling tongue of loud alarm:
Peace lies untroubled on the weary farm
Yet some sweet hours before the glare of day.

On to the forest huge in ghostly shade—
No brittle twig betrays his roving feet,
No leveret scutters to a dim retreat,
No shambling badger hurries from the glade.

Leaping and coiling like a wisp of wire
The small sharp weasel chatters at his play:
The heedless dog-fox prowls his eager way,
A lean dark shadow swift with hungry fire.

The nightjar tumbles from the thicket deep,
A grotesque shadow flitting through the furze,
Bat-like she wheels, and in her flight she purrs
So faint she scarce disturbs the lightest sleep.

The owl breaks silence with a loud tu-whoo,
His round eyes blink upon the midnight dim,
No laughing echo leaps to challenge him—
Unheard, unseen, the moon-ghost passes through.

Through to the fields and past the secret pond
In whose deep darkness dreams the impassive pike:
The bullfrog sports and splashes in the dyke
Twisting and glittering through the marsh beyond.

On, on he goes for many a tireless mile,
Untouched, untroubled in his journeying,
Joyful, exultant in each separate thing,
Sight, scent or sound: and slowly all the while

His mistress moon sinks down: till, far away,
When from the East the first soft shadow breaks,
On his dim perch the red-eyed rooster wakes
And flings a crazy challenge to the day!

You Were So Sweet

You were so sweet at seventeen,
    So delicately fine,
That roses yearned to reach your lips
And sheathed their beauty in eclipse
    And dared no more to shine
Until, perchance, your finger-tips
    Should coax them from decline:
So sweet you were at seventeen,
    So delicately fine.

You were so sweet at seventeen,
    So exquisitely fair,
That when Selene rode the night
She trailed her fleecy fingers bright
    And traced them in your hair,
All silvery soft her shafts of light
    Came streaming down the air:
So sweet you were at seventeen,
    So exquisitely fair.

You were so sweet at seventeen
    For Phoebus to adorn
That myriad voices seemed to shake
From eager throats 'Awake! Awake!'—
    Such melody from bower and brake
    Up through the air was borne,
That the lily trembled in the lake
    And the dew upon the thorn,
Till the sun stole up the veiled scene
    To blaze a brilliant morn.

From the Hill

Here at my feet the rich and mellow earth
Of England rolls into the golden sky,
A land of twilight, drowsed with summer mirth,
Warm with the sun, and glowing hazily:

And each faint pulse, that, trembling upward, shakes
Softly this high hill where I dream alone,
Each pulse of thy slow heart, my England, wakes
A full though feeble echo in my own.

Ah, dost thou sleep, my England, dost thou dream
Of those innumerable hosts that strayed
Long since in slow and everchanging stream
O'er thy old soil by centuries relaid?

They trod thy lands, and fought and laughed and cried,
Kings, peasants, courtiers, the great and small—
Like streams that mingle with the ageless tide
Into thy bosom thou receiv'dst them all.

Oh, England, when the happy years have passed,
And I am old and tired, and sing no more,
And when my little stream has joined at last
That sad smooth river flowing to the shore,

Thou wilt receive me, too, that loved thee best:
Thine arms will open tenderly to fold
My ashes to thee, and thy gentle breast
Will warm again this heart in Death grown cold:

Thou wilt receive me, when my song is done,
Thy rich blood creep along my leaden veins,
Thy roots entwine and draw me from the sun
To live once more where thy dark spirit reigns:

Thou wilt receive me, and the little voice
That once was raised upon this old green hill,
Will with those other nobler choirs rejoice
That through thy vaults, my England, echo still:

Then one great song shall leave those myriad lips
And burst from thy dark vaults to which I pass—
One wild, high strain, thrown from the mountain tips
Through leagues of light to leap among the stars.

And when the mighty echoes of that song
Are drawn at last down to the voiceless deep
To perish there, then to the shadowy throng
I too shall sink, and with thy dead shall sleep.

Forest Evening

To-day in the heart of the forest
I have heard the wild bird's song,
And the noise of the crickets crying
In the bracken all day long:

To-day in the heart of the forest
I have seen the young hawk's flight,
The curve of his long swift swooping,
The flash of his wings in the light:

I have seen the butterflies chasing
On the drift of the careless breeze,
The bright-eyed squirrels leaping,
The lazy run of the bees:

I have seen the high sun streaming
In green and gold on the leaves,
The diamond's glint and sparkle
On the web that midnight weaves:

I have known all things that are joyful,
That are wild and fresh and free,
All things most young, most lovely,
Most glorious to see.

I have walked all day in the forest,
I am dusty and tired and sore—
And the voices I heard in the sunlight,
I hear them now no more:

And the things that I saw in the forest,
The lights and the shades and the dews,
The birds and the beasts and the flowers,
The dragonfly's myriad hues,

They are gone from the glade, they are sleeping
Where even the wind is still,
Where the mist of the sweet pale evening
Creeps with a gathering chill.

And now from the margin of shadows
The young moon wanders high,
And the scents that blow in the forest
Rise to the primrose sky:

And the dim white road goes winding
Past meadow and farm and pond,
Right through the heart of the forest
Over the heath beyond:

And the only sounds of the forest
Are the owl's and the nightjar's song—
But the crickets will still be crying
In the bracken all night long.

Towards the end of 1936 Julian's godfather, J. C. Snaith, died, leaving him a thousand pounds. On the strength of this he and Yvonne became engaged, an event which he announced in a characteristic letter to his godmother, Cordelia Curle.

Many thanks for your most charming letter, which please forgive me for not having answered before. Nor need you worry at not having heard the joyful news before, since I myself have not told anybody—not that I dislike telling people, but it makes me feel embarrassed. However the news is now out, so I see I must stir myself and bravely comply with your demands like the true gentleman I am.

I have had printed a circular for distribution among the inquisitives—you know, the old dears who rally round ceaselessly and beam at you and then go away and make nasty remarks about the happy pair behind their backs. It runs as follows:

Madam—Mr. Julian Tennyson presents his compliments and begs to enclose herewith a description of his *fiancée*.

Name. It wouldn't convey anything if I told you.

Age. Mind your own business, you old cat.

Height. Nothing unusual.

Pedigree. Go and look it up in Somerset House.

Figure. Damn sight better than yours.

Hair. By Clarkson and Son, 1s 6d. per strand.

Colour of Eyes. It depends on the light.

Teeth. They're her own, anyway. One up on you, ma'am.

Complexion. Quite natural.

Anything else you'd like to know? Well, you won't get it from me. That'll be sixpence please.

This circular, of course, is not intended for such as you, my Corkle. Only the undesirables.

The other day I was reading the German philosopher Dr. Schippen-Schopper (whom God preserve) of Hamburg. His views on betrothal seem eminently sound. He says:

'The young man, who betrothed become is, first the feet (his feet of course) upon the mantel place should and the door with bolt and key lock. Then from the drawer whiskey should he take (or Rhein-wein if it possible is) and pipes, and cigars, in order that he the illu-sion of bachelordom once more create may and his last supper in lonely happiness eat. If the sense of doom thus from him not lift should, may he himself further console with this thought, that at this moment his beloved probably the same thing does.'

A morbid man, this Dr. Schippen-Schopper (whom God pre-serve) of Hamburg.

But he finishes on a cheerier note. After a lot more in the same strain, all about morbid reactions, he says:

'First should the young man of the news inform:

His godmother.
His great-godmother.
His great-old-godmother.
His great-grand-godmother.
His grand-old-godmother.
His grand-old-great-godmother (whom God preserve).'

I don't know which of these is you, but I promptly sat down to comply with the Doctor's directions.

Since you asked for a description, I will give it you as best I can, tho' I never was much good at that sort of thing: it makes me blush.

Name (of girl). Margerie Yvonne le Cornu. (There's a mouthful for you, Corkie.)

Age. 19 yrs. 8 mths.

Birthplace. Jersey, C.I.

Height. 5 ft. 8 ins.

Girth. Haven't measured. Sorry.

Complexion. Very fair. Sweet.

Eyes. Corn-blue. Very large (and sweet).

Hair. Very fair and very long. Much longer than mine. Sweet also.

Interests. Literature, music, the country.

General Summary. First class.

Sorry, but can't do any more. My face is quite crimson already. Hope that will satisfy you.

As to weddings and all that, that will occur when and if I get a job which doesn't chuck me out on my ear just when the money is coming in nicely, at present there seems every chance of her getting one before I do! . . .

In the spring he succeeded in getting employed (again 'on space') by the *Daily Mail*, and during the three summer months made eight or ten pounds a week. Then at the end of July, two months before the date fixed for the wedding, his appointment was suddenly cancelled and he was once more out of a job. It was a severe blow, but this time there was a mitigating factor, for Messrs. A. & C. Black, on the recommendation of Eric Parker, who had seen the great promise of his contributions to *The Field*, invited him to write a book on rough shooting, a subject very near to his heart.

He immediately retired to Peasenhall and set to work with enthusiasm. Pen and he spent many hours discussing the plan of the book, and Pen, with the help of Mr. Bland of King William IVth Street, undertook (anonymously) the chapter on guns. Julian's practical experience, in the Isle of Wight and in Suffolk, supplied the foundation for the book, but more important than all was the co-operation of Alec Bloomfield. Many were the afternoons and evenings which the two spent walking about the woods and heaths of Scots Hall near Dunwich, where Alec was now keeper, or discussing fine points of practice and natural history in Alec's little cottage or at 'The Eel's Foot' at East Bridge. Once again his friends saw with amazement the concentration and methodical precision which Julian, so dreamy and erratic in the ordinary affairs of life, brought to his work. By 27th September, the day of his wedding at Old Chelsea Church (of course with Pen as best man), the book was well under way.

*　　　*　　　*

During these years preceding Dooley's marriage both he and Pen had continued to live in their parents' house in London, and Pen's cheerfulness and courage had done much to help Julian through his trials and disappointments. The conditions at Shepherd's Bush and in Fleet Street had many similarities, and the two boys were able to share a common love of literature and a common appreciation of the humours of London life in its varied manifestations. But in some respects their tastes had begun to diverge. Julian retained his passionate love of the countryside and would steal away to Suffolk or to the Isle of Wight whenever opportunity offered. But Pen, with the gradual diminution of opportunity, began to lose his interest in shooting.

During his early days at Shepherd's Bush, sailing continued his principal hobby. He kept a cruising boat at the mouth of the Thames and used to go down there for the day whenever he could.

He took immense pains with his boats, improving them at considerable cost, without any hope of recovering what he had spent, but in order to test various theories and for the artistic pleasure of making his craft as good as possible.

He grew very fond of the Thames Estuary and loved to roam over the flats and islands, finding unexpectedly lovely villages and inns. He also enjoyed the hearty contrast of Southend on a Saturday night, for he delighted to see people enjoying themselves without restraint.

But in time he began to find the handling of this type of boat by himself too heavy a job after a week's hard work in the studio, and as he no longer cared for dinghy sailing, he sold his boat and reverted to his old sport of riding. Soon he was hunting with the Essex Union, hiring from Brentwood.

Then he began to buy horses and keep them at a farm in the district, and finally went into a kind of partnership with the farmer. At one time he even had ideas of taking up horse-dealing on a considerable scale, but further experience dissuaded him from this. Sometimes, when he could get a few days off, he would ride in the New Forest, of which he was exceedingly fond.

When not working late he liked to go out in the evening, often to a studio party or to see a film from which he thought he might learn something, or a Shakespeare production at the Old Vic, or a play with a promising young actor, and, when possible, he would finish up the evening at the Café Royal. Whether it was a pleasure party or a 'busman's holiday', he enjoyed every moment of the evening with an electric energy and gaiety.

Then on Saturday or Sunday he would be off quite early in his car to sail or ride. He had a succession of horrifying little cars, which he acquired from friends in the trade. These were always

P

breaking down and being exchanged—generally for something smaller, faster and noisier. He seemed determined to get all he could out of life and never allowed himself to be deterred or depressed by ill-health, or any other obstacle.

Peasenhall proved rather remote for him in those busy days and there were no foxhounds to tempt him in winter. But he came when he could to shoot with Julian or go sailing or wild-fowling with Jerry on the Alde. Sometimes he would drive to Blythburgh, and hire a horse for a gallop with Hallam over the great heaths which stretch away to the south and east, and by which George Crabbe used to ride from Aldeburgh to court his 'Mira' at Beccles.

But Peasenhall was never quite so much home to him as his large attic room in London with the unstained bookshelves decorated (so characteristically) with Corinthian pilasters and beautifully made, but never quite finished, by the studio carpenter; his Hogarth and Alken prints and long copper coach-horns on the walls; his gramophone, with 'swing' records specially sent from America; his riding breeches thrown over the back of a chair, and the trousers in a press against the wall (he was always very particular about his clothes out of the studio); a volume of Herrick or a Surtees novel open face downwards on the divan; sheets of some script or 'treatment' lying about on writing-desk, chairs, and even on the floor, and Randolph Schwabe's drawing of his step-grandfather Augustine Birrell looking down on it all with a genial but rather combative smile from over the electric fire in the corner.

After the completion of his short pictures of York and Sandwich, Pen had passed through a strenuous term of apprenticeship. He had hoped that he might be sent abroad to make some 'interest' pictures on more intelligent lines, but this idea was given up and instead he was lent to a small company which hired the studios to make a series of cheap films. This was a very unpleasant experience. In an effort to keep down expenses, the team was driven inexcusably hard and Pen often worked fourteen or sixteen hours at a stretch, coming back more dead than alive at five or six in the morning. One picture had a Russian background and he had to toil day after day in some horrible chemical which was used for snow and which exhausted the atmosphere and made work intensely tiring. For another picture he had to be down at the London Docks by 6.30 in the morning to collect three hundred black men whose names no one knew, and very few of whom could speak English, and bring them dressed (or undressed) to the location at Uxbridge by nine o'clock. It was a very great relief when this phase ended and he went, in September, 1936, as assistant on 'Farewell Again'. The story of this picture took place entirely on board a troopship and Pen was fortunate in being given sole charge of the 'atmosphere' shots—a very responsible job. To get what was wanted he had to travel out to Aden in H.M. troopship *Somersetshire*, with cameras and camera-men. From Aden he went to Alexandria and Cairo, rode on an Arab horse to see the desert and the Sphinx, flew thence to Athens and Rome and came back by train to England. The visit to Athens, though it only lasted a few hours, was one of the great experiences of his life.

After 'Farewell Again' he joined Alfred Hitchcock for 'The Man Who Knew Too Much'. This was a most important move for him. 'Hitch' was undoubtedly the best of all the British directors and Nova Pilbeam was in the cast, though, as she was only fifteen, nothing except a man-and-child friendship then arose between them.

Working with Michael Balcon and Alfred Hitchcock was the best possible training that the British Film Industry could have given Pen, and before long he was 'Hitch's' first assistant and known as the best young man in the British studios. He was also known as a leader in trade politics.

About a year and a half after he joined the Gaumont British Company the Association of Cine-Technicians was formed, to be the trade union of the technical employees in the British Film Industry, and Pen became one of the earliest members. The Association met with a certain amount of opposition from the studio managements, and Pen was one of those who helped to break this down. He took a leading part in negotiating the Association's first agreement with the Gaumont British Studios (the first agreement ever made to regularize the salaries and working conditions of British film technicians), became the Association's Secretary in the Gaumont Studio, and was a member of the Council for three years—1936, 1937 and 1938—only giving this up when he started direction on his own account and so ceased to be eligible for membership.

His work in the studios and with the A.C.T. strengthened his democratic tendency. He began to chafe at the stodginess and complacency of Conservative statesmen and the ineffectiveness of Labour leaders. In the Abdication crisis he was an ardent supporter of Edward VIII, to whom he had come to look as one who might be at once King and National Leader, strong enough to shame politicians into throwing aside party manoeuvres and tackling, directly and courageously, such problems as the distressed areas, the slums and the low-wage industries.

When he had made five pictures with 'Hitch' there happened what seemed a disaster. Gaumonts gave up producing at Shepherd's Bush. However, Micky Balcon persuaded M-G-M to start an important producing unit under his management and took Pen with him. This gave him the opportunity of acting as Assistant Director under first-rate American directors for three big pictures —'A Yank at Oxford', 'Mr. Chips' and 'The Citadel'. When the latter had been completed M-G-M decided to reduce their British activities, and once more Pen began to think he was going to be on the street. Micky, however, as always, proved his friend and took him over to Associated Talking Pictures at Ealing, where at last he was to be given the chance of showing what he could do on his own responsibility, for Micky persuaded the Ealing Board to allow him to direct a picture himself. He did not succeed in this without a struggle, but he knew Pen's natural ability and the varied experience which he had crammed into the preceding six years. The early days in the Gaumont Studios had shown him the dangers of extravagance and lack of preparation. Working with the smaller companies taught him (by warning, not example) how to handle staff. From 'Hitch' he learned the importance of fresh and lively handling of detail, and his experience with M-G-M gave him the final drill and polish which can only be acquired in a large and highly-organized concern. What was even more important, he had learned by hard experience to adjust himself to the peculiarities of others, to make a virtue of necessity and use persuasion instead of protest.

All the time he was, as usual, observing shrewdly and commenting vivaciously, as can be seen from an article which he wrote for the *A.C.T. Journal* a few months after he himself had become a director and completed his first picture:

Madness and Movie-making

I have always held the view, based on a considerable and chequered experience as an assistant director, that all film directors are mad and that most assistants must in due course become so. The two most clearly recognizable types of directorial maniacs are:

1. The 'Hunted' Director who suffers from an advanced form of 'Persecution Complex'. This type is convinced, in spite of abundant evidence to the contrary, that everybody is conspiring to prevent him making a good picture—artists, producers, writers, technicians, and even his wife, should she venture to remind him that he is a human being as well as a cine-technician. This species may be recognized by a slightly shifty eye and extreme reluctance to make any decisions, a conviction that he is always ill, a refusal to eat food at the accepted times and an alternating belief that the film he is working on is either 'lousy' or 'terrific'. Advanced cases frequently have clearly defined physical mannerisms. They twitch, pick their noses, carry small sticks about, etc. Most good directors belong to this class. I hope to qualify for it myself as the years pass, if my digestion deteriorates and my imaginative powers ripen.

2. The 'Dictator' Director, who suffers from an inflated 'Power Complex'. This type finds everything dead easy. He snaps off decisions like a Bren gun, while his iron nerves and business sense enable him to weather crises which prostrate the 'Hunted' type. He has points to recommend him, but in the end his 'Power Complex' begins to infringe seriously on his natural sanity. He takes to directing in fancy dress and expects life to be a 'montage' of technical and histrionic impossibilities over which his own face is continually double-exposed wearing an expression of non-stop domination.

The assistant directors' manias are less harmful, although equally clearly defined. They follow roughly the same classifications as the directors':

1. The 'Hunted' Assistant always looks as if he handled a large share of the rearmament programme as well as tomorrow's call. He seeks relief principally by calling everybody 'old boy' in a subconscious attempt to propitiate the unseen forces which he is convinced are working to encompass his downfall. He also drinks a good deal of whisky—if possible on an empty stomach.

2. The 'Dictator' Assistant is generally offensive to everybody except the Director. His 'Power Complex' invariably makes him refer to the films on which he works as if they were his own private property. 'MY last film', 'MY crew', 'MY floor', etc. An extra can

always get another day's work out of him by implying that he, not the director, really directs the films he works on.

As an assistant, I undoubtedly belong to Class 2. If I remain a director, I hope to qualify for Class 1. The reason for this transition interests me as do the basic causes of the manias themselves. After completing a picture as a director, I feel better qualified to try to analyse them. The assistant's hallucinations are so obviously caused by being responsible to and working for an entirely irrational being that we can dismiss them as secondary. Thus restricting our analysis to directors alone.

Many lunatics are credited with the belief that the rest of the world is insane and that they alone are supremely sensible. In the entertainment business we see about as much of the outside world as the small boy sees of sex who peers at it through the slot-machines on Brighton Pier. I think in some mysterious way that a film director's complete isolation from the world proper and his inevitable, if partial, isolation from even his own world of moviedom, are the principal causes for the collapse of his reason. An assistant is kept in an agreeable state of aggression and alertness by the resistance and offensiveness which he encounters on all sides. There is a dangerous tendency to treat the director with politeness. On the floor, unless he is careful, he finds himself being lulled into a sense of false security and remoteness by the aura of civility in which he moves. So there he is, severed by profession from the outside world, slightly estranged by his job from his own world of technical back-chat and shop, and with his head crammed and buzzing with the lines, lives and thoughts of the bunch of characters about whom he is trying to make a film.

Then, when he has completed his picture, if it is any good, well-meaning people astonish him by congratulating him on points and effects which he himself had never realized the film contained. While if it is bad, he wants to crawl away and shoot himself. That is, unless he is already in a state of palpitating agitation about the next one, in which case the last epic is about as fascinating as a dirty shirt. Or even less so, for a dirty shirt is merely uninteresting, whereas by the time a director has finished a film it seems to me inevitable that he should regard the whole thing with a dislike that amounts almost to nausea.

But the one thing that most people overlook about lunatics is also true about directors. For the most part they find life infinitely more diverting and exciting than do the sane. It is for that reason that having been fortunate enough to complete my first film, my one hope is that I may be left at large long enough to become involved in many more.

ACHIEVEMENT

His marriage seemed literally to make a new man of Julian. As Hallam wrote:

After his marriage his gentle irony and cheerfulness became a settled condition. But along with this he seemed to have acquired the gravity and dignity of one who had passed through a lifetime of experience. His low voice, his slow walk, the calm benignity of his expression belied the boyishness and simplicity that still lay just underneath, as well as the passionate sensitiveness and persistent shyness.

He and Yve settled in a very small three-roomed flat at 140, Elm Park Mansions, where there was just room for his cherished library, some drawings of Suffolk and his gramophone and records, including a complete series of Dvořák's 'New World' symphony, which he passionately loved. The rest of the year was devoted to the completion of *Rough Shooting*. Eric Parker wrote a foreword, and the book came out in March of 1938 with a dedication to

'My brother Pen
and all equally good sportsmen.'

The copy which he gave to Pen had an additional inscription, in acknowledgment of all the anonymous help which his brother had given him and especially the chapter on guns:

'With all my thanks for you know what,
but Mr. Black doesn't.'

The book was an immediate success, as it deserved to be, for it was thoroughly practical, easily and clearly written and, thanks largely to Alec Bloomfield's co-operation, admirably complete and accurate.

Julian and Yve had very little money to live on and he was still, in spite of many attempts, unable to get a job, but he was writing regularly for *The Field*, and began to do occasional reports for *The Times*, and reviews for the *Literary Supplement* and *Country Life*. With his marriage all inclination to write verse seemed to disappear—carrying out what Robert Nichols had said some time before, that though he 'could certainly make words dance' he would not find his true expression in poetry. Unfortunately, he loathed London. He enjoyed an occasional theatre, concert or café-crawl, but these meant nothing to him in comparison with the peace and natural interests of a country life. Worse than this, in London he found it almost impossible to write anything except the purely ephemeral.

Then, out of the blue, came the opportunity for which he was longing. A friend suggested to Messrs. Blackie of Glasgow that they should arrange with him for a book on Suffolk.

> If they accept [wrote Julian] it will be one of the happiest days of my life. Something sincere to write at last. But I've learnt not to expect anything too much.

But in the early summer Blackies did accept and he set about the book at once, giving up everything else, for it had to be finished by the end of November.

A good part of the intervening time he spent at Peasenhall, writing in his little solitary room, where at night he would call out of the window to the owls and make them answer him; or walking, cycling and motoring about the county. The publishers had in mind a descriptive book of the *Highways and Byways* type. But Julian was not to be tied down and *Suffolk Scene* (as the book came to be called) turned out to be very unlike the usual book about a county—full of personal adventure and experience, humorous, imaginative, direct and intensely human. Above all, every page glowed with that love of England which he had expressed, however crudely, in his poem 'From the Hill'.

The book was finished and delivered up to time in spite of the handicap of a wet autumn, which made the taking of the necessary photographs very difficult.

That autumn was ominous of things to come, for it was the autumn of Munich. When the crisis came, Julian insisted on joining the Territorials, though his family tried hard to dissuade him, partly because they felt—how wrongly!—that, with his sensitive temperament, he would never be able to stand the horrors of modern war, partly because he had at last found an attractive job, on the staff of *The Geographical Magazine*, and it seemed important that he should concentrate on this. But Julian felt too intensely the issues at stake for civilization and the personal responsibility which the crisis imposed on the youth of England. Some of his friends who had joined the anti-aircraft artillery urged him to go with them, but he had made up his mind to give his service in the infantry, the 'P.B.I.', upon whom, ever since war began, the burden of sacrifice has chiefly fallen. He joined the London Irish, solely because their Headquarters were at the Duke of York's School in the King's Road, within a mile of Elm Park Mansions.

The months which followed were for Julian months of intense experience. He still hated London and had little interest in the routine of territorial training, but he tackled both this and his job on the *Geographical Magazine* with his usual conscientiousness and common sense. These qualities, with the benign irony noted by Hallam, carried him successfully through, his humour and unselfishness making him a general favourite in the office and often enabling him to resolve difficulties where more serious and deliberate efforts had failed. One little incident told to me by the person concerned, may serve as an example. Julian had been teasing her one morning—perhaps not taking quite so seriously as she thought he should, some grievance against a colleague. Full of her new grievance she burst into the sub-editor's room, exclaiming, 'I can't stand Julian Tennyson!' There was a dead silence, then a still, small voice from the corner said, 'PIP! PIP!' and there stood Julian beaming at her benignly through his large round steel-rimmed spectacles.

In June came the publication of *Suffolk Scene*. There was a danger that reviewers might treat this as an ordinary guide-book and that it might pass unnoticed. But the title *Suffolk Scene*, printed in large type across the first two columns of the *Sunday Times* of 2nd July, with an enthusiastic notice by Desmond MacCarthy beneath it, set the tone for the reviewers, and there can seldom have been a book which received more general commendation. Moreover the estimate of the critics has been justified by events. *Suffolk Scene* has been reprinted every year since its first publication and is now in its thirteenth edition, a classic of the countryside which Julian loved so well.

The success of his book had an immediate effect on his position: within a few weeks he had invitations from the *Literary Supplement* and the *Sunday Times* to join their teams of regular reviewers. But before he could take advantage of these, war was declared and he had to join his company of the London Irish in an old school building in Wandsworth.

* * *

Pen reached the climax of his brief career almost exactly at the same time as his brother. Just as Julian was putting the finishing touches to *Suffolk Scene* in the autumn of 1938, Pen, at the age of twenty-six, was appointed to make his first feature picture as a film director—the youngest man ever to be entrusted with such a responsibility in the history of the British Film Industry. The subject chosen for his picture was from a novel called *There Ain't No Justice* by James Curtis. It was not a very strong story from the film point of view, but there was good characterization and dialogue in it and the boxing atmosphere had a strong appeal for Pen. He started work on the scenario with the author and Sergei Nolbandov in August or September, for he held very strongly that the director should come into the picture at the earliest possible moment, so as to mould the script to suit his own ideas and to get the details of it in his mind as completely and clearly as possible before he began shooting.

Sergei Nolbandov had been a Russian barrister and had fought in the Civil War, then come to England as a refugee, married a Scottish wife and been attracted to the movie business, in which he had served a long and varied apprenticeship—a brilliant fellow, full of ideas (Pen said that he never had one which was not truly cinematic), quite as obstinate as Pen, a great talker, a great worker, a great lover of life and a most loyal friend.

The partnership, which was to carry on through all Pen's three pictures, had its moments of uneasiness, but in time the two grew to a perfect understanding of one another. Sergei excelled in the generation of ideas and Pen in criticism, adaptation and construction. Both were tireless in perseverance and would never let go till they felt that the job in hand had been carried as near to perfection as they could take it.

Pen made up his mind from the beginning that he would have no star in the cast. He wanted it to be his picture and not a star's and, as he had not much money to spend, he felt he must use what he had to secure as level a cast as possible. But he chose his actors with the utmost care so as to fill every part with a really

suitable personality, and he and Sergei and Curtis worked un-
remittingly to build up life-like characters and a real cockney
atmosphere—for the film was to centre round the story of a
London working-class family whose son falls into the clutches of
a shady boxing promoter.

Shooting began in the middle of January and Pen was busy up
to the last minute. Forty fighting men had to be engaged to play
the part of thugs, spivs and stewards—also stunt artists, skilled in
falling at all angles and on all parts of their bodies without
suffering injury. The fights had to be rehearsed blow by blow
under the skilled direction of the famous Bombardier Billy Wells,
and Pen took infinite care to get the very best and most genuinely
natural acting.

In spite of much interruption from illness, shooting was
finished early in March and the picture completed in plenty of
time for the trade show on June 5th, 1939. It was excellently
received by the more intelligent critics, who were unanimous in
their praise of the director's natural and sensitive handling of the
cast.

The trade was, however, a little frightened of the picture,
which they seemed to think rather highbrow. Perhaps they were
dimly conscious of a touch of poetry in the direction and of a
sympathy with the underdog rather alien to Wardour Street.
They were also apprehensive that the absence of star names might
prove an obstacle with the public. In consequence, 'There Ain't
No Justice' failed to secure a West End showing, though it drew
full and enthusiastic houses when it was screened at the Paramount
Theatre in the Tottenham Court Road in August. But it was hard
for a British second feature to get very far in the 1930s however
sincere and sensitive its acting and direction. In December Pen
replied rather sadly to a critic who had written favourably of the
picture in a review of the year's films:

> I have always held that critics and producers or directors should
> keep well to their respective sides of the bed! All the same, I can't
> help writing to thank you for your very generous championship of
> our little picture 'There Ain't No Justice'.
> It is slipping so quickly and quietly into the vaults where all the
> other British second features stand in their forgotten hundreds,
> although audiences seem to have genuinely enjoyed it wherever it
> has been shown. But after eight years of travail in the movie business,

I can't help loving my firstborn with a blind fondness which has made me almost disproportionately pleased by the opinions of those people of intelligence who have liked the picture.

So once more, very many thanks for your eloquent and whole-hearted advocacy.

This was an unduly gloomy view of the achievement of the picture, which, in fact, had a reasonably successful career and made the trade and the critics look forward with interest to the young director's next production. Mickey had no doubt of its merits or of the promise that it held for the future, and as soon as Pen had finished with the negative he was launched on a new venture.

This time he was entrusted with the direction of a real star picture, for the studios had a contract with Paul Robeson and he was to be featured in the new film, the setting of which was to be in the Welsh mining valleys. Pen wished to make the story an epic of the dangers and hardships of the miner's life, with the title 'One in Five', that being quoted as the percentage of casualties amongst those engaged below ground in the mines. However, the management were opposed to this idea, so he had to think out some less harrowing use of the mining background. Then there was Robeson to be worked in, and of course he would have to sing. Obviously here was a collection of elements not very easy to blend harmoniously together. Moreover, Pen had little knowledge of music and none of the Welsh. To remedy this last defect, Jack Jones, the miner playwright and author of *Rhondda Roundabout*, which had recently enjoyed a considerable success on the London stage, was brought into the team.

The script finished, Pen had to grapple with the difficult question of locations. The Welsh mine-owners, one and all, refused to give facilities, and it was not until after shooting had already begun in the studio that the emissaries from Ealing got into touch with the Shelton Coal and Iron Company of Stoke, who threw themselves wholeheartedly and most generously into the project.

'The Proud Valley' was destined to have a chequered career in production. Shooting began in the studio on 23rd August, 1939. Within a week some of the technical staff were called up. On 1st September the unit lost its production manager, its second assistant director, a number of the shop staff and electricians, and one of the most important actors. There was loss of time through the necessity of releasing staff and artists, in order to enable them to deal with private emergencies due to the outbreak of war; through air-raid warnings; through the failure of artists to arrive up to time from Wales, and through the general distraction caused by the world crisis. In these circumstances it was a notable achievement for the director that shooting was completed within three days of the scheduled time.

Pen was surer of himself now and he had improved in the handling of his actors. He got on excellently with Paul Robeson (who had seen the merits of 'There Ain't No Justice') fitting him into the picture without letting him dominate it, and at the same time getting the very best out of him. The Welsh atmosphere, too, was miraculously well maintained—considering that the producer was a Russian and the director such an intensely English Englishman as Pen. Indeed, 'The Proud Valley' is still remembered in Wales as the Welsh epic of the screen. It was trade shown at the beginning of October and started on a successful career, in spite of the simultaneous appearance of a lavish production based on *The Stars Look Down* (a best-seller with a mining theme) and of a boycott by an important section of the Press, which objected to some speeches made by Robeson on his return to America.[1]

Early in August Pen became engaged to Nova Pilbeam. At first there was no talk of an early marriage. Nova was only nineteen and the idea was that they should wait till she was twenty-one, though those who knew Pen received this with some scepticism. Immediately after he had finished shooting 'The Proud Valley', he came to one of his impetuous decisions and announced that he would be married in a fortnight. Marriage for Julian had been the dawn of a new security and unsuspected horizons. For Pen it was simply the catching up of a kindred spirit into the orbit of his swift and sparkling progress. They were married quietly in October. Julian was still at Wandsworth and, to his great disappointment, could not get leave to attend the wedding.

Pen now had to decide what he would do next. There was no immediate prospect of his being called up for active service, though he had been a member of the Royal Naval Supplementary Reserve for about five years, having joined soon after Hitler's

[1] In 1943 'The Proud Valley' was one of the three pictures chosen for general release in the U.S.S.R.

accession to power. He had always been an uncompromising opponent of the Nazis and of the policy of appeasement, and had very early come to the conclusion that Hitler was bent on a course which must end in European war. But he had been so much in demand in the studios that he had never been able to find time for the necessary periods of training. In September, 1938, he tried to get permission to do weekly training, for he felt sure that the crisis could not be long delayed, but he was a month over the age limit and, in spite of the serious outlook, the Admiralty would not make an exception in his favour. In consequence of this lack of training the Navy declined to accept him at the outbreak of war.

Then came the great chance of his life—in the suggestion that he should direct a big naval film for Ealing. He was very doubtful whether he should undertake this, feeling that somehow or other he ought to get into the armed forces without delay, but he was much pleased with the confidence that Mick had shown in entrusting him with so great a responsibility, and gratitude and affection played their part in his decision to accept the offer.

He and Nova now took over Julian's small flat in Chelsea, for Julian had left London with his Company for Ashdown Forest and Yve was at Peasenhall awaiting her confinement. There he worked hard on the script with Sergei and Pat Kirwan.

Those few months of his marriage when he was writing and shooting his biggest and most successful picture, were the climax of his short life. The script was a difficult one, for he had to weld a human story into the big battle theme. But he was given a completely free hand to deal with this, not being tied down, as he had been before, by having to work from someone else's ideas.

The script was almost finished by the beginning of January, 1940, when Pen went in H.M.S. *Valorous* with a convoy down the East Coast from Scotland, to gather atmosphere, and shooting began early in March, just after the successful start of 'The Proud Valley' at the Leicester Square Theatre.

The direction of 'Convoy' presented much bigger problems than either of Pen's other films, for the technical difficulties involved were far more formidable than anything he had attempted before. A great deal had to be done with models, a type of work of which he had not previously had much experience. Then there was the continual worry of seeing that all was right from the naval point of view. However, with the help of a naval

adviser and of the Ealing technicians, all difficulties were surmounted and, though the picture did not give him quite so much
scope as 'Justice' and 'The Valley' for the human atmosphere
which most interested him, he produced a wonderfully strong
and convincing result. The story never flagged for a moment, the
dialogue was full of force and sparkle and the big moments tre-
mendously exciting. The greatest tribute to the battle scene was
paid during the trial show for the Admiralty, when at some crisis
on the screen an officer half-rose from his seat, trembling with
excitement and muttering 'Why the hell don't they try a torpedo!'

'Convoy', which was the first of the great British pictures of
the Second World War, opened at the New Gallery on 8th July,
1941, and there was never any doubt of its success. It ran in London
till the September blitzes began, and the Foreign Department of
the Ministry of Information immediately arranged for special
showings in Madrid and the U.S.A. Pen had the satisfaction of
knowing that he had accomplished something which would help
to spread the fame of Britain and the British Navy throughout the
Allied and neutral world, and that his achievement had raised him
to a position in the industry which no man of his age had attained
before. The greatness of this achievement was shown by the
account of him sent to the *A.C.T. Journal* by the Ealing Studio
Staff after his death:

> It is often said of people that success has not changed them. It was
> certainly very true in Pen's case. With his tousled hair and general
> untidiness he was always just the same boyish, friendly colleague. The
> only change in our attitude towards him was that our affection for
> him became tinged more and more with admiration, as he grasped
> all the aspects of film making and emerged as one of the most inter-
> esting as well as the youngest director in this country.
>
> We all realize that deeply though we feel his death as a personal
> loss, his death is an even greater loss to the British Film Industry in
> general. Pen was only twenty-eight, and at the beginning of his
> directorial career. Of the films that he directed all had shown him
> to be one of the sincerest and most imaginative directors the screen
> had yet discovered. Each represented a marked advancement in his
> technique.
>
> Pen would never have been content to settle down as an orthodox
> commercial director. He had a keen insight into social problems,
> which showed itself particularly in his first two films, 'There Ain't
> No Justice' and 'The Proud Valley'. His work would undoubtedly

have developed along these lines and the screen would have been the richer for it.

We all felt when working with him that he was seeking in the screen a medium of expression. Perhaps all of us could not understand it, but we all felt that sense of idealism about him in everything he did.

But he was not in any way a high-hat director. He was never a hard taskmaster. He spoke in a language that we all understand. We knew his problems and he knew ours. He had worked in many different departments before becoming a director and he never asked for the moon because he knew just what was possible and what was not.

We all respected his technical knowledge and we all had the feeling that he knew exactly what he was doing. We had confidence in him. He inspired that confidence in old stage hands, veteran actors and newcomers alike.

War

Pen and Julian began their officer training at about the same time, though they were not able to meet until the end of the year. Pen was so busy on the floor with the final stages of 'Convoy' that he could not come to the christening of Dooley's twins on 12th April, a great disappointment to him. He had been invited to be godfather, and it was typical of his large-heartedness that he was highly indignant when asked which of the two he would act for. He insisted on being godfather to both and scoured the antique shops of the West End to find them suitable christening gifts.

Julian was recommended for a commission early in 1940 and went to the O.T.C. at Colchester, a great delight, for he was able to rent a small furnished house and so have Yve and the twins with him. Then in May came the collapse of France. The O.T.C. was mobilized for coastal defence and the little house had to be given up. For Julian the weeks which ensued were a time of great emotional strain. He felt with all the force of his clear imagination and deep sensibility the terrible issues threatening England; the imminent horror of German invasion; the possibility of defeat for everything which he held dear; the chance that Death would blot out for ever the life which had come to hold for him so much sweetness and hope. But no such thought could shake his resolution. One evening he said to a friend, with whom he often talked till far into the night after the day's work was done:

'I don't care what they do to me—they can tear me to pieces, they can kill me now or next year, but so long as I die helping to stop them taking England, then I am satisfied.' He said this with a vehemence and conviction that amazed his friend and (to his surprise) made him 'feel incredibly happy'. But neither this conviction nor his unshakable confidence in England's ultimate victory (in Julian's mind it was always 'England' for which he was fighting) could save him from many hours of mental agony.

I do not believe England can ever be beaten [he wrote in a letter from the Essex coast]. This is perhaps my clearest belief of all; clearer than belief in my own life, clearer than belief in the ultimate security of ourselves. England will not lose. I do not believe in God, but I believe unshakably in the triumph of good against evil. I do not pray to God; I pray to the goodness of the earth and the goodness that is the rock of civilization and the foundation of all that is worth calling progress. These things can never be overthrown. England is the rock of civilization. If the rock is swept away from beneath us, what hope is there for us? There is none; and therefore I will fight and die that the rock may stand firm.

In July he was given a commission in the Oxford and Bucks Light Infantry, and a week or two later Pen, who had spent some happy weeks with Nova at Hove, taking a hurried and strenuous course in the *King Alfred*, was commissioned to an anti-submarine trawler which he joined at Hull.

They were to sail round the north of Scotland to Belfast, stopping on the way for gunnery trials. His first letter after leaving Hull was from Edinburgh:

Dearest Mother and Father,

I suppose its better than the Army. Its got periods of incredible discomfort and unpleasantness relieved by moments of odd beauty and quiet. We're lying in Leith, the port of Edinburgh, this evening and the trip up the Firth in the sunshine was lovely. Edinburgh and the hills around it looked gloomy, delicate and beautiful in an aura of sunset and smoke. I think its the most lovely town I know although I'm afraid there's no chance of a walk down Princes St. this time! We've only put in because the engine's giving trouble and we can't take on the trip round to the West until its been looked at. In some ways I'm very lucky, although I've no right to generalize about the existence until I've had a dose of a month or two's routine.

God knows what this little ship will be like in the North Atlantic. She rolled us all inside out in the North Sea. Half the ship's crew were prostrate with sea-sickness. No need to tell you what your eldest son was like. He outheaved, outstretched and outspewed the lot of them! But I hope and trust it will have more or less cured me. The crew and other two officers are all very nice human beings which is the devil of a help. The first lieutenant a vast, portly, imperturbable young chap of about my age. The skipper—the exact reverse—a very highly strung almost donnish little fellow who took to teaching navigation after he left the Mercantile Marine. He's had a bit of a bashing and is very anxious to get round to what we trust will be at least the comparative quiet of the Western coast. We were attacked by a couple of German bombers yesterday while in convoy. But they quite ineffectively dropped stuff on ships some distance from us. The one thing which is bloody shocking is the food. We have had one eatable meal since I came on board and that was just before I had gastritis so I didn't fancy it. The first Lieutenant would eat anything including his own belt, as he beamingly announced in answer to one of my protests! The skipper's too nervy to worry much about what he is eating! The lieutenant might slip the belt in the stew without his noticing it. Thank God however the cook has just gone sick, so we may get a decent meal now he has gone to hospital. The crew nearly all came from East Coast harbours, Yorkshire, Suffolk or Norfolk fishermen, very easy chaps to get on with. We have no Naval nonsense thank heaven and all slop about just as we want to. In fact if we can get to a sea where there are no bombers and discover a cook who can produce an occasional meal, everything will be hunky dory.

In September they spent a few days at Tobermory on working exercises, after some strenuous weeks at sea. Pen found that the routine of four hours on and four hours off duty reduced him to a complete shred after twenty-four hours, for in rough weather the little boat 'rocked and bounced like those celluloid balls you see on jets of water in shooting booths.' He was put in charge of the ship's principal armament, an ancient four-inch gun, and enjoyed 'encouraging people to ram charges into it' and 'the exhilarating uncertainty of target practice'. He was now almost 'master of his stomach', though it got out of control one night when he had to go on watch in a gale of wind.

At Tobermory he sent for Nova to join him and they spent some marvellous and delightful days together. Thence the ship sailed to Belfast, stopping a few days at Greenock, where Nova came to discuss the script of a film ('Spring Meeting') in which she had been offered a part; then to the Clyde and round the north of Scotland to the Firth of Forth and back to Milford Haven, after being caught in a severe gale and having to run for shelter to Holyhead. Soon afterwards Pen was asked by the Admiralty to take over their instructional film unit at Portsmouth, which was not working at all satisfactorily, and got a few days' leave in order to discuss the offer. At first he was very doubtful about accepting, although it would mean that he and Nova would be together again. Having started at sea and fought his way through the first few months of seasickness and discomfort, he did not like the idea of going back to a shore job, where he couldn't 'hit back at the bastards'. Also he felt that from the film point of view he would probably find the new job niggling and unsatisfactory. But his friends felt that he would be wrong to refuse an offer which would enable him to put his professional knowledge and experience at the service of the Admiralty. The job, though not spectacular, was an important one and there was obviously no one who could do it as well as he could. Eventually he came round to this view, and wrote that he would accept the post if the personnel and equipment at the studio were supplemented and if he was associated with the writing of the scripts in Whitehall as well as with the studio at Portsmouth.

In the middle of November he heard, to his surprise, that all his conditions were accepted, and it was decided that he should leave the trawler after one more trip. This proved a very bad one, with appalling weather and a good deal of enemy activity. The whole crew were as sick as dogs and Pen pronounced complete disagreement with Neville Chamberlain on yet another topic—his statement that 'boredom is better than bombs'. He now felt that he 'would gladly exchange all the bombs in London for the monotony of those damp, heaving, tedious weeks at sea', and when the decision was taken he began to rejoice in the idea of getting back to his proper job.

> I'm longing to get near a movie camera again [he wrote], even if its only to photograph guns, mines, etc. Though I don't know, this is a strange, unsettling, chaotic sort of world and I shall probably be hankering after a more active life again in a month or two.

He felt keenly parting from the crew of his trawler.

> I had some affecting farewells with various chaps in the crew.
> They were a grand lot and it has been a privilege to live and work
> with them.

Early in December he was installed with Nova in a boarding-house
at Havant.

One great advantage of the new job was that it brought him
close to Julian, whose battalion was now stationed at Rockley,
near Newport in the Isle of Wight. Pen was able to go and see
him, once bringing a reel of 'Convoy' and giving his men a talk
on film production, and Julian got over to Portsmouth and was
shown the studio.

Julian had taken kindly enough to life in the Battalion, although
the agony which he had felt at Colchester was never far beneath
the surface. He knew that what he was doing accorded with the
deepest feelings of his nature. He liked his fellow-officers and the
men under his charge and, in spite of his complete inability to con-
form to the conventional pattern of a British infantry officer, was
soon a popular figure in the mess, where his sense of humour, 'the
homely roll of a farmer in his walk', and the impression which he
gave of never having been in a hurry in his life, soon made him a
marked figure. Moreover, he had been put in charge of the mortar platoon and had in the spring passed through a course on the
subject with distinction. Buster, also, was a respected member of
the battalion, leading the platoon with his master on all ceremonial
occasions and often helping him to supply the mess with a hare or
a brace of pheasants. One night when there was a false report that
the Bosches were landing and the Oxford and Bucks were rushed
to the danger point, Julian caused great amusement by emerging
from his vehicle in full battle-dress—with his shot-gun and Buster
—having failed to find his revolver at the critical moment. But
what did more than anything else to establish his position in the
mess was the discovery of his dramatic talent. The full range of
this was not known until it was decided to organize a revue,
in order to relieve the tedium of waiting in the Island, week
after week, for the invasion which never came. To everyone's
surprise Julian, in spite of his shyness, which, it was thought,
would prevent him from facing the footlights, became the leading
figure in every comic sketch, many of which he wrote himself.

From that time he was the star turn whenever the Battalion gave
a concert or the officers or sergeants' mess threw a party. His
greatest triumph was when the Battalion staged their revue at
Ryde to an audience of 1,200. It had been the kindly habit of his
friends to prime him with two stiff whiskies before he went on the
stage, for he was still apt to be nervous. The stage manager (the
Battalion's Quartermaster), who insisted on a rigid stage discipline, strictly forbade such an indulgence on this occasion.
Julian took the centre of the stage for his monologue 'Old Bill'
without a protest. Then, as soon as the curtain went up, and he
knew that he was out of the Q.M.'s reach, he drew a large flask
from his pocket and, amidst the cheers of the audience, took a
deep and stimulating draught before beginning his soliloquy.

Unfortunately Pen's work did not allow him much time to
visit the Island. He found the studio very inadequately equipped
and staffed and immediately began building sets, ordering scenic
backgrounds, circulating the industry with inquiries for second-
hand equipment, and generally straightening things out. Then his
work was held up through destruction of part of the studio in an
air-raid, and later the electric current was cut off by enemy
bombing. During one of the German raids he was in a hotel
lounge in Portsmouth and he was astounded and encouraged by
the way in which the guests stood up to the experience.

The lounge of the Hotel was very comic when the blitz began. It
was filled with those odd human relicts who pass their lives in sea-
side hotels out of season. 'Filled' is the wrong word. There were
half a dozen of them dotted amongst the palms and big red sofas. A
man with grey drooping moustaches sucked a pipe and read *Blackwoods*, somebody's elderly aunt knitted her naval nephew a pullover,
an old clergyman snoozed over his coffee. Nobody interchanged a
word of conversation. Then the blitz started. It really does sound
like hell let loose if you are near a big military objective. We were
opposite the barracks. The clergyman woke up with a little start. I
wondered what they would all do. I pictured a rather dignified and
deliberately leisurely descent to the air-raid shelter on the next floor.
But nobody stirred a muscle. The clergyman closed his eyes again,
the Aunt's needles accelerated to a slightly irritable tempo, the man
with *Blackwoods* commenced contemplatively to chew one end of
the drooping moustache. We went below an hour afterwards when
the power station was hit and all the lights went out. Up till that time
nobody had moved or spoken—with the exception of the elderly

aunt. She complained to the porter about the incompetence of the management in failing to provide a sufficiency of candles, when the latter was endeavouring to relieve the darkness of the lounge with a couple of candlesticks!

Towards the end of February he was summoned to London by the Admiralty to arrange the production of a propaganda film for American armament workers. He had only three days in which to write the script for a three-reel picture, and two days were spent in viewing available material (from news reels and so on) and arguing with various people concerned in the development of the story. 'I find the blind, determined, confused convictions of amateurs much harder to shake than the more reasoned professional obtuseness of actors and producers,' he wrote sadly.

By March he had finished his first picture, which, to his great relief, was well received by the Admiralty.

> You never know with Service people—a man salutes when he shouldn't salute, or, equally horrible thought, fails to salute when he should salute, and the fat is in the fire. However, it was the first picture they have ever made here which was cut at a modern tempo and the band of the Marines produced a thumping full orchestral score skilfully blended from Wagner and sea shanties.

Early in May he finished a second picture and had planned a third and fourth. For one of these he would need to work with very large ships, which could best be done at Scapa Flow. For the other, which was to deal with sailing boats, the location chosen was the Isle of Man.

The visit to Scapa was much hampered by bad weather, but it contained a good deal of excitement and tragedy, for while he was there the destruction of the *Hood* and the chase and sinking of the *Bismarck* took place. The loss of the *Hood* affected him deeply, for he was working in her and lunched with the officers only two days before it took place.

> I cannot yet believe [he wrote], that the whole magnificent ship and all those hundreds of men have just disappeared. They were all very good to me and most helpful. The sudden dissolution of the whole terrific steel edifice and the entire crew is a possibility one can't quite absorb.

The delays caused by weather and ship movements made it impossible to carry all his work at Scapa through at a stretch without waste of time, so he decided to go to the Isle of Man and come north again later, telegraphing Nova to join him. The time which they spent together in the Isle of Man was crammed with hard work and enjoyment. Pen felt almost guilty when he realized his good fortune in being able to be so much with Nova while Dooley and Yve and so many other young couples were separated. 'However I salve my conscience by working as hard as I can and infuriate the film unit by insisting on their sitting over the cameras, even on the most unpropitious days.'

One day he and Nova nearly lost their lives. He took her sailing, and when they were well away from land a violent off-shore gale got up and, as the tide was against them, they found themselves being carried out to sea. To make matters worse, poor Pen was so sick that he could hardly manage the boat. Fortunately their danger was seen from the shore and the lifeboat put out and brought them in.

In the interval of all these activities he began to work on a novel.

> I find it hard work writing in hotel lounges and ward rooms with intermittent leisure [he said]. However, I think I shall finish it some-how, since it is a complete conception and once I get down to it, the track lies ahead as clear as a long stretch of railway lines. Nonie has set the seal of her approval on the production to date, though she is worried about censorship. Don't be perturbed—it's horses not humans!

He finished up the visit with a mild attack of influenza, which he also enjoyed, finding Nova a delightful nurse 'although rather apt to overdo the washing stuff—never a favourite process of mine'.

Soon after the middle of June he had finished his work at Douglas and now had to return to Scapa to complete what he had begun on his previous visit. He and Nova travelled together to Carlisle, where they parted.

On 29th June he wrote to Yve from Scapa:

> I am still shooting the half-dozen films I started in the middle of May, although thank Heaven they are nearly finished now and I ought soon to get back to edit them. Scapa is a deadly place. . . . I rush around the harbour when the sun shines in a herring drifter

bristling with cameras and film technicians thinly disguised as naval ratings. Since I got going in March I have succeeded in turning out a picture a month and now that I have got another camera man in the crew, I may be able to increase the rate of striking. . . . I have bought a Chippendale writing cabinet for £25 in Lancashire. In a career of foolish financial gestures, it is probably my most stupid. It is a lovely piece and worth £40 in London. But I shall probably never see it again since

1. I bought it off an Irishman.

2. I have nowhere to put it so he is storing it (gratis) but without any sort of check.

3. If he doesn't make off with it I anticipate it will probably be blitzed.

'I am nearly through my savings now . . .'

On Monday, 7th July, he telegraphed to Nova:

'Will be with you to-morrow
evening—Cheers.'

Immediately afterwards he and four others set off in a Fleet Air Arm 'plane for Rosyth, where he was to catch the night mail to London.

Within an hour the 'plane had crashed into a mountainside and that brilliant, loving, lovable spirit had ceased to be.

*   *   *

To Julian the shock was crushing, for he looked up to and loved his brother with rare intensity. So deeply did he feel what had happened that he could not bear to have a photograph of Pen in his room. The shock redoubled his desire to escape from the monotony of Home Defence and to get to grips with the enemy. But the chance of real action seemed to be indefinitely postponed by the instruction, which he received from the War Office in the middle of October, to go as mortar instructor to the Battle School at Woolacombe. The choice was no doubt due to his success at the course in the spring, but he did not at all relish the compliment. 'I do not want to leave the Battalion,' he wrote, 'and I do not want above all things a non-combatant job.'

He and the Colonel both protested as strongly as they could, but the War Office was adamant and he had no choice but to go.

The next few months were a time of acute frustration. When he reached Woolacombe he found that no equipment had been provided for his course, nor did visits and letters to H.Q. at Salisbury produce any practical result. In these conditions it was impossible to start work effectively. Fortunately he liked his colleagues, particularly the C.O., who backed him strongly against the authorities at H.Q. in his refusal to begin a half-baked course without adequate equipment, and by the end of the year he had found a house on the front 'full of lodging-house furniture and pictures of Stags at Eve and kittens', where Yve came in the first days of the New Year with the twins, a nondescript puppy called 'Bloggs' and 'Moaning Minnie', a Siamese cat. No serious work was yet possible, but he spent much time on Exmoor looking for suitable practice grounds, and set about building a beautiful model landscape in the lecture-room for demonstration purposes. He was only able to start his first course with very inadequate equipment nearly five months after his urgent removal from the Battalion in the autumn.

At the beginning of April, he wrote with delight that he had found a bungalow cheaper and pleasanter than the house on the front. On the 19th, thirty-seven men arrived for his second course. Of these he promptly returned thirteen as unsuitable, and a day or two later set off to Netheravon to discuss the situation with the authorities.

Just after the course had started came a fateful and wholly unexpected letter from him, dated 17th May:

> Now some rather startling news. I leave here within ten days. It has come about like this.
>
> The Bn. were ordered to I . . . a on the very day I left them. The Col. at once tried to get me back, failed and was told that the move was indefinitely postponed. Last week the Adjt. wrote to me that it was on again and said the Col. would move heaven and earth to get me back if I wanted to go. I said I did. To-day the old man told me that they have succeeded and I am to leave here almost immediately, as soon as they can rake up a successor. Probably within ten days at most.
>
> My reasons for wishing to go do not spring from any fatuous

heroics or misplaced enthusiasm. You know what I have always felt about this war, that I would give up anything to really get down to it, and nothing will alter my feelings. I know there are scores of arguments against it and probably I am just an ass. Yve has always known and understood all this . . .

Things appear to be urgent at the other end. They won't even allow me to finish my present course, which I've just started. So it really does look as if something is about to happen and I shan't find the usual programme of sandbag-filling, etc. when I go back. I shall be absolutely furious if it is all a fuss about nothing, but I'm sure it isn't.

Well, there isn't much more to say about it at the moment. Those are the bare facts and the halcyon days of Woolacombe are at an end. I cannot help feeling terribly sorry about it although in my heart I am quite sure I am doing the right thing.

A day or two later he wrote again:

My heart is very heavy. However, I have thought it all out over and over again, and I cannot but feel that I am doing right; perhaps I am quite wrong, but I alone can judge. This is no blind plunge, but something that I have considered coolly and calmly for many months. I've worked this course up to something really good, though I say it myself. The C.O. is, I feel, really sorry to see me go— ironically he had just arranged to keep me another six months. He has offered his place in Dorset to Yve—a rather hopeless proposition I'm afraid. He has been quite extraordinarily good to me all along and has backed me nobly in a job that hasn't been at all easy. It has been quite wonderful to be here with Yve and it is tragic that it has to end like this. It is entirely my own doing and I hope and pray that I am right.

He rejoined the Battalion at Andover on 22nd May and wrote next day:

Of course when I got back last night I suffered the most dreadful agonies of remorse. I thought of you all and Yve and Pennie and dear Simon and I felt that I was just an appalling fool. But it is passing off now. The conflict in my mind has been awful. I cannot write about it. I suppose it will long continue so. Sometimes I think I must be mad to do this. Yve of course has been quite wonderful. We never discussed it. There seemed nothing to gain by doing so. We just pretended that nothing was happening. Her courage is unbelievable.

INDIA

By the middle of June he was on board the transport, and before the end of the month had begun his voyage to an unknown destination, which ultimately proved to be Bombay. From Bombay, where they landed in mid-August, the Battalion went by train to a camp in Southern India, which was to be his head-quarters until the middle of 1943. The primary object of the division (the 25th Indian) to which the 6th Oxford and Bucks were attached, was the defence of Southern India against an anticipated Japanese invasion. The Battalion was part of the 74th Brigade, the remainder of which was composed of Baluch and Hyderabad battalions. Their camp was at Attur, near Pondicherry, where the most important aerodromes in Southern India were situated. As the threat of invasion was considered urgent, the Division was plunged straight into formation training on a grand scale, without the preliminary individual company and battalion training which it would normally have received. Julian lived in a rush hut 'built' (as he described it) 'by the natives without the use of a single nail (price £2) visited periodically by lizards, mongeese, tree-rats and dogs of various affiliation'. Life was at first fairly monotonous, relieved only by an occasional week's leave at Ootacamund which, with its 'sweet, half-English' air and scenery always fascinated and refreshed him. 'There are oak trees in the garden,' he wrote, 'and the flowers are those of my native land and never seem to fade.'

There he could get a little rough shooting, for he had met, and borrowed a gun from, a Suffolk friend, who was quartered only a few miles away. Sometimes he went duck-shooting on the reservoir near the camp; sometimes he represented the Battalion in a game of cricket against a neighbouring village. Greatest solace of all was the leisure which his new life gave him to read. He bought books (including some old favourites—George Borrow and Richard Jefferies, De Quincey's *Opium Eater* and *The Ballad of Reading Gaol*)—whenever he could visit Madras, and friends helped him to build up his stock with presents from home. The gift from Robert Nichols of his *Selected Poems* pleased him greatly. Before long he could write, 'I have quite a library now, balanced precariously against the rush and bamboo wall of my shack.' The greatest solace of all he found in Shakespeare, especially the tragedies—*Macbeth, Othello, Hamlet, Romeo and Juliet,* and *King Lear,* which he read again and again. 'So long as he and Yve are with me, I shall be all right,' he wrote. He needed solace sorely at this time, since his army life offered him few consolations for his separation from everything that he loved. He longed intensely 'to tear into a few Japs and come home again as quickly as possible and forget the whole idiotic business'. Moreover he felt keenly the fact that he was passed over for the promotion which had been more or less promised him when he left Woolacombe. A number of regular officers had joined the Battalion before it sailed from England, and this had blocked promotion for the subalterns who had raised and trained it since its inception. Julian had the courage and independence to lodge a formal protest. This only resulted in a rather humiliating rebuff, the Adjutant being instructed to inform his Company Commander that he was not considered enough of a regimental soldier.

> This, [writes one of his friends] was typical of the attitude of the regular commissioned officer to the emergency commissioned officer. Julian certainly did not look a soldier, nor was soldiering his bent. However, he possessed a profound knowledge of man-management, his men would follow him anywhere, and he had a brain of which he could make use in his specialist's job.

It was in this direction that he found consolation, for he was soon after given back his old charge of the mortar platoon. It was perhaps not altogether surprising that a regular infantry officer should find it rather difficult to adapt himself to so unconventional a junior. One incident became famous among the British troops in Southern India. On making an unexpectedly early visit of inspection one morning, the Colonel, who was always insisting on the importance of the Battalion setting an example of the utmost efficiency to the Indian troops with whom they were brigaded, was staggered by discovering a bird's nest under the radiator of one of Julian's vehicles. The Company Commander was equally surprised, but not so Julian, who calmly explained that the bird, an Indian robin, had built the nest in a single night and he had given orders that until the eggs hatched the nest should remain, being carefully removed when the carrier had to go out on exercise, and put back in the engine as soon as possible after the vehicle's return.

In 1943, the Battalion's training became more intensive. There was a succession of schemes and manoeuvres requiring great endurance and often lasting three or four weeks. Julian, to the astonishment of his friends, showed extraordinary stamina. Indeed, he had only two periods of sick leave during the whole of his two and a half years in the East, and those were both for the extraction of impacted wisdom teeth. No fatigue was too much for him and, at the end of a long day's march, he was always to be found sitting cheerfully among his mortars, sipping a cup of hot and very sweet tea, brewed by his cockney batman, Charles Porter, who was his faithful and much-loved companion during the whole of the campaign.

The Japanese threat to Southern India had now receded, and it was decided to employ the 25th Indian Division in the projected attack on Burma, as follow-up troops to an assault landing. This meant a complete change in their training, for they must now be capable of fighting their way through twenty miles of jungle, and subsequently deploying for mobile warfare in open country. As the neighbourhood of Attur contained hardly any jungle, it was arranged that the troops should move to the Madras district, where conditions are more like those in Burma. At the end of June the move was made. It proved most unwelcome, for the new camp was wretchedly dilapidated and the climate hot and unhealthy. Julian described the condition of his new life in characteristic letters.

July 8.

New camp pretty lousy. The site and the shade are all right, but the climate is quite dreadful, it reduces one to a pulp, and we are mixed up with a native village. Boy, does it smell. A terrible place . . . My corner of a shack is right on the village—I can pull 'em in thro' the window by the hair. I refer to my peculiar neighbours as the Robinsons, and have laid a double wire fence to keep them out. To make the place look more like home I bought straight away some curtains and tablecloths and got a bookshelf up and hung my portrait gallery. Really I was quite pleased with it and almost asked the Robinsons to tea to hear their views on the colour scheme. Then, presto, they say we've got to go away in the jungle and live in tents and use this place only as a base (we've only been here a few days) and furthermore they shoot me off to Madras to-morrow on a five-day course on educational welfare! ! (nobody else being available),

and postpone my leave. Ah me, this Army. Sometimes its methods
leave me speechless! So altogether I'm a bit wild and in a slight whirl.
The mess sergeant has just told me that I look ten years older. I
wonder if I do. Things get a bit trying out here now and then. I was
horrified when the native barber cut my hair the other day—going
jolly well silver now, but I'm fit and well and feel pretty sprightly
in mind and body and can easily put up with the discomforts of this
most loathsome country and far worse things than that. I've great
faith in the future.

You know that I love you all most dearly and think of you always.
Take care of my beloved little family for me. They are all my
life and world. This is only an interlude, however unpleasant it
may be.

I had the most delightful letter from Alec Bloomfield, simple and
sincere as ever. 'Was at home for Christmas. Didn't go much to the
"Eel's Foot". Sat at home and told funny stories to Lorna' (she'd
had a baby two days before) 'and kept the children amused.' Can't
you picture him? Sometimes I feel that his friendship is the most
valuable one I have.

P.S.—I think I'll call my shack (if they ever let me live in it)
'Locksley Hall', the House of the Future.

July 19.

I'm staying at a small station in the hills, fairly near our old camp
site. At the moment I'm in a bungalow on a coffee estate in the
middle of the jungle (dear old jungle!) having a very quiet time
indeed. I think I must be getting old, parents mine! The idea of
staying in an Indian city and drinking gallons of bad whisky attracts
me not at all; I want to get as far away from both as possible. And
as I don't care in the least about Eastern culture, architecture or customs (really I'm getting more English every day) I try to live as
nearly as possible as if I were in beloved old England. Up here I read
and write and potter and think. I am delighted to find that I am in
the mood to appreciate the tremendous beauty of Marlowe, whom
I bought in Madras. I even did a bit of writing yesterday—grue-
some and cynical but none the less my own. Grand news from Sicily.
How I wish I was there, instead of messing about in this horrible
country.

The 'bit of writing' mentioned in his letter of 19th July showed
how bitterly the madness and cruelty of the war preyed on his
mind in his moods of introspection. It was called

Forever England

He knew that it would come that night. It had nearly come the night before, he had smelt it, felt it near him, but he had shouted to the man lying beside him, the man who feared nothing, and the man had laughed, shouted an order and fired his rifle. Then it had crept away, whispering, rustling, defeated; but they had only postponed its coming, for in the morning the man who feared nothing had said: 'This is the last day. Christ! some bloody Crusade!' He had rolled on his back, his eyes wide and fixed and his mouth twitching. He lay as if in a trance. Sleep on, better never to waken again.

And now he knew that it would come that night. Well, he had waited for it long enough. He dragged his fingers through his knotted hair and pulled the earth from his beard. Too much beard for a week. Was it a week? It might have been a month. He didn't know or care. Years ago, in a distant, friendly land, a Great Someone had said: 'Men, you are going forward to a Crusade. The eyes of the world will be upon you. . . .' 'Christ! some bloody Crusade!' had said the man lying beside him. 'And whose eyes? A lot of little men like apes. They'll be watching us all right. Nobody else.'

Then he had seen them grow old, those Crusaders, they who had been gay and hopeful and arrogant; he had seen them grow old from fear, from hunger, from disease, from shock of battle, from loss of friends. Old men with eyes glazed by bewilderment and minds dulled beyond emotion. He and the man who feared nothing had left them and gone out alone. A week ago? Too much beard for a week. A month ago! He didn't know or care. He couldn't see himself; but he saw his own image in the man lying beside him, wide, feverish eyes and twitching mouth. He didn't care. The weakness of his body didn't matter because his mind was quick and clear. Words bubbled to the surface of his brain:

> '. . . . . *Think only this of me:*
> *That there's some corner of a foreign field*
> *That is forever England. There shall be*
> *In that rich earth a richer dust concealed.'*

Where was that written? In the middle of some bloody Crusade?

'Forever England' in the rich earth of the Tropics, dank, steaming, fetid. 'A richer dust'—oh God! no richer dust of his. There was something to take care of that; something that trailed an ugly, restless shadow which quartered the ground like a hunting dog. He laughed at it, and the bird looked downward with hard, cruel, calculating stare. It soared beyond his sight. He knew that it would return within the hour, but he didn't care.

The sun climbed steeply up the blinding sky. A sharp, hot pain seared his hands when he touched the sides of the rock beneath which he lay. Because his brain was clear he did not whimper, only cursed. He did not care, because he knew that it would come that night.

Why was he waiting for it like this? Less than thirty years ago another man had waited, waited for the same thing, grimly shivering in a hole in a mangled, ravaged country. 'Men,' they had said, 'this is a great Crusade.' And afterwards, when that other man waited no more, a woman looked upon her little world with darkened, fearful eyes. She lived to hear them say again: 'Men, this is a great Crusade.' And when she heard that, she hid her face and murmured: 'No, oh! no.' He had smiled upon her pityingly, and now he waited in his turn.

Soon another woman would look down the years with desperate eyes.

When this vision came to him, he beat the rock beneath which he lay and cried, because his brain was clear: 'No! No! Not that!'

Perhaps in another thirty years another man would wait. . . .

Once more he beat the rock and cried: 'Ah no! Not that! Not that!'

The bird glided again above his head, glancing down with bright, cruel stare. He laughed at it. He didn't care. He knew that it would come that night. And because his brain was clear, he asked why, why, why was he waiting for it like this?

A mighty cloud gathered in the west and rolled towards the sun. The hand that moved it cast a mantle over his brain, so that his thought was dimmed and his earthly visions fell away from him and he never knew why he waited.

It was almost night when the rain stirred him, the wild, crushing rain, spouting off the rock beneath which he lay. Feebly he lifted his face and drank, closing his eyes, and letting the rain tear the clogged earth from his beard that must have been more than a week old.

And then suddenly he knew that it was coming: Above the deadening rain he could hear it, whispering, hissing, rustling towards him. Calmly he wriggled back beneath the rock. He looked at the man lying beside him. Pale, piteous face, eyes wide and vacant, mouth hideously open, mumbling a sentence. 'Christ: some bloody Crusade!' The lips twitched no more. Maybe asleep. Maybe dead. He didn't care. Sleep on, better never to waken again lest you should know fear at the last.

He lay on his stomach and pushed his rifle out before him. And as he stared into the gloom his fingers relaxed their grip, his lips parted and his face sank gently down upon the damp, steaming earth.

'Forever England.' Men, this is a great Crusade.

In September the new Colonel, who had recently taken command of the Battalion, gave Julian his long-deferred promotion. He announced this in a letter, replying to one reporting Buster's death and telling him about Robert Nichols's anthology of war poems, with its prefatory dialogue between the poet and Julian (described as 'a conscript'):

Sept. 28.

I was very interested to read your remarks about Robert's anthology. A *conscript*—oh, Robert, Robert, that hurts me deeply—careless devil. Pretty comic about the *News Review* and the photograph. I only wish I was 'a representative poet'. Alas I fear I'm not very representative of anything, and if the war goes on much longer I shall not be even the 'younger generation'.

Poor old Buster! Its a good thing we can't foresee the future. Six years ago to-day I was about to be married. Our new Colonel has *made me a Captain*. I get a bit more money, which I shall be able to turn over to Yve, and I feel it is some reward for my very negligible services. But all I want to do is to finish the whole business and get rid of my insignia for good.

The longer I'm away the more I think of you all and the more do I love and miss my own sweet family. But I know I can hang on all right and I feel the deepest conviction that one day our own small world will right itself—there are things in it which cannot be destroyed.

Heigh ho, my wedding eve,

Bless you all,
Your devoted Dooley.

It was immensely to his credit that, in spite of his distaste for the routine of military life and the long postponement of official recognition, Julian had worked solidly and devotedly at the building up of his mortar platoon. At the end of a year in India, when the then C.-in-C. came south, he was informed by H.Q. Southern Army that the best British unit in Southern India was the 6th Oxford and Bucks, both for its general efficiency and for the efficiency of its specialized units. The unit most in demand for

R

demonstration to other battalions, both British and Indian, was the mortar platoon. Their accuracy of fire and speed in action, with the contributory factor of the carrier-drivers' skill, were recognized as outstanding. Moreover, Julian had trained two of his sergeants so effectively that either of them was capable of deputizing for their officer, whether in or out of battle.

At the end of November the Battalion moved to the Wynaad jungle, whence he wrote to his godmother:

> I understand that, after studying various snapshots of me, you asked querulously why I didn't send home a few of myself—did my whiskers alter me so much? Never mind, they're off now; the Viceroy accepted them gratefully for his private museum in Delhi. They were a fine growth while they lasted and I still think of them with a twinge of regret.
>
> Life is no more grim than usual. We are away from the plains and the incredible heat for a while and in the jungle, where the days are like August and the nights distinctly cold—some jungle too, Corkle. I never thought that I should come to this: living in a home-made hut of bamboo and elephant grass, with the wild beasts all around me. Ye gods, what a comedy—that's the only way to look at it. Soon I shall be like the locals with uncut hair and a large bug-filled beard. What a place to spend Christmas in. We are farther from civilization than we have ever been before. The sun shines splendidly all day, but it has a job to get through the teak trees and elephant grass. The crazy English prepare for war in their own extraordinary way. Snakes—blimey they killed a fourteen-foot python down the road a week or two ago—and the tigers still come and have a good laugh at us at night.

In February, 1944, the Division was moved to Bangalore, 200 miles to the west, where, soon afterwards, mobilization for war was hastily completed and the Division travelled to Madras, whence they sailed by successive brigade groups to Chittagong, a voyage of about 1,000 miles. During the train journey to Madras, Julian read the privately printed *Memoir* of Pen, which his father had written and sent him.

> My dearest Father, [he wrote], I want this to be chiefly about the memoir, which I have read mostly cooped up in a 3rd Class Indian Carriage and not alone as I should like to have been. I have to wait until the train stops before I can write, and perhaps I should wait until I get to the other end; but its going to be such a long time and

I want to write now. I was glad to find that after a while it did not distress me too much and that I was able to feel almost detached while reading it. . . . It is all there, his robust humour, his zest for living, his deep affection, his courage and independence of spirit, his keen intelligence and brilliant mind, his great kindliness. All the Pen whom I loved with all my heart. Truly I think that I loved him more than my own children. Since his death, and perhaps before it, I have felt that if one of us had to die, then I would rather that it were I, because he had so very much to give the world. These are not idle and pretentious words, but a real and true feeling. When Pen died, something in me died too; I know that no one else can ever fill again his place in my feelings. I don't know why I write this to you now when I've never written it before. Often I remember him with a brilliant clearness for no apparent reason and through no special association of ideas, and find myself so affected that my eyes are stinging with tears. . . .

*   *   *

So ended Julian's experience of India. To his friends it seemed strange that with his keen imagination and sensibility he should have found so little to interest him in that marvellous country. To remonstrances on the subject he would reply briefly that he had very little leisure and that what he had was fully taken up with thinking and reading about the things which he loved at home: that he had no interest in the East and no desire ever to go further east than Thorpeness in the future. What his critics did not understand was that beneath the surface of his life a great integration and massing of his deeper self had been taking place, which alone could enable his sensitive and introspective nature to endure the hardships and miseries of separation from all he loved. There all the time, steadily and brightly, burned his faith and passion for the life he longed one day to lead. He would not come to terms with circumstance and spread his emotions and interests thinly over half a world. Rather he went inside himself, found the truth there, and stuck to it with magnificent obstinacy.

BURMA

The voyage to Chittagong gave Julian his first direct experience of the brutal horror of war. I will describe the incident as far as possible in his own words. The convoy had been at sea three days,

R*

and was steaming in a cloudless, soundless calm up the coast of Burma. The sea along the coast is so shallow that it seemed impossible for any enemy submarine to lurk there. Julian and some of his friends were leaning over the rail on the lower deck, watching the ship next to them, a sturdy grey 10,000-tonner, the handsomest ship in the convoy of six. They could see the line of khaki figures leaning on the lower deck rail, after the manner of men in troopships all the world over. One of them waved a handkerchief in greeting. Suddenly there was a shattering explosion. The great grey ship seemed to split in two, as a cloud of smoke shot up from the water-line below the poop deck. Débris was hurled high into the air; smoke and flames enveloped half the ship. When the smoke cleared, the stern had disintegrated and disappeared and the maimed vessel turned away, burning, drifting and helpless. All round her the sea was strewn with rafts, boxes and broken fittings, with men seated on upturned lifeboats or struggling among the floating wreckage. In Julian's transport the men had pulled on their lifebelts and rushed to their boat stations, waiting for the next shock which all felt sure would send them to join their shipwrecked comrades; but no shock came. The sinking ship drifted astern, smoke hanging thickly above her in the windless air. Far away to starboard the little corvette, the only escort, turned and raced towards her. An old Dutch tanker, the last ship in the convoy, moved across to wait for the end. The rest of the convoy steamed slowly ahead, without altering speed or course. The minutes dragged by. The men murmured among themselves. The passage of their lives was suspended. The tragedy that they were watching seemed impossible and unreal, too monstrous to assimilate. Far behind they saw a boat put off from the ruined ship, then another and another; four, five, six, seven, eight, nine. No more. Suddenly her bows reared up into the air, like the nose of a giant whale. For a fraction of time she appeared to balance vertically, black against the first golden tinge of the early tropic sunset. Then, without a sound, she slid quickly and smoothly beneath the surface—less than a quarter of an hour after the first explosion. Save for the scattered lifeboats, not a sign marked her vanishing.

A Japanese submarine had been lurking in the one narrow inlet where the water was deep enough to hide her, and the torpedo had no doubt been aimed at Julian's ship, which was leading on the port bow. Only the narrowness of the inlet, which allowed no room for manoeuvre, prevented the firing of a second torpedo and enabled Julian and his comrades to escape.

Their ship docked on the following afternoon. Up to the last the sea remained benignly calm, its colour unsurpassable in depth and purity. It did not seem that its smile of divine contentment could ever change.

Such was Julian's introduction to the last act of his life's brief drama—the Arakan campaign of S.E.A.C.

The object of this campaign was to clear the enemy from the Mayu Peninsula, which occupies the north-western coast of Burma, on the eastern side of the Bay of Bengal. Just a year before, British troops had fought their way over the same ground with the intention of capturing Akyab, the island at its southern-most point, and had been pushed back by the Japanese, in a drive for Chittagong. This threat had been defeated and a violent counter-offensive by the Japanese repelled at Maungdaw in early March, but the enemy were still full of fight and holding the Arakan country in considerable strength. The backbone of the Arakan is the Mayu range of hills. This runs north and south, reaching 2,000 feet at its highest point, with a knife-edge crest seldom more than a few yards in width, and falling precipitously away on either side. The whole is covered with impenetrable jungle, where movement without cutting is impossible. The whole of this range gave the Japanese ideal defensive positions. On either side of it are rice-growing plains, thickly inhabited. The western plain (four miles wide at Maungdaw in the north and narrowing to a few hundred yards at Foul Point in the south), is covered with a succession of paddy fields intersected by a large number of tidal creeks or *chaungs*. The climate is one of the hottest, dampest and most unhealthy in the world.

When the 25th Indian Division arrived in Burma, at the end of March, there were still some weeks of fighting in prospect before the expected onset of the monsoon at the end of May. The Oxford and Bucks were given the temporary job of defending Head-quarters, and their introduction to Burma was discouraging. To quote a correspondent of the *Bicester Press:*

> Heavy black rain-laden clouds filled the sky as the British troops hastened to build jungle shelters that would give them some protec-tion from seven months of torrential rain. Battle litter, unburied

bodies, collapsed bunkers, rotting food, scattered enemy equipment, and old latrines, black with flies, a legacy of earlier fighting, had to be cleared away before new homes could rise on the unhealthy sites of the old positions. Bodies were burned or buried; latrines filled in and sealed over; areas tidied up; new latrines, and soakage pits for cook-houses were dug; benches, made of bamboo and saplings, were erected for 'dining-rooms'. 'Jugger', a home-made word for a cross between a jungle *basha* and dugout, were provided for living quarters. Riveted with bamboo, fronted with grass thatch and roofed with tarpaulins, the jugger became the soldier's monsoon home.

By the middle of April the Battalion had been moved south from Maungdaw and was playing an active part in the fighting. On 6th May they made a raid in strength on the village of Thayegenbaung in the western plain, killing many of the enemy and gaining valuable experience in the difficult art of operating across the network of tidal creeks with motor transport. In many of the Battalion's activities Julian's mortars played an active part. Indeed, they were constantly in demand to assist the infantry because of their remarkable accuracy of fire. Once when the Oxford and Bucks were holding an isolated post behind the enemy's lines, they were continually troubled by the Japanese equivalent of an eighteen-pounder, sighted up a valley and defiladed, from the British position, by the hills overlooking the sea. In the dark of one night Julian took two of the mortars right up to the mouth of the valley. When day broke and the Japanese gun began to fire, a careful bearing was taken on the flash. The mortars opened up in the half-light, and firing at an extreme range of nearly a mile put down a quick succession of twenty-four bombs. With the echoes of the bursts still filling the valleys, the teams of both weapons packed up and ran to the nearest cover, carrying their heavy burdens with them. The Japanese gun was silenced and never spoke again.

The monsoon was expected to break at the end of May and the Japanese withdrew southward to their monsoon quarters, leaving our troops in occupation of Maungdaw and the surrounding country. Monsoon conditions in the Arakan will never be forgotten by those who lived through them—the ceaseless four months of rain and mist, the leeches in the jungle and the mud which clogged feet on slippery hillsides; the *chaungs* in spate, that had to be crossed with ropes; the socks that shrank to nothing because they were never dry; the whiskers that grew on boots overnight, and the fungus that obscured binoculars. But every effort was made to secure the comfort and morale of the troops: huts were built with more or less waterproof roofs, though more often men had to live in holes in the ground, covered with tin or tarpaulin. A mobile cinema was established at Maungdaw, the hardier ENSA parties now and then appeared on the scene, there was a certain amount of sport, and one Divisional concert was given, in which Julian appeared with his usual success.

On 11th June, when news of the landing in Normandy had reached Burma, he wrote:

> Well its truly under way by now and the tension and excitement are terrific even out here, so what it must be like in England I can hardly imagine. I feel so proud of England and I love it more than ever. I pray for a speedy success for this enormous and dreadful enterprise, so that the world may return to some kind of sanity and decency again. . . . I've no doubt about the final result, only I hope that it won't drag on. I know that this must be the thoughts of all of you too, and I pray that you will be spared any horror and suffering that is to come. It is difficult for us to imagine the gigantic scale on which it is being done. This little war is so puny by comparison. . . .

On 15th June he wrote to Cordelia Curle:

> Corkle mine, You mustn't be horrified at my being in Burma. Its a splendid country I don't think. . . . What dreadful times these are, my Cork, yet there is still something great about them, even for me in this sorry exile . . . and you, my cherished Godmother, are you still your twinkling, indomitable self? I bet you are. My parents seem pretty well—I wonder whether they have aged much. As for me, I'm still my old unshakable self, and you need have no fears for my health and sanity. I seem to escape all the foul diseases that ravage this glorious land, also the Jap bullets and shells (only just, sometimes). How long this will last I cannot say. Of course its all pretty bloody, but what would you? I just laugh and let the war roll by. I never let it get me down. We get plenty to eat and life is not entirely unalcoholic. But, oh my Cork, I look forward to the end. Its gone on too long, you know.

Preparations were now in hand to drive the Japanese out of Arakan and capture Akyab. The task allotted to the 25th Indian

Division was to clear the Mayu Peninsula, and the 74th Brigade, including the 6th Oxford and Bucks, started to spread southward over the western plain and foothills of the Mayu range. There followed a long period devoted to individual and unit training, for the Japanese had discreetly withdrawn from contact with our troops, and considerable preparations were necessary before the difficult task of negotiating the jungle and hills on the east, and the *chaungs* and marshes of the western plain, could be attempted. Meanwhile the monsoon had passed and the hot weather was beginning. Julian had still little leisure for letter-writing although, of course, his thoughts were never far from home, and most evenings he and Charlie Porter would contrive to spend an hour or so smoking cigarettes and talking of their respective wives and families. At the end of October he sent a letter describing the conditions of his life:

Oct. 28.

Very little news to give you from here. Our initial skirmishes have died down and we find it a bit difficult to contact any Japs at all at the moment; all is peace and quiet, more or less! No doubt the storm will break again soon, but I think we've a few weeks of calm yet. The monsoon is over, thank God. The heat by day is almost stupefying. But I, of course, am feeling very fit and good for a lot more yet. No need to worry about me, and I hope you aren't. I'm perfectly comfortable in this delightful jungle and take it all in good part. . . . Lord, when I set foot in England again, I can't imagine what my feelings will be. I only know that there will never be a moment of greater happiness in all my life. Yve and I have great plans for our life at Peasen and I hope we shall be able to set them going. I read a lovely article on Suffolk round towers in *Country Life* —made me dreadfully homesick.

A month later he wrote to Cordelia Curle:

I'm my usual cheerful self, still keeping clear of disease and shot and shell. . . . We did quite a bit of battling for two months and are on the verge of doing a lot more. I'm all in favour of basting down these abominable Japs. Horrid sub-human creatures: you'd be horrified if you knew how they treated the villagers. Life has plenty of laughs—one morning when we were being shelled, I was *attrapé avec mes pantalons en bas! Comprenez?* Well my sweet Goddam, time to finish. Look after yourself and write to me again.

On 11th December the 74th Brigade started its offensive. Brigadier J. D. Hirst, who was in command, took his own portable bridging to cross the innumerable waterways which intersect the Peninsula. He left no supply line behind him for the Japanese to cut, but was fed from the sea by the Army's Inland Water Transport Service, while destroyers of the Australian Navy shelled the way ahead of him. During the whole forty-two-mile advance not a gun or vehicle was lost and, although the troops were occasionally shelled by Japanese warships, battle casualties were negligible, for Brigadier Hirst decided—as it turned out, wisely—not to play the game the Japs would have liked him to play and fight them in the hills of the Mayu range, but to push on and leave them behind to rot. Myinhlut was reached within the appointed time and it was decided to seize Donback before the point could be reinforced by the enemy. The 6th Oxford and Bucks were chosen for this enterprise and they reached their objective unopposed after a night march of over twenty miles. 'This long march,' said the history of the campaign which was afterwards compiled at Divisional Headquarters, 'completed within the space of a night, by men carrying everything they needed on their own backs, through unknown country, along a sandy beach, with the possibility of an enemy ambush ever present, was an accomplishment in keeping with the highest traditions of the light infantry soldier.'

By the 27th December, the whole of the south of the Peninsula was reported clear of the enemy and the Brigade began to concentrate for the assault on Akyab. The Brigadier's orders had been to seize Foul Point by the 15th January, or just over a month after commencing his advance. His whole task was in fact accomplished by the 29th December, or within a period of seventeen days.

Indeed, so rapid and complete was the British success that the enemy did not wait to defend Akyab, and our troops, when they entered it on 3rd January, found both the island and city deserted.

Everywhere was destruction and decay, [wrote a historian of the campaign], testimony to the grim work of the R.A.F. in over two years of bombardment. Not a civilian walked the streets, nor was there any sign of recent habitation; for even the Japanese had avoided the town and taken to defences on the outskirts. Once fine gardens were now a wilderness. Rank, tropical vegetation had overgrown many of the ruins, softening their aspect and lending an air of antiquity to their decay. By night the melancholy howling of jackals bespoke the utter desolation to which this once-proud city had been reduced.

The Battalion now enjoyed a few days of comparative quiet. There were no Christmas festivities, though at 4 p.m. on 29th December the Battalion, seated on the ground outside the cookhouse, consumed a meal of goose, duck, chicken, potatoes, cauliflowers and cabbages, followed by tinned plum-puddings and fruit salad. 'I don't think I ever saw men eat so much at a sitting,' wrote one of their captains, 'it did me good to see it.'

Meanwhile, Julian had celebrated the defeat of the enemy with an outburst of derisive ribaldry, entitled

Happy Christmas

'*Twas Christmas day in Arakan,*
The day in all the year,
There were hundreds of Japs all around us,
The beggars had smelled out the beer.

The snows lay deep over Burma,
The icicles hung from the trees,
The poor old brass monkey was shivering,
He was froze from his neck to his knees.

They carried him into the guard room,
His teeth were fair chattering with cold,
He said 'Gimme a month's leave for Chrisake!'
The poor sod looked a hundred years old.

They were warming him up by the fireside
When the Colonel came in and said 'Boys
'*There's a gallon of beer for each fox-hole,*
'*Let's all make a hell of a noise!'*

'*Here's a bottle of whisky apiece, boys,*
'*I hates the horrible stuff!'*
Then he sent the Adj: off for the turkey
While the R.S.M. went for the duff.

Then a Jap put his head round the doorway,
With his section and all alongside,
He shouted 'Hands up! You're all plisoners!'
But the Colonel said 'Buzz off! outside!'

He said 'Don't you blokes know it's Christmas?
'Ain't you chaps got no manners at all?
'If you want, you can come in and join us,
'If you don't, you can buzz off, that's all.'

The Jap disappeared pretty quickly,
He didn't seem keen to remain,
But he showed his head once through the window
'Flicking British,' he said, 'tight again!'

The party got wilder and wilder,
Beer flowed like the Severn in spate,
So the Adj: tried to close the proceedings
'Cos he thought it was getting too late.

He said 'Sir, we've a battle to-morrow,
And what'll we do if we lose?'
'Which one?' said the Colonel. 'Oh that one!
'Blast the battle—get on with the BOOZE.'

So the party went on till the morning,
It was still in full swing the next night,
And the Japs jiggered off, tired of waiting,
'Flicking British,' they muttered, 'still tight.'

N.B.—The reader is invited to vary the epithets and expletives according to his taste and experience.

THE END

Soon after this, news reached Julian of the sudden death of Robert Nichols. He felt it deeply, for their friendship had been a source of great pleasure and encouragement to him. He did not

know that one of Robert's last acts had been to write to Lord
Wavell, asking him to see if some work of a literary kind at
Headquarters could be found for Julian, whose talents he felt sure
were being wasted in the merciless routine of the Burma front.
Lord Wavell made inquiries about Julian, and was told that he
was an exceedingly good regimental officer doing very well with
his Battalion. He then wrote to the D.P.R. on the Commander-
in-Chief's staff, putting forward Robert's suggestion. The D.P.R.
happened to be away and the letter lay unopened in his office for
some weeks. Before action could be taken on it, Julian had been
killed. Even if there had not been this delay and work at Headquarters had been offered him, his friends know that he would not
have accepted it. He had made up his mind to go through to the
bitter end and nothing would have changed his determination.

It was now clear that the enemy had no intention of making
any counter-attack, and was hoping for nothing better than an
orderly withdrawal eastward to the Irrawaddy valley. The
British task, therefore, was to follow him up as quickly, and
harass him as severely, as possible. The Myebon peninsula to the
south-east was occupied by 18th January, after some fierce fighting
and most difficult amphibious transport operations carried out
with great skill. By 17th February the British had, after a month's
continuous activity, captured Kangaw, some miles to the west.
The Oxford and Bucks were not involved in these operations.
They had been sent north from Myebon to harass the retreating
enemy and came successfully through some sharp fighting, during
which Julian's mortar platoon was often sent to bolster the fire of
other regiments which found themselves in difficulties. On one
such occasion, four of his mortars fired 236 bombs in fifteen
minutes under the nose of a Jap .75, which they knocked out in
the process. When the position was captured, twelve tail units
from the bombs were found in the gunpit itself, a striking testimony to the accuracy of the shooting.

There followed a period of regrouping, preparatory to a move
southward to Ruywa and An, on the way to Mandalay. Julian
now had some days of quiet and, as usual, his thoughts turned
homeward. The splendid progress of the Eastern campaign and
the good news from Europe and the Pacific made him hope that
before another year had passed he might be home again. He was
also encouraged by a letter from the *Geographical Magazine*,

offering him the sub-editorship, with a salary of £800 a year, as soon as he could be demobilized.

Immediately afterwards the Battalion was sent southward to take part in the Ruywa operations. The approach had to be made by boat through miles of tidal waterways, half hidden amongst thickly wooded islands and banks of mangrove swamp, quite uninhabited and, indeed, uninhabitable. As soon as they had landed they marched north to seize Tamandu on the Dalst *chaung,* which was still strongly held by the enemy. It was essential that these operations should be carried through as quickly as possible and the speed of the Oxford and Bucks Light Infantry served them admirably, as it had done in the night march down the Mayu Peninsula. They overran several enemy positions and, by 5th March, had reached the neighbourhood of Tamandu, where the Japanese were strongly entrenched on the high ground. The 7/16 Punjab were ordered to attack these positions over precipitous country, covered with thick bamboo which made it extremely hard to detect enemy positions without entering fire lanes covered by machine-guns. The Japanese defended, as always, with maniacal tenacity, and the Punjabis soon found themselves in difficulties. Julian, accompanied as usual by the faithful Charlie Porter, was, therefore, sent with his mortars to their support. The mortars were established in what seemed a safe position, and Julian, as was his practice, went forward to a more exposed point by himself, to make his observations and direct the fire. Immediately his 3-inch mortars opened up, the Japanese countered with their 4-inch weapons. A piece of shell, the size of a little finger-nail, pierced his heart and he fell dead instantaneously.

The fight continued all that day, the two sergeants carrying on with the discipline, skill and courage which he had taught them, and it was largely due to their efforts that the position was captured. Then the platoon carried his body down to the plain, and buried him by the sandy road which passes below the foothills to Tamandu, the capture of which marked the end of the 25th Indian Division's campaign in Burma. Had he lived he would have been proud of the special order of the day, in which the Corps Commander recorded the achievements of their twelve months of warfare:

> I congratulate all of you on the very successful conclusion of a whole year's uninterrupted campaign in Arakan.

You came at a difficult time and had to take over a wide front south-east of Maungdaw during a period of Japanese offensive. You not only held your ground, but turned him off the strongest mountain-tops which he had held for two years or more.

You will always remember the Arakan monsoon. I shall always remember that you patrolled and fought aggressively all through it in spite of the appalling conditions, and that you came through the ordeal with your morale high.

You have to your credit the clearance from the Mayu Peninsula of the famous 55th Japanese Division and the capture of Akyab and clearance of the surrounding districts, the Myebon operations and the surprise landing and resultant decisive battle of the whole campaign—Kangaw.

You finished off your campaign to clear the Northern and Central Arakan of the Japanese 54th Division by the brilliantly executed landing at Ruywa, leading to your final capture of the enemy's base at Tamandu.

Throughout these operations you have shown magnificent fighting qualities and the highest morale. You have to your credit the successful accomplishment of probably the most difficult combined operations any British force has ever attempted.

You first came under my command on 12th November, 1942. We trained together and we have fought together. I could wish for no finer troops to command and I am intensely proud of you all.

*   *   *

After Pen's death there was found among his papers a sheet containing the following lines in his handwriting.

With them I feel that I can fitly close this brief memorial of five brilliant spirits, whose fragments of life were intimately linked with mine by ties of blood and friendship:

The advent of death is like the coming of a great wind: no man knows whence it is nor where it goes. Its visitation is often without reason and its action without intent the understanding may perceive. One thing alone it shows. By his death man sets a seal upon his life and in the manner of his dying is revealed the strength of his spirit. For the spirit of man is formed in the secret places of his will and shaped by the private utterance of his desires. He himself knows not its ways nor perceives the manner of its growth. And in life few achieve the full expression of the spirit, compassed about as we are by the world and its implications. But if the spirit be set upon high things then in death it will be without fear, not as the foolish who know not solemnity, but with courage, dignity and consideration.

Index